# FAEROES' CHILD
## *a life in exile*

## Antonia Stephenson

FAEROES' CHILD
Copyright © Antonia Stephenson 2005
First published by Zeus Publications 2005
http://www.zeus-publications.com
P.O. Box 2554
Burleigh M.D.C.
QLD. 4220
Australia.

ISBN: 1-9210-0555-6

National Library of Australia listing:
**Stephenson, Antonia.**
**Faeroes' Child**

This book is a work of non-fiction. The author asserts her moral rights.
Copyright © photographs: Antonia Stephenson, with the exception of the
*SS Tjaldur* on page 21, courtesy of National Museum of the Faroe Islands.
Copyright © drawing: Aase Bømler Olsen 2005

*No one knows in the morning, where the evening will find him a guest*

*Faeroese Proverb*

## About the Author

*Antonia Stephenson was born in Italy to a Serbian-French mother and Bosnian father. Most of her working life has been spent in the international airline industry. She lives in Sydney and has one son. Faeroes' Child is her first book.*

## Author's Note

*The interpretations and any errors in this book are entirely my own, while the people and their names are as real as their personalities. I have attempted to portray them faithfully.*

*I have used the old spelling of the Faeroe Islands throughout this book as that was the spelling used in my time there in the 1950s. Today, it is more common to see the islands' name spelt as Faroe Islands.*

*For Andrew and Roger*

# ACKNOWLEDGEMENTS

I am enormously grateful to the Sivertsen family of Tórshavn, who so generously allowed me to print details of their personal family history. Without their valuable cooperation this book would not have been possible.

In particular, I am indebted to Sjúrður Sivertsen, his wife Eyðhild, his sisters Rachel Jensen and Anna Maria Pavia, their brother, the late Júst Sivertsen and Sjúrður's daughters-in-law Guðrið Holm and Ann Mari.

My thanks also to my special Faeroese friends, Laura Joensen, Guðrun Haustein and Jorún Arge, who helped me to fill in the gaps in my childhood memory.

I also owe my gratitude to Jógvan Arge for his data on Faeroese history, to Símun Arge for making available his archeological findings, to Heinrik Vaupel of DFDS for archival shipping information and, to the professional staff at the Faroe Islands Tourist Board.

My dear friend and American author, the late John Minahan shared his insight and knowledge for which I am grateful, as did Australian author, Maggie Hamilton.

Special mention must go to Faeroese artist Aase Bømler Olsen, who helped bring the Faeroes to life through her astute comments.

My thanks to Roger Stephenson for his encouragement and infinite patience in performing the long task of reading and correcting several drafts of this book, and immense thanks to my skilful editor, Anouska Jones, who has transformed this book for the better.

Finally, I must acknowledge my friends - you know who you are - for your moral support.

## Prologue

My early childhood years were spent among the age-old survivors of the Vikings on a group of islands in the middle of a vast, hostile ocean. There I lived with my mothers, none of them my own. I had no direct contact with my real mother. All I knew was that she lived at the opposite end of the world, surrounded by oceans that were much calmer than ours. Our backgrounds were vastly different, that much I also knew. Mother had spent her childhood in the landlocked state of Serbia in a cultured Slavic society.

For a long time, I had accepted but never understood the notion that my mother and I had to lead separate lives. Mother had mastered the art of concealing her past and only rarely did she disclose her true feelings. For my part, I had knowingly wiped out all memory or even any reference to my childhood. I lost any desire to unravel the threads of my past. But that would soon change.

So it was that I found myself, some forty years later, flying towards the Faeroe Islands, islands so small that they are often omitted from maps, appear as an ink smudge or are not even named. What I found out there was as unexpected as it was astounding and it required a major revision of the memories of my early childhood.

I had chosen to fly rather than take the ferry service that was still operating from Denmark. My first tortuous passage across the North Sea, when as a child I had spent the entire trip being seasick, was etched indelibly in my memory. For the two-hour long flight on Atlantic Airways from Copenhagen, I had purposely asked for a window seat on the port side of the aircraft, as I wanted to catch sight of the islands as soon as they came into view.

Except for the English businessman seated next to me, the other passengers seemed to be locals, not all flaxen-haired but all with distinctive Viking blue eyes. Impatiently, I watched the unusually calm sea for any sign of land. Then I noticed a swirling mass of reddish-grey mist in the distance. I pressed my face against the window. Yes, there it was - the protective layer of fog that holds the secrets of this ancient archipelago. As we came closer, the islands suddenly appeared as if by magic, jutting out of the mist like giant upside-down ice cream cones dipped in chocolate. These were the immense rock pinnacles of the Faeroes. We flew closer and more islands came into sight, their resplendent green mantle now clearly visible, but paled by the curtain of mist. These were the storm-tossed Faeroe Islands, situated in the bleak North Atlantic, halfway between Iceland and Shetland; the islands I had first come to in 1949.

## Chapter One

*I*N ORDER TO understand my curious childhood and the circumstances which brought me to the edge of the Arctic Circle, it is necessary to travel south to Italy, to the port city of Genoa, where I was born to unwilling parents some months after the end of World War II. Before stopping here, it is essential to journey further southeast to the former Republic of Yugoslavia to the home of my half Serbian, half French mother.

My mother was born in Stara Pazova, about half an hour's drive northwest from Belgrade, in the agricultural region of Vojvodina, where her family had a country estate. The youngest of five children, she grew up in a privileged household. The family house was in the city, complete with maids, valets, a chauffeur and cook. Mother was named Dušanca (pronounced Dushanka) but she was nicknamed 'Beba', as one of her brothers had trouble pronouncing her name.

Her paternal grandfather, Vjovoda (Duke) Radomir Putnik, was the well known Field Marshal and Commander-in-Chief of the Serbian Army, who led Serbia to victory in many battles and also served as Minister of War during the Balkan wars. Even though Mother had not known him - he died four years before her birth - she was immensely proud of the old Duke's character and war record.

Mother's Serbian father, Dušan Putnik, was a pacifist, a lawyer by profession and a patron of the arts. He played the viola rather

4

well and insisted that his children learn a musical instrument, which they did reluctantly. He was a founding member of the Belgrade Philharmonic Orchestra and every Saturday afternoon a recital was held in the music room on Jevremova Street. He was a strict father in the Victorian sense.

Her mother, Denise, was of French and Greek background. Her father was a Greek shipbuilder, but most of the family lived in Paris where Denise met Dušan. Whereas Dušan was severe, Denise was gentle and his cutting remarks and autocratic demeanour were balanced by her gentleness and benevolence.

Already as a child, Mother showed signs of having inherited her father's sharp tongue and wit, which pleased the old boy no end, so she was often let off the hook from extra music practice and disciplinary measures. She was bright and clever and her father adored her, as did everyone else, except possibly her older sister.

My mother grew up to be tall and fine-boned, with large brown eyes, flawless light olive skin, manageable thick brown wavy hair and a high Beethoven forehead that contained a lot of brains. She was amusing and very attractive. Papa Dušan insisted that all his children study law at the University of Belgrade, but Mother convinced him to let her study arts at the Sorbonne in Paris, where she stayed with her maternal relatives. Her favourite brother, Djordje became a doctor. Her other siblings, Bogdan, Sofija and Radomir obeyed their father and studied law. Djordje loved birds and used to carry them around in the pocket of his coat or jacket. The brim of his hats all had distinctive V-shaped beak marks. He had his own nickname for Mother, *Kobac*, Serbian for swallow hawk, which summed up her searing powers of observation that developed from an early age. From Mother's description, their country estate had more animals than Noah's Ark. Djordje had a pet owl there and, for a time, Mother kept a spider monkey.

Interesting and eccentric relatives would come to visit. Uncle Sava always arrived for lunch with a trunk – a trunk full of toys for the children. He was also the size of a trunk, hulking and avuncular with a broad noble face and a huge moustache. His slim son, Cornelius, became a spy during World War II. Mother's aunt, Ann-Marie, fell in love at the tender age of fifteen with a man in his forties. She wanted to marry him, but her parents would not allow it. So she went on a hunger strike until the family relented. Two other aunts, Radmila and Ruydoka lived for a time at the court of Tzar Nicholas II in Russia, returning to Belgrade before the February Revolution in 1917 and bearing interesting tales from the imperial household.

Mother's only sister, my Aunt Sofija, known as 'Pepa', flirted briefly with communism while at university, much to her father's despair and for a while took to wearing workmen's boots and walking in the mountains with the peasants as a sign of solidarity. She married Milutin Stojadinović, a doctor from a well-connected family. The Stojadinović family lived in a rather sumptuous villa in central Serbia in the spa town of Vrnjacka Banja, where the Romans built the first spa in the second century AD. They also owned a hunting lodge in the nearby Goc Mountains, where Tante Pepa would sally forth on her solidarity walks. All in all, our family could hardly be described as a dull clan.

Belgrade, the new capital of the first Yugoslavia, where Mother grew up in the 1920s, saw a great rise in cultural activities. A rich variety of immigrants from across the new state of Yugoslavia and Europe swelled the numbers of intellectuals and professionals. Dance, theatre and opera benefited from the flood of Russian émigrés fleeing the upheavals in their country, elevating the arts to Western European levels. Literary journals and publications abounded. The hundreds of cafés were filled with authors, artists and musicians, and restaurants on the Sava River served delicious Serbian specialties roasted on charcoal grills. The Terazije, a wide boulevard traversing Belgrade, was alive with a mixture of bohemian and fashionably dressed citizens.

In these flourishing times, Mother's future looked rich and promising. Heads would turn when Beba walked, no, made an entrance into a room. It seemed she had the world at her feet. Then at 7.15 a.m. on 6 April 1941, without warning, Germany invaded Yugoslavia. Belgrade, previously declared an open city, was savagely bombed. In an instant, Mother's cosy world fell apart.

The German bombers continued their attack for four days, killing over 2,300 people and wounding even more. The Germans destroyed churches, hospitals, schools, the Palace and most of the residential houses. Many fled the city. Mother and her immediate family were initially unharmed even though they lived in the centre of the city. With the entrenchment of German occupation, the situation grew more dangerous by the day. The Germans took control of all urban centres and all cultural life quickly came under their control. Soldiers from the Yugoslav army were deported to prisoner of war camps in Germany. A special police force made up of *Volksdeutsche* was hastily established. No one was safe, and concentration camps around Belgrade were soon set up for offenders. Mother desperately wanted to get out of Yugoslavia.

My father, Branko Pavlović, came from a humble background. He was born somewhere in Bosnia; I have been unable to find out exactly where. Ten years older than my mother, also tall and good-looking, he had already been working as an architect in Belgrade where they met at the introduction of her brother, Radomir, at the start of Word War II. Branko was also keen to leave his country and had the connections and means to do so. My parents were married in Belgrade in the autumn of 1942 shortly before Mother's 21$^{st}$ birthday. The Nazi occupiers continued their aggression on the citizens of Belgrade. Mother's cousin and his Jewish wife were captured and put into a concentration camp, where they perished. Given the deteriorating circumstances, my parents decided to leave Yugoslavia.

'Your father was a commoner, but he was my ticket out of war-torn Belgrade. He had excellent connections in the black market.' This was how my mother would later describe my father to me. 'He was very diligent, just like you. My family adored him'. Mother always maintained that her family was intellectually active, but physically lazy. This about summed up the information

7

that Mother was willing to reveal about my father, occasionally adding little gems, such as: 'He made his money during the war from dealing arms.'

Early in 1943 my parents left Belgrade for Vienna by plane and from there continued by train to Trieste. My father had somehow got hold of, or been put in charge of, transporting King Petar of Yugoslavia's Cadillac on the train. It was an overnight trip and my parents slept in the Cadillac. To me, this story is only plausible because my parents knew King Petar, who had been driven into exile. My parents lived in Trieste in great comfort according to my mother.

'Lovely theatre. Performances continued uninterrupted, despite the war.'

Mother was referring to the lovely Teatro Verdi with its splendid recital hall and neo-classical façade, similar to that of La Scala in Milan. Trieste was a melting pot of culture and ethnicity, so perfectly suited to my parents, except for the matter of the war, which forced them to move to a safer country. They decided on neutral Switzerland, where they tried to gain entrée as political refugees, but were refused. However, after offering the requisite financial encouragement, they were accepted and took up residence at the lakeside Bauer au Lac Hotel in Zurich. Mother always managed to be stylish even in adverse circumstances.

How my parents got from Trieste to Zurich remains vague, but it would not have been without danger. Mother loved to tell the story of an incident that occurred on a deserted alpine highway before crossing the Swiss border. A Gestapo agent stopped the car my parents were driving and demanded they get out of the car. It was the middle of the night and pitch black. Mother showed her courage by taking out her Baretta handgun, which was conveniently strapped to her upper thigh. According to Mother, my father cowered in the car while Mother got out and, well, finished the guy off. They proceeded without further incident.

At the end of May 1945, six months before my birth, my parents ended up in Genoa for reasons unbeknown to me. The stories of their war exploits changed frequently over time. The year of my birth was a busy one. Germany surrendered on 7 May.

In August, the US dropped atomic bombs on Hiroshima and Nagasaki, and the United Nations was established in October. My grandmother Denise died in Belgrade shortly before I was born. Her family decided not to tell my mother about it straight away as they feared for the safety of her unborn child. But this concern was indeed a strange irony, as Mother did not want to have any children, realising correctly that she was not maternally inclined. My father had been in an aircraft accident, from which he had fully recovered, but had been told that he was unable to sire any children. Somebody got it wrong, because much to Mother's horror, she found herself pregnant and went off to a trusty doctor who informed her that, at four months, it would be far too dangerous to have an abortion.

I entered this world on 10 November 1945 in the Ospedale Evangelico Internazionale in Genoa. Here Sigrid Sivertsen first entered my life. Sigrid, from Tórshavn, the tiny capital of the Faeroe Islands, worked as a paediatric nurse and attended to my mother and me during our hospital stay. She had previously been in the employ of a Danish diplomat in Copenhagen, where she had worked as a maid. When the diplomat was transferred to Genoa, the family took Sigrid with them. Sigrid had attended nursing school in Denmark, so ended up working in a hospital instead of continuing as a maid. When Mother left the hospital, Sigrid came to live with us as my full time nanny, or so I was led to believe.

My memory of Sigrid is vivid, with her light brown wavy hair, fair skin and grey eyes like the sky in winter. She smiled at me a lot and smelled of talcum powder. I mainly remember her wearing a uniform. A nurse's uniform that is. White for summer, black for winter, complete with a starched veil with a red cross on the headband just like the iconic Red Cross that seemed to be on many trucks around Genoa. Her friends who came to visit us all wore

9

the same uniform. Sigrid was always with me day and night. I know that I never went anywhere without her.

Besides Sigrid, my mother also employed an elderly cook called Philippe. He was French and came with impeccable qualifications, having been a pupil of the famous French chef, Escoffier. In the Belgrade household, there had been no need for my mother to cook or keep house. However, being multi-talented, Mother soon learned from Philippe to prepare exquisite French meals 'like a chef, not a cook' my mother would stress.

The first three years of my life were spent in Genoa. The city had sustained much damage during the war, but the old quarter, dating back to the Middle Ages, was intact. I have no idea where our home was.

In the summer of 1947, my parents, Sigrid and I went to a lovely beach town on the northern coast of Tuscany, Forte dei Marmi - the Fort of Marbles - so called because it was used to defend the area when ships were loading marble from a nearby quarry. Now the fort overlooked the fashionable summer beachgoers.

One day as I was playing inside our villa, I decided that Mother's sparkling jewellery made interesting playthings, so I proceeded to throw them out the window. A few photographs taken of us printed as postcards have survived. There is a lovely one of Mother looking terribly glamorous, even on the beach. There is also a telling photograph-postcard of me on the beach playing in the sand. It is addressed to Mother's sister in Serbia and what she has written on the back expresses her maternal detachment rather well:

'My dear Sister,
As you can see, this child adores the water and sand. We are going to stay here until the end of the month. Hugs and kisses from Beba.'

'This child adores the water' describes rather well my mother's ambivalence towards her nameless daughter. It was to become a source of pain for me in later years.

My father does not appear in any photos from this time, perhaps an indication that he may not have been with us. Of him, I have no memory whatsoever.

One of my few memories of when I was three years old is of my mother's two Great Danes, called Bim and Boom. They were patient dogs and tolerated my playful antics, one of which was trying to put my hand down their throats to see what was going on. One day Bim, or Boom, who were about three times my size, had had enough and picked me up by the collar and dumped me at my mother's feet. Mother would tell me later that she felt this to be an excellent way to discipline children. On another occasion, I was standing outside a shop with Bim and Boom seated closely on either side of me. A stranger came by and asked if the dogs belonged to me. In response I introduced them formally, 'Posso presentarle Bim Pavlović i Boom Pavlović.' Allow me to present Bim Pavlović and Boom Pavlović.

Just like the war stories, the post-war stories were just as difficult to assemble. My mother stayed in Geneva for some weeks at a time, where she had trained as a simultaneous translator for the recently established United Nations. She always came back to Genoa, or maybe it was Torino - I had found a photo of my parents taken there - and then would return to Geneva for a spell of work when she needed the money. Judging by her stories, my father had many girlfriends.

'He had a Jesus Christ complex and wanted to save every woman he met,' Mother would scoff later.

Accordingly, Mother had many admirers and lovers, which was not difficult to believe, and she seemed to move in sophisticated circles. There were trips to Nice, Monte Carlo and supposedly a brief meeting with Prince Phillip from whom she bought a dog.

Photographs were also taken of Mother at Villa Anna in San Vicenzo on the Tuscan coast, depicting her in shorts, which show off her long tanned legs. Despite this evidence, I believe my parents must have suffered some hardships, being refugees. However, their life of travelling between the Italian and French Rivieras was typical of my mother, who never strayed far from her path of upholding the privileges of her birthright.

In the European spring of 1949, my parents emigrated to Australia. It was decided that I would not accompany them, but instead should go to live in the Faeroe Islands in the middle of the North Atlantic where Sigrid's older sister was going to take care of me. Being a three-year old, I had no idea what was going on, otherwise I might rightly have asked: 'Hey, why are you going to Australia without me?' As with much of the information about my early years, the real reason would only be revealed to me much later.

## Chapter Two

*A*T THE SAME time as my parents left Italy for Australia in 1949 so did Sigrid and I, though for a destination that could hardly have been further away from Australia. It was to be the longest journey of my young life.

Sigrid and I left by train from Genoa. It was April, I think. Our Thomas Cook itinerary took us to Milan, Basel and Frankfurt. The trains were so crowded; the whole of Europe seemed to be on the move. We were fortunate to have a wagon-lits carriage and the narrow bunk beds were welcoming, though unfamiliar. The airy bedroom that I had shared with Sigrid in Genoa had had such a high ceiling that it seemed to touch the sky. But now, in the tight confines of the sleeping car, I could almost reach the bunk bed above me with my small arms. Others were not so lucky. They spent the entire night standing in the narrow passageway, most smoking endlessly, or sitting on their suitcases as the only means of getting some sleep. Sigrid kept me well away from this unkind reality. Many people were still displaced, searching for lost family members or simply searching for a new life. Above us, the British and US aeroplanes were continuing to airlift supplies to Berlin, in response to the Soviet's closing of that city from the West. The North Atlantic Treaty Organisation had just been set up to provide for the defense of Western Europe and North America against the perceived threat of the USSR.

After a brief stop in Frankfurt, we broke our journey at the Danish frontier station of Padborg, where we stayed for two nights with Faeroese friends of Sigrid. They lived in a flat, over the Padborg post office, and their daughter, Annelise Hansen, later sent a photograph of me taken in her parent's garden. I am wearing a smart coat and matching hat, unmistakably of Italian design. Annelise wrote:

'You and your mum were on the way from Genoa to Tórshavn and stayed with us in Padborg as my parents knew your mother from Tórshavn.'

It was not my real mother that Annelise was writing about, but Sigrid, whom she understood to be my mother. Sigrid always referred to herself as 'Mamma Sigrid', both in speech and correspondence to me. I always assumed that I must have entered Denmark as her daughter, as I had no passport and was stateless like so many in Europe at the time. This technicality would remain a puzzle for a long time.

Sigrid and I spent a couple of nights in Copenhagen before boarding the old passenger steamer, the SS *Tjaldur*, owned by the Faeroese Shipping Company. Earlier, the Faeroese had been reliant on Danish shipping services bound for Iceland, where Tórshavn was an intermediate stop. Desperately in need of their own regular service to and from Denmark, the Faeroese purchased an old passenger steamship that had been plying the West Indies and proudly christened her *Tjaldur,* oyster catcher, after the Faeroese national bird. Sigrid had sailed on this ship when she had left Tórshavn to work in Denmark. However, on a calm summer's day in June 1946, the *Tjaldur* ran aground in thick fog about a kilometre off the coast of Eysturoy Island and sank to the bottom. Only one man was drowned, but the loss of his life and that of the first Faeroese-owned ship was described by the newspapers as a national tragedy.

The vessel we were to sail in was the replacement *Tjaldur*, a second-hand steam ship, originally built in 1915 in Reykjavik. I watched with Sigrid as a large amount of cargo was loaded. I was soon to learn that almost everything had to be imported into the

Faeroe Islands, even basics such as flour, fruit, vegetables, coal, timber and tools.

We had our own cabin with bunks just like on the train. There was, however, a peculiar smell on board. It was not the salty sea air, but an unctuous combination of engine oil and rancid cooking grease. It made me feel sick, even before we sailed, but as the *Tjaldur* began to roll unmercifully in the heavy seas, I became horribly seasick. Sigrid seemed fine and kept smiling at me. Our cabin had a porthole with a view of the grey frantic waves. I lay in bed for the entire sixty-five hour journey watching the frothy spray against the porthole, tormenting me as I continued to throw up. All the while Sigrid kept wiping my face with a flannel.

The Atlantic was still rough as we approached the misty treeless islands that, unbeknown to me, were to be my new home. Anyone who has spent a winter in these storm-ravaged islands will soon understand why they are completely devoid of trees, outside of the odd sheltered garden. I was born in a Renaissance country, surrounded by centuries of exquisite architecture, paintings and music. I was coming to live in a barren country, surrounded by fog, a lot of grass, moss and rocky islets or skerries - a term used by my new neighbours, the Scots, some three hundred kilometres away, to describe their similar topography. Remoteness and isolation were the stuff of this place, typified by a family that lived on the island of Stóra Dímun whose farmhouse was protected from the gale force winds by two stone walls reinforced with steel wire.

The sea was calmer as we entered Tórshavn harbour, but a thick fog encircled us. I, too, was in my own fog of uncertainty; I had no idea of what was happening, least of all that I would be living here without my parents and especially without Sigrid, from whom I had never been separated for even one day.

15

## Chapter Three

AS SIGRID AND I disembarked from the *Tjaldur*, I had difficulties finding my land legs, having spent the whole passage in bed. Sigrid took me up to a strange man, who was standing next to a car. He was dressed differently from anyone I had seen in Genoa, with his knee-high breeches and soft brown shoes that looked like the slippers. Sigrid said it was her brother, Júst (pronounced Yoost).

'It's only a short trip from the pier to Bakkahella 4, where my sisters live,' Sigrid told me gently, as I must have looked bewildered. Júst soon stopped the car outside a black house. We got out and walked towards a brown door. It opened immediately. I was about to meet my new mothers.

I held tightly on to Sigrid's hand as we entered the black house. The entrance hall was painted brown, with dark brown trimmings. I remember this most distinctly. And there in the gloomy corridor stood another stranger, who Sigrid said was Mia, her older sister. Mia spoke rapidly to us in a startling tongue. Her voice was gravelly. I didn't understand a single word she said as I could only speak Italian. Then Mia came towards me and bent down, putting her pale lined face close to mine as her light blue-grey eyes eagerly searched mine. I wanted to cry, as I was afraid of this stranger and the unfamiliar surroundings. Mia, short for Marie, was to be my new mother and the black house, my new home. Her dark grey hair was pulled tightly into a bun at the base of her neck. Thin

16

strands of hair were sticking out here and there giving the appearance of a broken spider's web. She had a thin upper lip and a thick chest. I thought she looked old and I didn't like her unfamiliar smell. I was used to Sigrid's talcum-powdered scent.

Yet another pale stranger appeared in the hallway. Sigrid said this was her youngest sister named Louisa. She was also old. It was not that I was able to discern their ages in actual years, it was just a sense that I had. I didn't think that Sigrid looked old, even though there was little age difference between the sisters. However, coming from a country of mainly brown-eyed and dark-haired people, I suppose too that I noticed the stark physical contrast. Louisa was called Visa and was of slight build. Little did anyone know that one day her name would be carried on a small plastic card by millions of people around the world.

We proceeded into the kitchen where I was given something to eat that was unfamiliar and I looked up at Sigrid and shook my head. I had not spoken a word since our arrival. Then Mia showed me a jar containing something red. I recognised it as being *conserva*, jam, and she spread it on some bread. Suddenly I was feeling very hungry and was pleased to be eating something familiar, all the while slipping off the chair and edging wordlessly towards Sigrid.

I have little recollection of my first couple of years in Tórshavn. Soon after we arrived, Sigrid left to go back to work in Italy. Some weeks later, in a postcard to me from Genoa, dated 3 June 1949, she wrote in Italian:

'Dearest Gugghi I am looking forward to seeing you soon. I miss you. With lots of kisses Mamma Sigrid.'

I confess that after a while I didn't miss her much, though for a long time it felt strange going to bed without Sigrid's familiar, 'Buona notte, Antoinetta,' or 'Gugghi', her pet name for me. No one spoke to me in Italian any more and soon I became fluent in Føroyar, the Old Norse language of the Faeroes. I never addressed Visa or Mia as 'Mamma'. I may have called Sigrid that as a baby and I naturally loved her as I had been with her since my birth, but Sigrid was no longer with and me and neither were my parents. It was all very confusing.

Mia worked at the Telephone Exchange, not far from our house in a drab modern building, and Visa was a teacher at the local school, which was made out of lovely basalt stone. While they were at work, I was taken care of by Ulla-With-Bright-Yellow-Hair, the daughter of a friend of Mia's. I was happy to have such a young and colourful substitute. Ulla's hair was dead straight and her fringe looked as if her mother had ironed it into place each morning. My hair was dark brown and very curly. Ulla's mother, Lisa undir Kletti, which translated into English as Lisa Beneath Rocky Ground, also worked at the Telephone Exchange.

On arriving home from school, I was more interested in heading straight for the pantry, where Ulla-With-the-Bright-Yellow-Hair poured out a glass of milk for me and gave me biscuits, which were kept in an old Danish biscuit tin. Then it was upstairs to the Bedroom of the Dolls where I lost myself in making up interesting games until Mia came home.

Ulla-With-Bright-Yellow-Hair played with me inside the black house as the weather was mostly stormy. It never stayed calm for long. Growing up on these islands, I was soon to realise the thousand-odd kilometres of coastline were ceaselessly pounded by the mighty Atlantic waves, so much so that the enormous rock pinnacles had been worn unevenly to form weird and wonderful shapes with equally weird names. 'Dog's Tongue', 'The Troll's Head', 'The Witch's Finger', and 'Shag Pond'. Folklore has it that these are solidified giants - giants after all, being identified with the creation of the world. It was common knowledge that The Troll's Head was the leftover body part of a giant troll, who fastened the islands of Nólsoy and Streymoy together with his hair, which he used as a rope, his intention being to make one large island out of two. The giant went into the sea, dragging the two islands behind him. Unfortunately, even his huge neck proved too weak for the task, and his head broke off and promptly turned into a rock with the first ray of the sun.

I was told one winter that in some areas the mighty waves had lifted enormous rocks and thrown them onto the shore, requiring the strength of two men to remove one rock. I recall only too well many winters when wild storms raged for days on end. I would watch the giant waves crashing against the shore, sending spray up so high that it would reach the front row of buildings in the harbour. It didn't matter where I stood, I could always hear the Sea Voice calling, sometimes soft and gentle, but mostly loud and threatening. At first, I didn't understand what it was saying until I stopped and listened intently and then I understood every word:

'The islands will be worn away by the power of my waves and slowly I will sink them as well.'

I wanted to tell someone about this threat, but I was unsure if other people knew about the Sea Voice, so I kept it to myself.

The mighty Atlantic waves had already done considerable damage to the westernmost island of Mykines. No one I knew ever wanted to go there and only a few people were brave enough to live there. It did not have a harbour, only a landing site and there was a good chance of having one's boat and oneself smashed to bits against the rocks. Here vertical basalt cliffs soared to great heights. We called them *fuglabjørg*, bird cliffs, because every summer, they became home to thousands of birds, all seeking nesting ground with a dress-circle view. For the birds, the island was perfect, in contrast to the few humans living there, who struggled to make an existence.

Being hardy survivors of the early Viking settlers, the Faeroese that I lived among were used to battling the elements. In Faeroese, the name for the Faeroe Islands is *Føroyar* (pronounced 'furr-ja') meaning Sheep Islands, presumably because the Norsemen found the islands stocked with sheep, but no one knew why for sure. *Faar* in Scandinavian means sheep and *oy* is island. However, some scholars believed Føroyar was derived from a Celtic word similar to Gaelic 'fearan', meaning the 'Far Islands'.

19

Most outlying villages and hamlets remained isolated and the islands themselves were isolated to a great degree from the rest of the world. Our nearest neighbouring country required a couple of days' rough crossing. I was isolated from my real family, both geographically and emotionally. There was no quick way for me to get out of our archipelago and I came to realise that except for Sigrid, no one from the outside would come to visit me. My isolation was complete.

Antonia's parents, Branko and Beba, in happier
times shortly after their wedding,
Belgrade, 1943.

Antonia and her mother, Beba, outside the Ospidale Evangelico Internazionale during a quick hello-goodbye visit. Genoa, January 1948.

*SS Tjaldur (*ex *Guilfoss),* berthed in Tórshavn Harbour in 1949.

## Chapter Four

*O*UR TWO-STOREY BLACK house that was now my home did
not sustain much damage from these frequent storms, though it
groaned and creaked and the rain made a terrible noise on our
corrugated iron roof. The house seemed very big for just the three
of us. Some time in the past, there must have been more occupants,
though I had not been told about them. It was not unusual in
Faeroese families for members of various generations to live under
the one roof. There was 'Our Side' of the house, where we lived
and the 'Other Side', a later extension, where no one lived, except
for possibly a ghost. I liked to imagine that the Other Side had
been built for Mia and her future husband, who had died shortly
before their wedding day.

The kitchen on Our Side had a black cast-iron coal-burning
stove in the far corner, under the steps, which led up to the second
level. As coal was often scarce and expensive, peat was a common
substitute. Mia told me that when she was young, there were still
homes in some of the villages with ancient chimney-less hearths in
the middle of their one and only room, which had no windows. To
increase the heat on our stove was not a matter of simply turning a
knob. Instead Mia had to take a series of cast-iron rings off with
tongs to enlarge the opening, a function only performed by Mia
and Visa for safety reasons. In the morning, before the stove was
re-lit, I would help Mia to empty the grate of ash. All ironing had
to be done in the kitchen, as the only way to heat the flat iron was

on top of the hot stove. I could tell the iron was heavy by the way Mia lifted it up and brought it down with a thump.

We had running cold water in our kitchen sink. Outside town, I had seen houses with a pump in the yard, so I was proud that we had such a modern facility. There was no fridge, but there was really no need for one, as the cool larder off the kitchen seemed more than adequate for our food storage. We even had a hand-cranked wall telephone in the hallway. Mia had to turn a lever once or twice and the operator at the telephone exchange came on the line. I could hear Mia shouting into the phone to be heard and the operator, who had a rewarding job, could always listen in to the call.

A tiny sitting room led off the kitchen, where we retired to every evening. Here Mia sat in the same wicker chair for the greater part of her life, in the same V-necked nylon dress with a small white printed pattern on a black background. Mia liked to smoke cigars, which she did every evening. When the cigar was nearing the end, she would get out her pocketknife and insert it into the cigar, so that she could smoke it all the way down. Mia was an expert at blowing out smoke rings and could do so on command.

'Oh Mia, please make three rings' I would beg. And sure enough three perfect rings would escape one by one from her mouth, which she formed into a sort of fish orifice in order to perform this feat. Mia was also able to smoke her cigar at least halfway down without the ash falling off. I watched the ash on the cigar grow longer and longer and sometimes mischievously wished for it to fall off, but it never did. Mia knew exactly how long she could go before giving the cigar that certain flick with the thumb over the ashtray. On one occasion as Mia was dozing in her wicker chair, her cigar fell out of her hand and down her V-necked frock. Mia had to stand up quickly and shake the dress in order to avoid getting burned, the ash from the cigar falling from under her dress like dead skin. I was terribly amused. Mia understandably was not and gave me a rare disapproving look.

Books were precious. I gathered this because Visa was often bringing books home with torn covers and loose pages in need of repair. I sat next to Visa as she proceeded to restore the books. I watched intently as Visa cut to size lovely paper with wavy watermarks in different shades of brown with just a hint of blue and green. Sigrid had brought these decorative end papers with her from Italy and I was told that they came from a special place called Florence. Carefully, Visa applied a white paste on the outside of a book, gently placed the paper over it and patted it flat. Much to my delight she let me help her with the patting down and I learned to love books even before I could read them. I treated them as gently as though they were porcelain dolls. Then onto the spine Visa placed a strip of cloth on which she afterwards wrote the title of the book with a long scratchy pen, constantly dipping it in ink. Some of the old books were written in the Gothic script, which Visa taught me to read when I was older. I would practice for hours writing the capital letters since I found these very fancy. I used a brown pencil and purposely smudged the rest of the page with the brown lead, as I believed this gave it that authentic medieval look.

We hardly ever used the dining room and even less the living room, which pleased me, as it was far too dark for my liking. On one wall hung numerous framed photographs of the Sivertsen clan, both past and present, watching my every move. Only two items drew me to this room. A table lamp with an unusual oblong shade on which was painted a scene of Venice, a present from Sigrid, and an album in which were kept photographs of my parents.

Even though there were four bedrooms on Our Side, Mia insisted that she and I share the same bedroom. The rectangular room was long and narrow and our single beds were placed at opposite ends against the wall that was no more than the length of the beds. There was a washbasin near Mia's bed on 'Her Side'. We had no bathroom. A large window on 'My Side' afforded a lovely view of the harbour and the Nautical School across the bay. The branches of a solitary tree reached up to the window, so that in summer I could watch the little brown wrens with their erect tails, hopping quickly from branch to branch, singing sweetly. In winter, they lived in a birdhouse nailed to the outside wall and I would put bread out for them. We called them 'mouse's brother', because of their similar size and colour to the mouse and their habit of darting about from one place to another. One autumn, I watched from my bed as the hurricane force winds tore the leaves off that poor tree in just one day.

I hated sleeping in the same room with Mia, hence the necessity for me to divide the room mentally into Her Side and My Side. I pleaded with her to let me move into one of the smaller bedrooms where my dolls were kept, but she would not hear of it. I disliked her intensely because of this. Despite Mia's good intentions and care, my bed was not a place of deep childlike sleep but rather of frequent nightmares. To top it all, Mia had a wooden board fashioned to fit the length of my bed, preventing me from falling on to the floor, as my frequent tossing and turning found me many times out of my bed rather than in it. I resented this sensible arrangement and regarded it as similar to being tied to my bed. I found her constant vigilance to be suffocating.

One night I was about five years old and afflicted with a childhood disease; I think it may have been measles. I was burning up with a high fever and woke up suddenly from a bad dream. In my delirious state I called out, 'Mamma, Mamma.' Mia was promptly at my side, given the short distance between our beds. She leaned over me. 'Here I am.'

'I don't want you,' I almost shouted, 'I want my Mamma.'

'I am your Mamma now,' she replied, putting her lined face close to mine and I was immediately repulsed by her unpleasant smell.

My response was immediate: 'No, you're not. You're too old and ugly.'

I didn't want Mia or Visa or Sigrid to be my mothers. I didn't want their love. I just wanted my own mother. That night I came to the awful realisation that my mother was not part of my life any longer. I was about to cry, but stopped myself, as I didn't want Mia back at my side. Why had I been taken away from my mother,

I asked myself? No one had ever explained anything to me so I was left to conclude that Mia was entirely responsible from my present circumstances. All of a sudden I missed Sigrid and her talcum-powder smell. I missed our sunny room in Genoa that I had not minded sharing with her. I longed for the real mother I did not know.

My pillow was warm and damp from perspiration. I turned it over so that the coolness of the other side would keep me awake a little longer. I wanted to think about the photos I had of my mother in the album, looking young and beautiful. My father, too, was very handsome. I was extremely proud of their looks, though I didn't remember them at all and had no direct contact with them. I had no idea what kind of life they were leading in this town called Adelaide in South Australia, and neither did Mia.

I had arrived in Tórshavn with several photos of my parents, which Mia placed in the album. I would study these photos over and over and constructed my parents' character according to their looks. My favourite photograph was of my mother seated in an armchair, wearing a lovely short-sleeved dress with dark piping and a matching belt. She is looking lovingly up at my father who is sitting on the armrest holding her hand and looking adoringly at her. I concluded that they were as sweet, loving and tender towards each other and everyone, as they would be towards me one day. I was way off the mark! Another photo depicts my parents seated at a table set under a tree in a garden. They are with several friends. It looks like some kind of celebration. My mother is wearing a soft patterned dress. I liked to think it was red. She is very tanned and her long thick hair is curly and shiny. My father is in a beautifully cut double-breasted suit. Everyone is laughing. Taken after the party, another photo shows my parents leaving in an open carriage. Mother has put on an elegant cream-coloured coat over her dress. Where did I fit into these pictures? I didn't and so I closed my eyes. My parents went back to being remote images.

26

Mother would write occasionally to Mia. Since Mother and I had no language in common, as I had forgotten the Italian of my infancy, we did not correspond ourselves. Mother also paid Mia for my care. How much I do not know, but she kept that financial sustenance going for all the years I was in the Faeroes, even during those first difficult years in Australia, when she was no doubt stretching to make ends meet herself.

Adelaide, where my parents settled, must have been a disastrous choice for a sophisticated couple, not to mention one with their fiery Slavic temperament. Their marriage had been failing ever since day one and the quiet, non-cosmopolitan city of Adelaide did not help matters. Among serious complaints about my father's infidelities and lack of financial support, possibly all valid, Mother would complain later that, 'One couldn't even get a cup of coffee in *that* place... and those awful soft white sandwiches.'

Fresh coffee was not available in the shops and had to be ordered from Sydney and mailed to Adelaide. An outrage for coffee-loving Serbs. A considerable number of Yugoslavs and Hungarians had settled in Adelaide and, according to one of them, my parents started a restaurant. Even if this were true, my mother would never have admitted to it. However, my parents were in good company, as a photograph shows them seated in a restaurant - possibly theirs - with Yugoslav artist Stanislav Rapotec. In 1951, while still in his figurative period, Rapotec made a charcoal painting of my mother in which he captured perfectly her shapely legs.

About Adelaide, Mother was tight-lipped, except to offer that my father returned to his profession as an architect. In fact, my father's degree was not recognised and he became a building contractor, again something that my mother failed to tell me. Being multi-lingual, Mother was able to find work as a translator in the courts.

A few years later, Mother moved to Sydney, where she lived in financially improved and happier circumstances. I had no idea what happened to my father as he was never mentioned in

Mother's letters to Mia. I suppose that I would have last seen him in Genoa before leaving for Tórshavn, but possibly I didn't, since according to Mother, he did not acknowledge me as his daughter.

'It was to avoid taking any responsibility for you,' was the explanation.

However, there is a strong physical characteristic that proves his fatherhood. On his left hand his small finger was slightly crooked and he could not straighten it. I have the same characteristic and so does my son, Andrew.

After Mia had tried to 'masquerade' as my mother, I decided that henceforth, I would have as little physical contact with her as possible. I felt that this course of action was my only resort. Someone had to be punished for putting me in this parent-less situation. Little did I realise that I was punishing myself as well. Consequently, I spent the rest of my years in Tórshavn, in a self-imposed un-hugged state. I only allowed Sigrid to hug and kiss me on her holiday visits to the islands. I learned to sustain myself emotionally but did not enjoy my isolation. I longed to be part of an ordinary young family. It was painfully obvious to me that all my school friends had parents who were considerably younger than my mothers in the black house. With no regular contact from my own mother, none at all from my father, and my own virtual rejection of my carers, I had to turn to myself for solace and courage.

It was not easy for any of us. Mia, a spinster in her late fifties, had suddenly been entrusted with the full time care of a young child. Her sister Visa was in failing health. In the absence of Sigrid, who visited us every year, Mia became the dominant force in my new life, yet I could not love her. I knew that my parents were alive because I had photos of them, proof enough I reasoned. I was not an orphan, I concluded, and therefore I decided to reserve my love for my real mother.

## Chapter Five

*J*ÚST, THE BROTHER of my mothers, his wife Tulla and their four children lived next door to us in an unpainted cement house. Even though their children were older than me, I enjoyed being with them and they didn't seem to mind at all that I hung around them. Beautiful looking Rachel (pronounced Ra-quel) was the first-born and several years older than me. Rachel had poise and charm and I admired her tremendously. I could not imagine that she ever got her clothes soiled like the rest of us, an easy thing to do with the constant rain and mud. Then came the two boys, Júst (it was traditional for the first born son to carry his father's Christian name) and Sjúrður (pronounced Shoo-rour), both with the same aquamarine blue eyes as their father, and the youngest girl, Anna Maria, the closest in age to me, though still a few years my senior. Completing the family was Per, the black and white Border collie.

I never found out why their house was not painted, but this deficiency certainly added to its unattractiveness; a true example of the dreary but functional architecture of the post-war era. The ground floor of the unpainted house was given over to the workshop and garage and outside steps led up to the first level of the living quarters. There were a few cement houses in our immediate area and even though the others were painted, it did not noticeably improve their appearance and they looked out of place among the predominantly small, black-tarred, single-storeyed wooden dwellings, many roofed with sod. The houses stood close together, divided by narrow twisting lanes. The window frames were painted either white or red and the front doors faced straight onto the street.

Despite our age differences the Sivertsen children included me in some of their games, or rather I included myself in theirs. Being allowed to play with the Sivertsen children, without Mia's supervision, was a great source of relief, providing some respite from the constant watchful eye of Mia, as family were deemed to be safe company.

Every winter, with the first fallen snow, they would help me to build an igloo next to our house under the window of our hallway or, more accurately, I helped them. I loved the crunchy sound of the snow under foot and how it was easy to shape in my hand when making the bricks for the hut. Although it would have failed Eskimo building codes, the igloo looked really magnificent. It was beautifully rounded and had a small tunnel opening. However, Per could never resist leaving his luminous yellow calling card on the side, which spoiled the appearance somewhat. We always built the igloo in a hurry, as with temperatures only remaining below freezing for a short time, the snow would never stay on the ground for long. Nonetheless, this mildness of temperature was hardly noticeable because the wild storms of winter raged for many days bringing cold bitter winds and driving up the wind-chill factor. Even the calm Faeroese would be driven to near madness by the savage winds that rarely abated.

The Sivertsen children had a wooden sled, whose design had not changed since Viking times. An identical Viking one, though larger in size, was on display at the Oslo Museum. The sled fitted only two of us and we would go flying down the gentle slope. Neighbourhood children would join us on their sleds and Mia allowed me to participate in these rides provided I only rode with the Sivertsen children. She would watch me through the kitchen window, forever vigilant. Spring brought some almighty snowstorms, but we soon grew tired of building igloos after each snowfall.

When the snow was finally gone, we would play in Júst's rowing boat. He kept it on the pebbly stones of Bakkahella when not in use, as he was concerned that his children might be tempted to take it out on their own. Instead, we contented ourselves with climbing on board the land-bound vessel and pretended that we were sailing on the high seas in a beautiful big boat with plenty of food and no adults. It was a safe adventure that relied on our collective imagination rather than the hard realities of local waters. Most people owned a rowing boat, which was used as both a means of getting from one settlement to another and for catching the family's dinner. The Faroeman is born with an oar in his hand, so the saying went.

The old part of Tórshavn, where we lived was called Reyni, meaning Stony Ground. There was no shortage of stones. I especially liked going down to the flat rocky peninsula that divided the harbour into two bays: the East Bay where the ferries came in and the West Bay, over which my bedroom window faced. Though close to home, Mia only allowed me to go to the harbour if the Sivertsen children promised to hold me by each hand.

The peninsula has always been known as Tinganes (Assembly or Parliament Headland), as in the times of the first Norse settlers, the *ting*, an assembly for law and communal transactions, representing a form of democracy Viking style, was most likely held in the open on the outermost point of this peninsula. Carvings could still be seen in the rocks, indicating the rightful place held by the different chiefs in the *ting*. The Viking chieftains settled with their families and thralls – just another name for slaves – on the main islands where they built farms. Once a year, the Viking chiefs travelled from all over the Faeroes to meet *al fresco* in Tinganes in late spring or early summer. The *ting* was set within ropes, held together by poles and the setting holes are still visible. There were no buildings then, so it would have been impossible to have parliament 'sitting' in winter. Even these hardy Vikings would have been blown into the sea.

The early Norsemen most likely chose the peninsula as the best place for their annual meetings on account of its central location in relation to other islands. Gradually the meetings fostered a market place, which by the Middle Ages had developed into a permanent trading post with warehouses. Tórshavn grew from a population of one hundred in the 1580s, to around 5500 when I lived there in the 1950s. To me, Tórshavn seemed like a big village, there were few cars; ducks and chickens ruled the roads, and every corner of it could be reached by foot in a short time.

Tórshavn is named after the Norse god *Thór* and *havn* or *havnin* meaning harbour. The official symbol of the city is Thór's hammer, which has the characteristics of a boomerang, for when he hurled it in the air against giants, or whoever, it returned to his hand of its own accord. Thór created a lot of storms and thunder, which Tórshavn experiences rather often. His father was Oðin (the All-Father), a one-eyed patriarch, having exchanged one eye for wisdom.

Tórshavn was not a natural harbour. Besides being at the mercy of Thór wild storms from the southeast, the harbour had only a short breakwater and a modest quay. In fact, it had been dubbed, rather unkindly, 'the port without a harbour'. There was not enough space for the ships and I used to watch the lighters ferrying goods and passengers ashore. The ocean liners in particular, that stopped there for a day, were too large to come alongside and had to stand off in the harbour, while passengers were transferred by small tenders to the quay.

The flat rocks of Tinganes occupied a small area of the harbour, but for me they held a vast playground of intrigue and history. I liked stopping at one place in particular called Krákusteinur (Crow Rock). I would stand on the very spot where Visa had told me the parliament used to burn the beaks of predatory birds that had to be collected each year to satisfy a 'beak duty tax'. This bizarre impost dated back to early times when, in the interest of protecting the sheep from birds of prey, a law was introduced whereby every male person on the islands between fifteen and fifty years of age (residents of Tórshavn were exempted) was bound to pay a tax in the form of beaks. The minimum was one raven's beak or two beaks from the eagle or hooded crow. Each year, the beaks were sent to the *løgting*, parliament, in Tórshavn, where an official counted them and imposed fines on districts not meeting their quota. Thereafter, one of the annual duties of the parliament was to take the beaks down to these rocks and to burn them with great ceremony. The beak tax was abolished in the late nineteenth century, by which time the Faeroese had almost succeeded in eradicating these bird species.

This was the town of my childhood, with its ancient traditions and beliefs.

## Chapter Six

AS MUCH AS I loved playing with the Sivertsen children, I loved even more being with their mother, Tulla, especially when she was preparing food, which seemed to be most of the time. I was certain that Tulla would live in my memory forever, because of her wonderful cooking. Mia was, well, a rotten cook really. So I was always pleased when we were invited next door where Tulla would prepare memorable meals. In between invitations, I would find any excuse to visit, just so I could sit in her kitchen.

Tulla impressed me from the beginning by creating a dessert consisting of a half-peach sitting on a bed of whipped vanilla cream, resembling a fried egg. I thought it terribly clever of her to do it this way. Tulla possessed an enormous amount of energy, despite her heavy build, continually busying herself with housework and cooking and never seeming to sit down except at mealtimes. She had a slightly ruddy complexion, as if she had been rushing around all day, which she probably had. Her kitchen was a steady hub of culinary activity and I loved to sit at the table and watch the goings on whenever I could.

The girls helped Tulla in the kitchen, while the boys were in the workshop below. Sjúrður was a good little carpenter. He made me a miniature doll's pram while Júst Junior had a talent for anything mechanical.

As Mia worked all day, we used often to buy home-cooked food from Frøkun Ellingsgaard, who ran a pension. Júst Junior would obligingly go to Frøkun Ellisgaard to pick up the food for us in a tiffin carrier. It had four aluminium containers stacked neatly on top of one another with a handle on the very top for easy carrying.

When the sheep were slaughtered in October, Tulla made use of every part of the sheep, in keeping with good Faeroese practice. The blood was collected to make blood sausages, or 'black pudding' as the English call it. Blood was also used for making *blódpannukoda,* a pancake made of blood, flour and tallow mixture. I did not much like any of these specialties, but I still loved watching Tulla prepare them with a great sense of style.

The making of blood sausages was especially fascinating. First Tulla would cut open a lamb's stomach, rinse it well under cold water and lay it flat on a wooden board. Then she cut it into equal parts and, with needle and thread, deftly sewed each part into a pouch, leaving a small opening. Next, in a bowl she would mix blood, water, salt, flour and chopped up tallow, the hard fat enclosing the lamb's organs. Once the mixture had thickened and passed the spoon-can-stand-up-in-it test, she proceeded to stuff the pouches with the mixture, but never more than two-thirds full. Then she would nimbly sew up the opening with her scrubbed-to-the-bone-fingers, prick the pouches, which now looked liked sausages, with a pin and place them in boiling water. There they remained for over two hours, while the blood mixture congealed.

Other sausages, using the intestines as casing were prepared from various items of sheep's offal such as the heart and liver. Nothing was wasted. Tulla would scrape off the thin layer of meat covering the ribs and then cut this meat into wide strips. Next she rolled each strip up with some onion and other things I don't recall and secured the individual rolls with string. The *rullupylsa* was then placed in a big pot to be given the usual two hours' boiling treatment. This seemed to be the standard time for most boiled foods. Even the bladder was put to use, not to eat, but to be filled with air to form a little balloon. It was tied with a string and hung up as a decoration at Christmas. It was yellow, of course, and lasted a long time, before shrinking.

Tulla also prepared delicious sweet soups. One of them was made with sour milk that she served with raisins and sugar. *Fiskaknettir*, large fish balls containing minced haddock or cod and lumps of sheep's suet, was another favourite dish of mine, but only if prepared by Tulla's fair hands. When Tulla made the Danish recipe *fiska gratin*, fish with melted cheese, we were eating 'Danish food' the name we gave to the style of cooking, or anything not grown or slaughtered on the islands.

From my seat at the kitchen table I would also observe Tulla's husband Júst, whom I secretly called The Silent Man. Much as Tulla hardly ever sat down, Júst hardly ever spoke. The harsh and hazardous life of the islands bred rugged and reticent men. The women were strong and serious, or so it seemed to me, though they were more talkative. However, Tulla was not as earnest, to my mind, as either Mia or Visa.

Júst was always dressed in Faeroese clothes. Black jodhpurs with metal buttons at the side and long dark grey socks, a knitted dark blue jersey, over which he wore a short collar-less jacket adorned with metal buttons. On his feet, he wore home-made skin shoes, the Faeroes answer to Indian moccasins: sole-less slippers, made out of tanned cowhide or sheepskin and tied with woollen strings. He made them himself in the workshop in the garage. Being worn outdoors, meant they wore out quickly, so he was frequently fashioning new ones. I used to wonder how Júst could tolerate walking on our streets that were covered with all those lumpy stones.

Perhaps, however, Júst's feet didn't pound the pebbly pavement as much as I imagined, as he was in the car transport business. In those days, there were no public buses or taxis as private companies ran most transport routes. People either walked along well-trodden, often slippery paths, marked with cairns set up at regular intervals, or went by open rowing boat from village to

36

village, though a ferry service run by the Smyril Line, was operating between the major islands. Júst was the first person to have a car on the Islands, a Model-T Ford, which he and another man bought together in May 1922. The road system was still undeveloped. The roads were narrow, without any permanent surface, covering only the main islands and were broken up into numerous segments. It was not unusual for a stretch of road to end abruptly. The roads were really just an extension of the sea routes. That first year Júst could not have driven his Model T Ford any further than 32 kilometres out of town. Later, Júst expanded his transport business with the purchase of a lorry and a Ford Consul replaced the Model-T Ford.

On his head Júst wore the distinctive dark blue 'liberty' cap, folded down to one side. As a young man, Júst had worn a black and red striped cap, but on the death of his parents he had changed to a dark blue one, as was the custom. The cap had not changed much over the centuries, but the way of wearing it had. The old cap was roomier and was often used for carrying tobacco and matches on top of the head, whereas the new caps are worn empty and folded over to one side.

Sjúrður knew a story about a crafty Faeroese, who during hard times had acquired some butter that he hid inside his cap. On the way home, he met a friend and they stopped and chatted a while. The butter began to melt and he had to pretend to be wiping sweat off his brow. His behaviour was frowned upon and he was teased about it for months afterwards.

I loved to watch Júst as he took out a jack knife, something that all men carried, and went into the *hjallur,* situated off the kitchen. I would promptly follow him. We still would not have spoken one word to each other. The *hjallur* was a small outbuilding off the kitchen, made of upright wooden slats with narrow spaces in between, in which meat and fish were wind-dried by air draughts passing between the slats. Here, hung by its hind legs from a wooden rack was the prized *skerpikjøt,* a skinned uncooked carcass of lamb. It was split completely open and the ribcage was on full display. It had been air-dried for up to a year and was considered ready to eat when one couldn't stand the smell any longer! Júst would cut a thin sliver of this dark meat and chew on it thoughtfully at the kitchen sink. It had a rather pungent taste and required a good set of teeth and an equally strong jaw to chew. Air-dried mutton was considered a delicacy and of value for its nutrition and energy content. Also hanging in the *hjallur* were thick strips of whale meat and legs of lamb that had only been dried for a few months; these Tulla used for making soups and other cooked meat dishes. In years past, before food was imported from Denmark, air-dried mutton and salted whale meat would sustain families through the barren winters.

When visitors came, they were always offered a slice of *skerpikjøt*. It was always fun watching Danish visitors politely struggling with a tough piece of *skerpikjøt* in their mouth. Air-cured birds were another specialty. Fish was also hung to dry on rafters outside, under the eves of the roof.

Finished with his slicing, Júst would wipe his knife clean and, ignoring my watchful eye, start to chew his snack food. On returning to the kitchen, he took out a match, and with the aid of his cleaned knife, fashioned the perfect toothpick and proceeded with the maintenance of his healthy gums, all the while at the kitchen sink. Sometimes he would sharpen his knife and the kitchen knives with a stone and water. I wished that I would be able to do this one day, though I instinctively knew that it was man's work.

When I returned to our house the kitchen was usually empty. Visa would be resting in her room and Mia would be listening to the radio, smoking a cigar, each resolutely removed from her least favourite room in the house. Sometimes, a sweet smell would draw me into the kitchen. Mia had not been idle. On the stove simmered a large batch of rhubarb, freshly picked from our garden. Rhubarb stew was a staple diet in most households.

Our house did not have a *hjallur,* only a larder where all the food was kept. Here Mia would pour boiled milk into a large wide rimmed bowl and cover it with a cloth. Every morning, I skimmed the thick yellow layer of cream that had formed on top of the milk and placed it into another bowl. After a few days, we had beautiful clotted cream that I ate sprinkled with sugar. Sometimes Mia added the cut up stalks of angelica, our local source of vitamin C. It grew wild on top of the bird-cliffs, but was also grown at home in gardens. The larder was also where Mia kept the vile-tasting cod liver oil, which she had to force feed me once week. The thick rich oil made me feel quite ill afterwards. A cube of sugar was my reward for undergoing this ordeal.

A cow, which was kept in a dark small shed next to Júst's house, provided our daily milk supply. I so wanted to help milk the cow, but was always gently turned away from the task, as the few times I had been allowed to try it I would go into uncontrollable fits of laughter every time I squeezed the teats. Thankfully, the cow's hind legs and tail had been tied up; otherwise, I am sure she would have kicked over the bucket and sent me flying in the process. The best part was dipping a tin mug into the bucket and drinking the still warm milk. Each day on his way to school, Sjúrður took the cow to pasture in an area up from the West side of the harbour. The distance could be covered in only ten minutes, or so Sjúrður assured me, as the cow always went at full gallop. What a funny sight they made, the earnest little schoolboy running alongside a crazy galloping cow.

## Chapter Seven

AS IF RAIN, storms and year-round fog were not enough
Tórshavn had its share of fires. Not surprising for a town built
almost entirely out of wood.

One might wonder in a land of no trees, why most buildings
were constructed of wood. The first settlers found masses of
driftwood that had accumulated from shipwrecks over the
centuries. Much of it had been carried by the strong currents from
Norway and even as far away as Siberia. But this natural supply of
flotsam eventually ran out and wood was then imported from
Norway and the British Isles

In May 1950, a year after my arrival, a major fire broke out in a
building on the point of Tinganes. It was the Skansapakkhus,
Skansa Warehouse, which dated back to 1749. It happened late in
the evening. Guðrun, Tulla's niece (Guðrun's father was Tulla's
half-brother) was most fortunate to witness it and provided a
breathtaking first hand account the next day. Guðrun was by then a
young teenager, so I did not see her much. Guðrun told us she had
come home from a confirmation party that evening and was
preparing to go to bed:

'And then I looked out of my bedroom window, the sky was
red. I saw huge flames and very dark clouds forming.' She
continued excitedly as all eyes were on her. 'I went out to have a

better look but the firemen prevented us from coming too close, as there was so little land between the burning building and the sea.' None of us in Bakkahella 4 had seen the fire, as our bedrooms faced the other way.

A few weeks later in June another fire erupted. This time it was the Hotel Føroyar, the one and only hotel in town, if one could call it that. There were rooms for rent and guests had to get permission from the owner to use the kitchen. The original building burned down, but the new addition survived. A Danish cleaning girl died in the fire and three people were injured. I begged Mia to take me down to the site, and as we walked towards it, we were greeted by a disagreeable smell and I was sorry that we had come. When we arrived home, Mia went over to the stove to get the fire roaring in preparation for boiling some fish. I saw the flames. They were not very big, but still I asked: 'Will our house burn down too?'

In a short time, the man who had started the hotel fire was caught. He was a Dane, who, as it turned out, was responsible for both fires. At each fire he had been the first person on the scene and was keen to help the fire brigade put them out. He was tried in the local court and found guilty. Guðrun went to the hearing, and reported that the court was crammed full of very angry people. The Dane was shipped to Copenhagen to serve out his sentence. That same year, well known local, Christian Restorff began construction of a new hotel in the garden next to his old house. The foundation stone was placed on 5 August 1950 and already the following year on 1 November, a week before my fifth birthday, the Hotel Hafnia was opened for business. Its new kitchen would soon contribute significantly to the diet of the inhabitants of Bakkahella 4.

Visa, forever the teacher, said that one of the most devastating fires to ever take place in Tórshavn was in 1673. At the time, the Faeroes were undergoing the bleakest period in their history, aggravated by the corruption of a feudal overlord. Emissaries were sent to King Frederick III, who responded by sending inspectors to check the Trade Manager's accounts. When the manager received word of this, he asked his assistant to burn all the records. Unfortunately, there was rather a lot of gunpowder stored beside the chimney, which blew up and caused enormous damage to the whole area.

The stone guardhouse *Myrkastovan* (dark house) did not burn and was still standing when I lived on the island. Its basement contained cells that had been occupied by anyone who offended the overlord. Armed with this information, I would always rush past it on my playful rounds of Tinganes, for fear of any lingering miscreant souls from that time.

Often after Sunday lunch, Mia and I would walk around Tinganes, but not before I had sat still for twenty minutes, 'in order to digest your food'. This was Mia's strict rule after a meal. There was a place at the back of Tinganes, called *Úti á Bakka*, best translated as 'Out on the Cliffs', where weathered and grey-looking wooden boats were kept on the wide flat rocks. I was convinced it was the Graveyard of the Boats, but it was really where boats were laid up during winter, spared from the torments of the merciless Atlantic seas. One of the boats had a gash in the side and I was convinced that a sea monster had caused it. I climbed into one of the other boats and called out to Mia:

'Please Mia, may I go out in one of these when there are no big waves?' Immediately spoiling my chances by stipulating this condition. Mia shook her head. Seafaring was a risky business and even a short trip was out of the question.

Whenever I ran ahead of her, Mia would call after me, 'Antoinetta, where are you going?' Mia's diligence in taking care of me was such that she never let me out of her sight, except when she was working at the telephone exchange. As I grew older, this was a constant source of irritation, as I did not understand her feeling of grave responsibility for her charge.

If the weather looked promising and Mia was feeling energetic enough, we walked all the way to a little plantation of white spruce and silver fir, planted over a hundred years ago by an optimist. A unique feature in a treeless land.

Families and young couples could be seen walking around there on infrequent sunny days. As was my habit, I ran ahead of Mia and came to a small clearing. A couple were lying closely next to each other on the grass. The sun was shining. As I drew closer, I noticed that they were kissing - on the mouth. I found it rather a puzzling thing to be doing and I was pleased that no such thing had ever gone on in our black house.

'Come back, come back right now.' Mia's anxious voice reached the couple, who stopped their odd activity. I ran back to Mia at once, much to her surprise and turned my attention to the pond where a family of eider ducks were of much greater interest.

## Chapter Eight

AFTER THE FIRES, starting school was the next major event in my life.

The Nuns' School, as it was known locally – the official name was *Sankta Frans Skúli* (Saint Francis School) – was started in 1934 by two Catholic priests and two sisters of the order of the Franciscan Missionaries of Mary. They had been sent to Tórshavn on the prompting of a certain Cardinal Van Rossum. When passing through Tórshavn on his way to Iceland, the cardinal had found, much to his distress, that there was no Catholic ministry on the islands and decided to remedy this oversight. There was considerable controversy among the pious Evangelical Lutherans at the beginning when the Franciscans first arrived. Letters were sent to the newspaper about 'these Catholics in the Faeroes', creating a somewhat hostile reception for these unsuspecting missionaries.

Ironically, for hundreds of years, the Catholic religion had been the only Christian religion on the island, but no sooner had Martin Luther nailed his 95 theses on the church door at Wittenberg than the days of the original faith were numbered. Centuries later in 1857, Father Bauer, a Catholic priest, set up a ministry in the islands. In a period of twelve years he succeeded in converting only seven souls. He left realising the awful truth that this had not exactly been the highlight of his career. But here, some seventy-five years later, the Catholics had triumphantly returned, albeit minuscule in number. Their timing was bad, as the Faeroese were in the middle of a heated debate with the Danish authorities on the use of Faeroese as a language of instruction in schools, an important mark of their national identity. The local authorities felt that allowing Danish nuns to speak Danish in their school, would water down the arguments for the use of the Faeroese language. Finally, in 1937, the Faeroese language officially became the language of instruction, and the arguments regarding the Catholic presence lapsed.

Initially, the Nuns' School operated as a private school, without public support and with only a small subsidy from the local council. The school's financial situation was poor at first and remained so until after World War II. The stoic nuns tried to manage by charging modest tuition fees, supplemented by donations from friends. However, by the time I became a pupil, the school had gained a reputation for its excellent teaching and discipline and was well established. I presume that I was sent to the Nuns' School at Mother's request. Despite being born in Italy and to Eastern Orthodox parents, until this time, I had received no formal religious instruction and was certainly unfamiliar with the Catholic environment. Mother may have been disinterested in religion, but not so in education and she sent Mia the necessary funds for the school fees. The Sivertsen children attended the municipal school, where Visa taught. I would have liked us all to be in the same school.

The nuns were well educated and came from diverse European countries, as was reflected in their names. Sister Grada was Polish. The English Sister with the un-English name was called Burga. Other sisters were called Vand and Duffa and I can't venture to guess from which countries they came. I do remember that one of them had round shiny cheeks, much like the polished red apples that came on the ship from Denmark. Mia would buy several pieces of this precious fruit as a treat. There was a ritual to peeling the apples– for some reason, the skin was never eaten - and it was important to be extra careful so that the skin came off in one piece. The long piece of skin would then be thrown behind one's back to fall on the floor, forming a letter of the alphabet. From this, one could deduce the name of a future boyfriend or, at the very least, a boy who really liked you. I never understood the significance of this game, but performed it with great enthusiasm, as did Mia.

The nuns all seemed to be thick-bodied women, even allowing for the many-layered curtains with ropes that made up their sisterly habit. They were fluent in many languages and spoke to us in Faeroese with an accent, just as we spoke Danish with a Faeroese accent. New nuns were kept away from teaching until they had mastered our language. And master it they did. Everybody was pleased, especially the parents. The nuns were sticklers for good grammar and writing. Danish was a compulsory subject and was taught thoroughly according to law. Consequently, we could speak and write Danish just as well as Faeroese. School books were printed in Danish, except for our Faeroese reading and grammar book and Bible history.

The first story from our Faeroese reading book was a simple little tale about a boy, Per, who has a dog called Snar (a popular dog's name meaning 'quick'). Per loves Snar very much and doesn't want to sell him (why would he want to sell him, anyhow?). One day, Per and Snar go for a walk on the moor, where Snar suddenly keels over on his back and promptly dies (no explanation is given for his early demise). Then Per did not have a dog (well, obviously not). Hardly your typical Anglo-Saxon happy ending for little children, though possibly something has been lost in the translation.

The Faeroese language that I soon spoke like a native belongs to the West Scandinavian subgroup of the North Germanic languages and has its roots in the Old Norse language from the first Viking settlers. Unlike so many small languages that have

46

disappeared all over the world, the Faeroese language is thriving and amazingly has done so, despite Danish having been the official language since the Reformation. In fact, the Faeroese language did not even exist in a written form until the middle of the nineteenth Century.

The language survived, because the ancient ballads were handed down orally. Naturalist and philologist, Jens Svabo, was the first to assemble a collection of these rich and wonderful Faeroese ballads and vocabulary. Finally in 1846, the Faeroese dean and linguist, with the wonderful name of Venceslaus Ulricus Hammerschaim – scholars spoil it for the reader by providing only the initials V.U. before his surname – set down what has become the modern reference to the Faeroese written language, with some later adjustments. Over the centuries, a large and elaborate vocabulary has developed, particularly in respect to surroundings, social and cultural activities.

The good sisters at the Nun's School put in place an intriguing coloured card system for measuring our schoolwork. Green cards represented diligence and good behaviour. Girls mainly belonged to this group. Yellow was for middle of the road, to which the majority of us belonged. Red cards were given to the bad and the lazy, and most of the boys fell into this category. In a spirit of fairness, the cards were re-allocated once a month. There was always hope for the bad and danger of falling from grace for the good.

Proficiency in reading and arithmetic was rewarded by allocation of stars. When a certain number was reached, one was rewarded with a small picture of Jesus Christ. As the Faeroese are religious people, one can only assume that this must have been viewed as a worthy reward. Some of these pictures ended up in our autograph books.

The nuns assured the anxious parents that the school was not a 'Catholic School' - with the possible exception of a few, all the children were of the Evangelical Lutheran faith – and that the Franciscan code of conduct respected people of other religious persuasions. On the other hand, the nuns stressed that the school was not indifferent to religion and that the pupils in their charge were taught to love God and to pray, and were encouraged to attend their respective churches on Sunday. A teacher undertook religious instruction in the Lutheran faith. The parents were satisfied. The good nuns further assured the parents that Bible history was taught in a neutral version, if there is such a thing.

As was the practice in all schools, the day started with Morning Prayer and a song. There were some that suspected the nuns of secretly indoctrinating us in the Catholic religion, though that was not the case. Nevertheless, the temptation to include some Catholic service was just too much; so every Monday there was a 'Children's Service' in the chapel after school and on the first Friday of every month another service, maybe it was a benediction, followed by a sermon given by Father Burla, a kindly priest, which started with: 'Dear Children'. The service was not compulsory, but many of us attended, as it was different from the Lutheran service.

Outside school hours, my time was spent at home. I was under strict instructions from Mia not to tarry. 'Go straight home from school, don't ever go to anyone's house,' were her firm instructions. At first I was resentful, as the other children seemed free to play in each other's houses or in the street, especially during the long daylight hours of summer. I was tempted to venture out and join them for a while, but it worried me that I would be found out. I was obedient. I walked straight home, and when I was older and taller, I took the key from the ledge above the front door and let myself into the solitary confines of Bakkahella 4. After a time, I became used to being on my own. As I grew older, Ulla-With-The-Bright-Yellow-Hair stopped taking care of me and by that time Visa had retired from work.

One day an unpleasant incident occurred just outside the school, when I was alone and defenceless. Some boys had peed together on a grassy area near where I was standing. Despite my proximity,

I remained oblivious to their little stunt. Suddenly, they grabbed me – four boys against one girl, mind you – and forced me down on to the revolting patch and rubbed my face in it, after which they fell about with laughter. I flew home and scrubbed my face almost raw. I even washed my mouth out with soapy water, a punishment that had once been dished out by Sigrid on a visit when she caught me chewing gum.

A far worse incident occurred when I was buried under the snow. It happened on a spring day after we had received a heavy dumping of snow from the last storm. I had just left the schoolyard when several boys grabbed me, held me down and proceeded to shovel snow on top of me. I closed my eyes and felt the increasing heaviness of snowy layers on top of me. It brought on an immediate panic attack as I thought of the horror stories I had read about being buried alive. When no one was holding me down any longer I fought my way out and raced home, up to my bedroom to hide behind the chair. I felt certain that I was the only person in Tórshavn to be singled out for such treatment.

A couple of years later, I was walking home from school on a dark winter afternoon. A piercing wind was howling down the streets, but I felt nothing due to the quadruple layers of clothing that Mia had dressed me in. I would alternate between two routes, though the one down the main street, parallel to the stream, was my preference. This time I took another street. I was not particularly happy with either of these ways, because I had recurring dreams about not finding my way home. In those dreams, the stream overflowed and I drowned in it. Or huge boulders appeared on the road, which I had to climb over, making it too difficult to make it home in one day.

All at once I was attacked from behind by a group of boys. I was not dreaming. I couldn't see my attackers, but knew they were boys by their distinctive squeals, different from the sounds us girls made. My arms were pinned behind my back and I was dragged to a telegraph pole. This was my worst nightmare come true. I started to scream but one of the boys clamped his hand over my mouth, though the area was deserted and no one would have heard my pitiful cries above the noise of the wind. The boys tied me with a rope to the pole and left me there. As soon as they were out of sight, I screamed my lungs off and within minutes a kind passer-by had untied me. I was frantic and raced home without offering my thanks.

When I told my school friend Laura about it the next day, she suggested that I had inadvertently moved into one of the gang's territory, hence my punishment. It was just bad luck. 'There are gangs of boys,' she said, 'each with their leader in different areas of town and nearby settlements. They carry homemade swords and spears and wage war on each other.' Often the police had to be called to break up their fights, she informed me. I had no idea such things went on and was greatly impressed by Laura's territorial knowledge. I knew that girls were not part of these gangs, though they had their own rival groups. I could not imagine the Sivertsen boys belonging to a gang. Although these were all isolated incidents, they loomed large in my nervous mind. I did not mention them to Mia, or to anyone else. I did not mind too much going to school, though because of my shyness, I would have preferred to have Visa teach me inside the confines of Bakahella 4.

By 1953, it seems that the nuns had recovered financially, as a new wing was added to the school, which included a new gymnasium. This meant that physical education was now to be taken seriously. I gathered this, as we suddenly had to wear special gym gear, consisting of short dark blue skirts with a double pleat in the back and a short sleeved white blouse with an 'SF' emblem. P.E. became my least favourite subject, after mathematics. I couldn't understand why we had to submit ourselves to walking on a raised plank, for example, wingless arms flapping about in the hope of acquiring some kind of balance, when there was already a nice level ground beneath our feet. As for jumping over the vaulting horse, well, it wasn't anything like a horse and I could never manage to jump over it. Inevitably, I got stuck on top, causing me severe embarrassment. Anyway, I wondered if I was to come across a real horse, would I want to jump over it? Of course not. I think that I missed the point of these classes.

My favourite subject was drawing. Mia kept me in plentiful supply with sketchpads and coloured pencils. Sigrid, who continued to work in Genoa, had sent me a small watercolour set from Italy, which I treasured. Practically everything, except for some foods, had to be imported, so even as children we were appreciative of anything given to us over and above our basic needs. The set came with a little paintbrush, which kept losing its hair and I pretended that the lid was a traditional painter's palette. I felt that I had made it as an artist by colouring in my drawings – no modesty whatsoever!

Sometimes Sjúrður's older brother, Júst, would come to our house to help me with my maths homework, as already at an early age I showed signs of having a complete anti-talent for this subject. Any calculations beyond the scope of the abacus were a mystery. We would sit side by side at the kitchen table while Júst patiently erased my awful work and carefully took me through the calculations. I loved the smell of the lead as he sharpened my pencils with his pocket-knife. I longed to own a pocket-knife, but when I asked Mia for one, she nearly freaked out at the thought of this clumsy child in her care operating a sharp instrument. I was grateful for Júst's help and felt confident that my homework would not be returned to me with the unsightly corrections marked in red ink that had occurred before his help and which I dreaded. As he was leaving, Júst would cast an eager eye on the radio in our sitting room. I could tell that he was dying to take it apart. Had he done so, he probably could have built a better one. He was very clever at that sort of thing.

Even though I spoke Faeroese at school and at home, for some reason I had a preference for Danish. Sigrid always wrote to me in Danish and in a postcard dated Genoa, 20 November 1953, she wrote:

'Dear Antoinetta,
Have you received the bracelet? What do you think of it? Write to me now that you are a big girl. Soon I'll be coming to visit you. Hope you haven't forgotten your Mamma Sigrid.'

The Italian bracelet was a present for my eighth birthday. It was made of delicate interlocking filigree hearts in white and yellow gold. I only wore it on special occasions, as it was not the sort of thing one wore when climbing over rocks or scooping up whale blubber, the more routine pastimes of local life.

Mother would also send me presents for my birthday and I particularly remembered that for a previous birthday, I had received some beautiful pale pink silk material with matching ribbons and trimmings. It was totally impractical for our lifestyle, but Mia dutifully had it made up into an exquisite party dress. I couldn't wait for it to be finished, as wearing it would surely help me lose the 'ugly duckling' image that I had of myself. Finally the dress was completed. I wore it just once when Mia took me, not to a party, but to a photographer's studio, where I posed for some time, hoping to look 'pretty in pink'. We returned home and the dress was wrapped in tissue paper and put in a drawer, never to be worn again. This was not at all disappointing. I forgot all about it as soon as the drawer was closed, as waiting for me in the kitchen was an almond cake, baked by Tulla.

*Chapter Nine*

*A* PROLONGED AND severe storm had kept us indoors for days.
Mia said it was one of the worst storms we had encountered in a
long time. Power lines were down and from my bedroom window
I could see a sloop half submerged in the blackened sea, her mast
broken. Mia had finally gone back to work and Visa was reading. I
had played every game I could think of and was becoming restless.
It was time to do some exploring. I had always been curious about
what lay upstairs on the Other Side. Even though nothing was
mentioned, I imagined this was forbidden territory.

I went up to the larger of the two spare bedrooms. Earlier, I had
noticed a second door, which did not seem to lead anywhere as far
as I could make out. I now opened this door with some trepidation
and found that it led onto the roof, which was surprisingly flat in
this section. Opposite was yet another door. Gingerly, I walked the
short distance towards it. The flat section felt like moss under foot,
but smelled strongly of tar. I was nearly blown off in the near gale
force winds. I opened the other door with great difficulty and
found myself in a new-looking bathroom. It contained a bath and
washbasin, but a remarkable absence of taps and running water.
This led into a kitchen and a living area.

There was a brand new feel about the place as if it had been
recently unwrapped and put on display, but never used. Even the
air felt as if it had not changed. Another door led to the hallway,

with steps leading up to what I guessed must be the loft and stairs leading down to the front door of the Other Side and the formal living room. I stood at the top of the stairs, looking down and felt the air move, yet I was alone and everything was shut. Ah, the ghost of Mia's husband-to-be. How could I have forgotten?

As I quickly retreated into the kitchen and sitting area, I knew that I had found the perfect venue to invite all my dolls to a tea party. As soon as the weather was better suited to the roof crossing, I would give my first party. I had a lovely green 'English bone china' tea set made out of fine plastic. I poured out imaginary coffee and served delicate little cakes. 'Sugar or cream for anyone?' Conversation flowed even though I had to do the talking for everyone. There was never any spillage or crumbs to pick up afterwards and washing up was a dream. Transporting my dolls and toys between Our Side and the Other Side took several trips and I made certain that the afternoon tea party was over by the time Mia arrived home. I wanted to keep the Other Side as my personal realm.

I was already familiar with the formal drawing room downstairs on the Other Side as we used it on special occasions, such as Christmas, birthdays and receiving important visitors. This room was light and airy with windows overlooking the garden. The pattern on the wallpaper looked like flowers from the forest, or so I imagined. I would gaze with wonder at a large oil painting of a forest of pine trees, forests being quite exciting to behold in our treeless land. The drawing room was furnished with the best decorative pieces we possessed. Leather bound books, objets d'art and even a Kilim rug on the wooden floor. An ever-present smell of furniture polish hung in the air. Mia had thoughtfully placed on the sideboard some framed photographs of my family, namely Tante Pepa, Mother's sister, with Grandpa Dušan and my two cousins, Milica and Sofija, the daughters of Uncle Bogdan. Tante Pepa occasionally corresponded with Mia and they exchanged photos. I would give the family photos a cursory look as they meant nothing to me. I knew even less about these relations than I

54

did about my parents. I was very proud of this living room and felt certain that ours was one of few houses to possess such elegance. However, I never went there on my own.

Some weeks later, I mustered enough courage to explore the loft bedroom. It afforded a perfect view of the fjord and the entrance to the harbour. At first, when I was younger, I had to stand on a stool in order to see above the curtain rod, which was positioned halfway down the window. I would form my index fingers and thumbs into circles over my eyes and pretend I was looking through binoculars. I could see the fishing boats come in, escorted by a flock of kittiwakes wheeling overhead. 'Ah, yes, a good catch.' I spoke these words aloud as if I were some fishery expert. This would also become my vantage point from which I used to watch my favourite happenings, such as the whale hunt and the boat race on St Olav's Day.

Despite my successful expeditions to the Other Side, I could not wait for summer time and to leave behind the wet fog of winter, known as *skadda* - Scotch mist as they call it on the Shetland Islands – a shadowy dark mantle from which there was no escape. It awakened a dormant feeling of unhappiness, which I never dared express to anyone. Mia was the last person to whom I wished to confide any dark feelings. It was bewildering being parentless, especially since I was not an orphan, and confusing that I had chosen to make myself sole confidante for all my emotional burdens. As I saw it, Mia and Visa were outside my family and I was not part of theirs, and however caring and tender, they were never going to replace my own kin. It was a fundamental feeling I always had and it was never changed by their behaviour.

## Chapter Ten

NORTHERN SUMMERS ARE typically fleeting but brilliant. Faeroese summers, while brief, were full of promise; a sensation no doubt shared by most other winter-worn inhabitants. The grassy fields were ablaze with colour; large patches of meadow buttercups and marsh marigolds seemed to appear overnight as if they knew that it would only be a short growing season. The smell of the damp fog was gone, replaced by a sweet aroma of red currant jam and haymaking.

Everyone's garden was in full bloom. Ours in Bakkahella 4 was transformed from a barren square plot into a crazed mixture of every type of flower that could grow here – Sweet Williams, Iceland poppies, Scottish bluebells – all attended by numerous slugs. None of these plants were native. Our seeds and bulbs came from Denmark. Tiny daisies also covered the stepping-stones in our garden. Even foxgloves grew here, in a stunted form. The rhubarb patch was begging to be turned into compôte. The currant shrubs were overloaded with tiny red berries. The wrens were already eyeing them, but so were we.

The seas around the islands swarmed with squid and fish. In the fields, the high grasses swayed in the breeze as if intoxicated by sudden bursts of sunshine after 300 days of cloud cover. Everything and everybody was on the move. The clouds rushed across the sometimes-blue sky at great speed. Although this was not the Land of the Midnight Sun, it stayed light until eleven in the evening. Lighthouses and streetlights were switched off. The young and the old were energized. The population increased by the millions, due to the arrival of migrating birds. Even the smell of seaweed was delicious, and in the best tradition of reuse, would later be turned into fertilizer.

My winter woollens were gratefully discarded for cotton dresses, though temperatures didn't exactly raise the mercury to dangerous levels; on a good day, the average would be about ten degrees Celsius.

Despite these relatively mild days, the fog was always with us. The *skadda* was replaced by *mjørki*, the fine rain fog of summer. I would wake up to the sound of the foghorn and find our house enveloped in fog so dense I couldn't even see into the rhubarb patch. The birds were silenced by it and the only sound came from the foghorn moaning its warning down by the lighthouse. Enveloped in the *mjørki*, it seemed that our house was the only one in the world, sitting on top of bright clouds. I liked it this way, as I had become used to my solitude.

Soon the fog would lift and the sun would shine brightly on us for an hour or two. Then, just as quickly, it would disappear to make way for a bit of rain, or *terradropar,* dry weather drops, as the Faeroese call it. The temperature would fall and we would don the ubiquitous cardigans that were always close at hand. Just as we changed clothes with the frequent changes in weather throughout the day, the light changed too, ranging from aquamarine blue to gloomy charcoal grey, an artist's delight.

The Sivertsens' farm by the sea, a short distance outside Tórshavn in an area called *Yviri við Strond,* meaning Place By the Shore. *Strond* also means beach, but the rocky coastline could hardly be designated a beach.

On the Faeroe Islands, farm tenure is separated into crown tenants and freeholders. All land is divided into *bøur* (infield*)* and *hagi* (outfields), or common fields, as they are known in England.

The cultivated infields are set around the village and are used for winter grazing and the growing of potatoes, barley and hay. The Sivertsens' farm was a freehold possession, on which they kept chickens, ducks, geese and sheep and grew an awful lot of grass between the boulders. The ruggedness of the land on the islands made it mostly unfit to plough. Walls made of rough stones and skulls from pilot whales surrounded the infields. The uncultivated outfields were used for summer grazing for sheep and a few cows that generally looked after themselves. The sheep instinctively took on the behaviour of mountain goats as they searched for fodder on the steep slopes. One false move, and, well, that was it for the baa baas.

The old process of inheritance of the freehold land almost bordered on the ridiculous. Each time the owner died, the infield was divided among all his children. As a result, a village might have multiple small plots, making them uneconomic to maintain on a commercial basis. Crown tenancies, on the other hand, were not subject to division, so they are really the only substantial farms still in existence.

I felt tremendous excitement as we drove in Júst's car for the haymaking days of summer. My parents' existence was temporarily forgotten. The sun would come out momentarily making the sea glisten. I would hear the smooth sound of the Sea Voice, becalmed by the gentleness of the summer's day.

We always set off early for the farm and would cram into the car for the short ride to the farm along the lovely coastal road. Sometimes we would have to make the journey by foot, while Júst waited for spare parts for his car, which could take weeks. Whichever way, it was always a joy to reach the farm, to experience the freedom, the proximity to nature and just the simple pleasure of being out doors. I looked forward to it each year. However melancholy my mood might have been in the preceding months, the sheer prospect of spending long days on the farm was a fillip to my spirit.

When we arrived at the farm, the tall grasses beckoned me onto the fields. I loved running unhindered through them before Júst and his helpers cut down the grass. Hay was a vital crop for winter fodder for cows and sheep. The grass was felled using a scythe called a *líggið*, fashioned with a long straight wooden shaft that had to be held with both hands, using an under-arm and over-arm grip. The men made reaping look effortless, but I knew that it required great skill to get the blade to skim evenly over the ground. I used to watch Júst and the other workers as they elegantly swept their scythes over the grasses with a half-turn of the body. Soon they got into a rhythm, and a melodious sound made by the cold hard blade cutting through the soft damp grass emanated from the fields. It filled my ears like the full orchestral suite that I listened to on the old gramophone, but without the scratchy sounds. Every so often the men would stop to hone the curved blade in order to keep it razor sharp. When they reached their late teens, Júst Junior and Sjúrður helped their father to cut the grass. As there was so much of it, only one area was cut at a time. As soon as the first section was done, the frantic rush to start the drying process began; after all, we had to take advantage of the average two months per year of warmish weather and halfway sunny days.

The smell of the freshly cut grass was intoxicating. Clad in overalls and armed with rakes, all of us swarmed onto the field to spread it out to dry. There was a certain procedure to this. First we spread the grass out evenly on the field. If the weather was good, we returned the next day to continue, but often rain would set in for several days. On the next visit the grass was turned over to dry on the underside. In the following days, we raked it together into swatches with a few neat strokes and wrapped it over a specially made wire fence that ran down the length of the field. Then we covered the grass with a net to protect it from the strong winds.

The coastal road cut through our farm, so to attend to the field by the sea, we had to cross the road, each carrying our personal rake over one shoulder, like soldiers on the march with their bayonets. Every bit of grass was cured for hay.

I enjoyed being part of all the stages of the haymaking procedure. It gave me a sense of accomplishment. There was also the added bonus of being with the Sivertsen children all day and eating Tulla's delicious lunch hampers.

On subsequent visits, the next area was cut and the whole drying process repeated. During those weeks, Júst and his sons went to the farm every day. Depending on the mood of our Viking thunder god Thór, the work was often not completed until the end of September or even the beginning of October, far beyond the usual season's end.

Being a pagan god, Thór would deluge us with rain on a Saturday and Monday, but allow the sun to shine all day on a Sunday; the day of rest, as prescribed by our Christian God. Our rakes were left idle; the hay left unturned as the sun shone brightly on the fields, while we attended to our devotions.

One sunny day in summer, back in August 1952, as I was eagerly looking forward to going to the farm, I went next door to check on plans for our departure, but Anna Maria told me we were not going for the next couple of days.

'Why not?' I asked disappointedly.

'The King of Denmark is visiting Tórshavn and my pápi has to drive him to all his appointments,' she explained.

Then Júst appeared, wearing his Sunday clothes and it wasn't even Sunday. He was driving King Frederik IX to the opening of an exhibition of products made in the Faeroes.

It was to be a memorable day for Guðrun. She was among a group of young girls who were asked to wear their 'Faeroese clothes' and to be at the exhibition place. Guðrun had told us that one of them was going to be chosen to present a bouquet of flowers to the King after he had made his opening speech. The girls quarrelled about who should be the lucky one. It was not Guðrun. However, while the King was inspecting the produce with the manager of the Føroya Fisasøla Company, the King stopped right before her. Much to Guðrun's delight, the king asked her to go outside and give the bouquet to Júst, who was waiting by the car. The next day, I went with Anna Maria and the boys to the main street where we knew the King would be walking. A crowd of people was standing on both sides of the street, so I couldn't see the King very well. But when I looked further up the street, I saw Júst standing next to his parked car waiting for the monarch to complete his walk. We all felt proud that Júst was involved in such important work. Later, King Frederik presented Júst with a medal in recognition of his services.

After our hard work in the fields, which I thought of as more fun than work, I would soak my feet in the brook's pure water. It was full of round pebbly stones, as this had been a river long ago. Someone had told me that at least one *nykur*, water nymph, had lived in it, and I suspected, still did. I knew that these water nymphs definitely lived in our lakes. The *nykur* was known to take on a horse-like form and was very strong. It lured young boys onto its back, after which it would jump into the depths of the lake, with the innocent rider still astride. The only salvation was for the victim to utter its name, preferably before being submerged, at which point the *nykur* would disappear.

I used to move the stones around with the rib of a sheep, part of my country toy collection, all the while hoping that I was not disturbing any nymphs. I was content to stay here until called away. I felt closer to the natural world than to people. The farm and its surrounds was alive with spirits and even though they sometimes frightened me, I was less shy of them than of human strangers, of which there were far too many for my liking.

Before the hay was cut, the fields were full of dandelions and I used to love to pick up one of these puffballs of white fluff and blow fiercely on it, as I watched the little seeds float away. Anna Maria and Rachel preferred to pick the daisies and pull off their petals all the while mumbling: 'He loves me, he loves me not, he loves me...' If the result was in the negative, another daisy was immediately picked. I copied the girls though the end result had no meaning for me, as who was 'he' anyhow? And did it really matter whether he loved me, or not?

After the hay had dried in each section of the field, we raked the haul to the middle and Júst and his men proceeded to make a large haystack. As it got higher, Júst climbed on top and expertly pressed the hay down with his feet and then with his knees. We threw a net over the haystack and tied it with straw rope. The haystack was left out until Júst was ready to bring it into the shed, where it was loosely laid. Often it was well into the evening before we finished, but there was plenty of light as the sun set late during the summer.

I had read in a book about frolicking in the hay. So one day I went into the shed, climbed up a ladder and threw myself on top of the hay. The consequences were unexpectedly painful as I came out in an awful rash. The book had made no mention of this possibility.

Repainting the little farmhouse and the sheds was almost a yearly task, as the paint never lasted long, following the assault of winter storms. One time, I was trying to be helpful by pulling out weeds that had grown up against the wall, when the younger Júst called out, 'Don't touch that, it's Poison Ivy and you can die if you touch it.' After that, I spotted Poison Ivy all over Tórshavn. It was easily recognisable as it grew upright and was hairy with whitish flowers. I was sure it was grown by the devil himself. Life was fraught with natural dangers. Nevertheless, I loved everything about the farm and it was the only time during my entire childhood that I felt truly happy.

My first sensation of power took place in the chicken shed. Much to my delight I was given the task of collecting the freshly laid eggs. I was certain that this required a lot of cunning on my part, although it was really just good planning by the chicken shed builder, who was none other than Sjúrður. With basket in hand, I approached the chicken shed with great caution. I put a hand over my nose, as the bad smell was powerful. I could hear the chickens clucking away happily in their individual cubicles, endeavouring to hatch little ones. I knew exactly what they were up to.

Fortunately, the shed was designed in such a manner that I had undetected access to the cubicles from the back. Treading softly, I quickly lifted the lid off each cubicle, surprising the unsuspecting hen, then shooed her off and collected a big warm egg. This process was repeated with each cubicle. I was pleased that it never occurred to the chickens to alert their neighbours to what was happening, so I always managed to fill my basket with many lovely large eggs. My reward was always one egg, which I was allowed to keep. I would take it to the kitchen and find two cups, as I needed to separate the egg white from the yolk. I knew that I had my mouth open as I was performing this delicate task because I was in awe of my own resourcefulness. I put some sugar in the cup with the captured yolk and whipped it furiously with a fork until it turned creamy and almost white. Then I ate it slowly, pleased that I had 'hunted' for my own food. I could now do haymaking and catch eggs. It was fun playing a farmer.

I so wanted to stay overnight on the farm, but the little house was not equipped for this. It consisted of a make shift kitchen, an eating nook and half a loft where the ceiling was so low that one literally had to crawl into bed. It could barely fit two people, least of all a whole family. A pump in the yard supplied the water. There was no electricity. It seemed like an idyllic place to live in the summer months and I was pleased that we had to go there so often.

Visa kept a small garden in front of the house. It was fenced off and none of us children were allowed anywhere near it. Beautiful flowers and even strawberries grew there for a brief period each summer. It was Visa's pride and joy.

An above ground bunker from World War II, which had been used by the British troops to store equipment, stood on our property. The boys liked playing in it but I didn't want to go anywhere near there. Close by, on the neighbouring infield, was a second British bunker, which had been a tracking station, Júst Junior informed me. I could tell that he was sorry that the bunker was now empty. It would have made an ideal mechanical toy for him. Both bunkers were just empty shells now, but I was certain that they held terrible war secrets and the ghosts of dead Englishmen.

As with most dwellings in Tórshavn, the farm overlooked Nólsoy, or Needle Island. Though none of us children had ever been there, we knew that Nólsoy had an unusual entrance to its harbour, featuring a high archway made from the jawbones of a single sperm whale that was conveniently found floating in the bay many years ago. Needle Island derived its name from a hole in solid rock at the southern end of the island, through which a boat could pass, we were told, provided the sea was calm, which was not too often. To me the island looked like a green reclining dog whose ears had been bitten off by sea monsters. During winter, the snow pocked dog-island looked as though it was suffering from a bad case of dandruff, but despite this affliction, Nólsoy was our protector from the northeast winds.

From the farm, we would see Russian fishing vessels moored between Nólsoy and Streymoy, our Stream Island. The early 1950s had seen an increase in Russian shipping vessels around our waters where they caught mainly whiting. We had only a three-mile fishing limit. Sometimes the ships would come to Tórshavn to carry out repairs or take on fresh water.

One year, a Russian ship was given special permission to anchor in our harbour. It was berthed at the wharf on the East Bay, and a rope cordoned off the immediate area, so that we couldn't get on board and be converted to communism and the Russians couldn't get off to lead a free life in the Faeroes. I was convinced this was the case, as all communists were bad. The Cold War was very real to us. Even though I did not understand it, I knew from listening to Mia and Visa that Soviet Russia (very bad) had the atomic bomb (bad); that Germany was divided into West (good) and East (bad); that the whole of China was now communist (very bad); and that North Korea (bad), supported by China, had invaded South Korea, supported by the USA (very good). With typical childish reasoning, I had everything compartmentalized into either

64

good or bad. And now we were told that the communists even had women on board working as seamen, or rather seawomen. In Faeroese society, this was strictly men's work. Trust those communists to force their womenfolk to perform such hard labour, I thought.

Curiosity got the better of me, so I went down to the harbour with the Sivertsen boys to look at these bad people. I strained against the rope, in order to get as close to the ship as possible, hoping to spot one of the seawomen. A number of locals had had the same idea, as there was quite a group of us gawking at the Russian ship. At first there was no sign of anyone. A constant low muffled sound emanated from the ship. Was it the engines, I wondered, or a chorus of the dreaded rats humming a Russian folk song? All of a sudden, someone came out on deck. I held my breath in anticipation of seeing my first communist. It was a woman and she was big, very big, even allowing for her thick garments. She wore a grey woollen cap atop a wide pale grey face. She bent down to pick something up – lifting a large barrel would have been no problem for her – and was about to go inside again, when she turned suddenly around and gave me a long hard look. I hurried home, somewhat shaken by having locked eyes with a communist.

Antonia posing with Anna Maria, Rachel, Sjúrður and Júst for a studio photograph, Tórshavn, 1949. The picture was taken for a story that appeared in the local newspaper, but no one remembers what the story was about.

Sjúrður, Antonia, and the dog, Per, in the rhubarb patch next to the black house. The garden bloomed briefly each summer thanks to Visa's green thumb. Antonia and Mia's bedroom window can be seen in upper right-hand corner, Tórshavn, 1950.

Anna Maria and Antonia on the farm outside Tórshavn, ready for a day of haymaking. Sjúrður specially made the wooden wheelbarrow for Antonia. The tiny farmhouse is to the left. Summer 1951.

## Chapter Eleven

*O*CCASIONALLY, MIA ARRANGED for me to play at my school friend Laura's house. My playtime with Laura was pre-arranged by Mia in consultation with Laura's mother. Mia would always drop me off and pick me up at a set hour, even when I was older, much to my embarrassment. Laura's house was in Jónas Broncksgøtu, a short ten-minute walk away. The street ran down to the ruin of the old fort of Skansin, next to the lighthouse. We learned at school that local hero Magnus Heinason had built it in 1580, to protect Tórshavn from pirates who had started to plunder the farm settlements. Evidence of this was still apparent as in certain areas one can find darker-haired and dark-skinned Faeroese rather than the predominant blue-eyed, flaxen-haired natives. There were also hiding places in the hills and it is told that one entire village was removed plank by plank to a safer area. The French razed the fort to the ground and during the Napoleonic Wars, the British naval rig, *Clio,* captured the fort. In 1940, the Royal Navy Command made it their World War II headquarters, this second time being on a much friendlier foundation.

Ernle Bradford, in a *National Geographic* article, tells a wonderful story of retribution recounted to him while visiting the village of Fámjin on the island of Suðuroy. A French merchant ship anchored off the shore there sometime in the eighteenth century. Two local fishermen rowed out to the ship to sell some fish to the sailors. There were two French women on board, who in true Gallic style were not prepared to buy the fish without a proper inspection. This required them to get into the locals' boats. No sooner had they done this, than the crafty fishermen rowed swiftly back to the village with their female 'catch' on board. One must add here that there was a desperate shortage of single females on the island at the time. Typical of Faeroese weather, it changed rapidly. A huge swell began to rise in the bay, making it impossible for the angry Frenchmen to follow the fishermen ashore. A storm broke out forcing the French ship to sail off. The French women were married to the two fishermen by the local pastor in a proper religious ceremony and, one hopes, lived happily ever after. To this day, the villagers give French forenames to their boys. It would appear the girls miss out, even though the association originated with the French women.

Whereas only three people lived in our house, Laura's house seemed to accommodate a large family. She had two sisters and two brothers and just as many cousins, who all lived under the one roof. Laura shared a bedroom with her siblings and I thought her very lucky. Laura's house was fun and noisy in comparison to our house, which was always deathly quiet. Her father and uncle ran a car and radio workshop called Firma John and Paul Joensen. Everybody referred to the brothers as one man named 'John and Paul' and the children were collectively known as 'the children of John and Paul', even after the business was closed and the families had moved on.

Occasionally, Laura was invited to our house for a specific hour, again set by Mia. When Laura came to my place, I would open up to her and prattle on about all the things I would do together with my parents when I went to Australia. I had absolutely no idea what Australia was like, or if I would ever join my parents there. Mia had told me that Australia was a very big island with beaches all around it and the weather was always warm – impossible to imagine. It had furry animals. I had proof of this as my mother had sent me a stuffed toy kangaroo and koala. The only furry mammals on our islands that I had ever encountered were the rats brought to the islands courtesy of the ships, and normal old cats, dogs and pet rabbits.

Sometimes Mia sent me by myself on errands to buy something we urgently needed or to deliver something to her friends. Súsanna, the daughter of Mia's friend, Hedvig, who also worked at the telephone exchange, was amused when one day Mia sent me to her mother with a Danish magazine *House and Home*. Even though Hedvig's place was only a few minutes away, Mia phoned Hedvig to expect me and made her promise to phone back when I was leaving to go back home. Mia was always concerned that something would happen to me. This must have had an effect on me, as I became very security conscious, running everywhere in the hope that no one would catch me. I started to imagine that strangers were lurking around every corner waiting to pounce on me. My favourite hiding spot was the greenhouse, situated between our house and the house next door, where the heavy smell of damp soil was calming. A few minutes of such treatment were all that was required to restore my composure. It was my secret refuge from both perceived and real dangers outside my cloistered world at Bakkahella 4.

There was definitely no danger of being run over by cars – in those days chickens and ducks ruled the roads. Sometimes I would find them on the sod roofs feeding off the tall grasses that grew there in summer. However, maybe Mia's concern was well founded as, one day, during the school holidays, I think it was near Laura's house, though she was not with me at the time, a few of us were playing hide and seek. I should have been at home as per Mia's firm instructions, but decided to risk going out for a spell.

At the time a man had recently been released from jail, where he had served a long sentence for killing a child. His release was reported in the papers. The children I was playing with told me that the man had cut up the child and hidden the remains in a cupboard in his house. When it came to my turn to cover my eyes and face the wall, I counted up to the required number. It never occurred to me to skip some numbers as others did. Suddenly I felt a presence close to me. I turned around and there he was – the one who had cut up a child. I knew it was him, as his face had been in the newspaper. He had light watery eyes and a pale puffy face; 'uncooked pastry' is how my mother would have described him, though I was not yet familiar with her insightful powers of observation and expression. He had a smug, ill-intentioned look. I screamed and ran home as fast as I could, straight into the greenhouse. The crime rate on the islands was low, so his was an unprecedented act of violence. There were only a small number of offenders in the jail located out on Tinganes, but we made up many horrific tales about them. As it turned out, the other children had fabricated this story about how he committed the actual crime to put the wind up me. But for me it was very real and this incident stopped me from ever playing hide and seek again, or from disobeying Mia's orders.

After this incident, I concluded that maybe Mia was right in not wanting me to play on the street. This led met to explore the loft on the Other Side more thoroughly, where I discovered one afternoon a strange heavy object that was to constitute my sole musical education on the islands. I reported to Visa:

'It's like a shallow box, but heavy; it's straight on two sides and rounded on the other and has lots of wire strings fixed tightly across it. What could it be?' Visa gave it a name. 'A zither,' she said nonchalantly, as though it were normal for everyone to have such a thing in the family loft.

The next day, much to my delight, I found music sheets in the exact shape of the zither; straight on two sides and curved on the other. Over the music score were heavy black dots, joined by lines. I took the peculiar looking sheets down to Visa, who explained that if I slid the sheet music under the strings of the zither, I would be able to follow the score, without any knowledge of reading music. Back in the loft, I plucked over the dots with the plectrum that Visa instructed me to place over my right thumb. It must have sounded terrible, as the zither was surely out of tune and I had no idea of tempo. It didn't matter; there was nobody around to hear my attempts at playing. I was very pleased with myself. I could read Gothic, play the zither, or so I believed, and I now also wanted to learn to knit. Laura already knew how to knit.

All women knitted their family's winter wardrobe; even Mia. In fact, knitted socks had been the main export product of the Faeroes in the seventeenth and eighteenth centuries. Mia would sit in her favourite chair in the evening and knit sweaters and socks - using three needles, I noted with fascination. Knitting was done either before or after the cigar, never while smoking.

At first Mia would not allow me to knit, as she feared that I would poke my eyes out with the needles. I suggested using pencils instead and this was allowed, though the quality of my knitting would surely have ruined the export trade. Later I graduated from the trainee pencils to real knitting needles and proceeded to knit clothes for my dolls. No human would have wanted to wear what I made. For her birthday one year, I gave Laura a pair of knitting needles with Walt Disney characters on the ends. She was a fine knitter and I reasoned would do even better work with the aid of Mickey Mouse and Donald Duck.

The wool we bought was wonderfully thick and I loved the earthy colours. It came in a long coil, rather like a coiled length of rope. Mia would put the wool around my outspread arms while she wound it tightly into a ball. Afterwards, we would play a game for which there is no word in English. A long strand of wool was tied to form a ring, which was twisted loosely around all ten fingers. The other person had to transfer the string to their hands by interlocking their ten fingers in the twisted strand on your hands. If this sleight of hand could not be achieved without the receiver dropping a loop, then they lost the game.

Life without sheep and their wool was inconceivable to us. Fishermen wore woollen sweaters and gloves which kept them warm even when wet. Tarred bands of wool were used for caulking seams of boats. Júst had knitted wool lining inside his sheepskin shoes. Thick home-knitted Faeroese sweaters gave

71

protection from the wild weather – the only thing that was wild in Faeroes – while at the same time being most distinctive in their design.

Every respectable household had a Bible and a copy of *Føroysk Bindingarmynstur*, a classic Faeroese knitting pattern book, assembled not by a dedicated female knitter, but by a tailor, Hans Debes, who had collected some unique designs. He was known as Tailor Debes, not be confused with Hans Jacob Debes, the historian, though Tailor Debes was himself a formidable storyteller of local lore and he wove these tales into his patterns. Many designs were in parallel bands and 'Walking the Dogs', 'Ring Dancing' and 'Goose's Back' had crazy zigzag patterns; 'Hens Pecking' and 'Grandmas Pecking' were not dissimilar in design; while the geometric squares of 'seawaves' and 'chess boards' all lent themselves perfectly to the Faeroese sweater style, and like the others, had a story to tell. Obviously a devoted citizen of the Kingdom of Denmark, Hans Debes dedicated his book to Her Majesty, Queen Alexandrine - he had included a 'King's Crown' pattern in special tribute. Guðrun's mother sensibly made a hard cover for this popular paperback treasure. Mia knitted me a light brown sweater with small white squares in the design. It looked as though it was intended to be 'Goose's Eye' but these came out looking unnaturally square. Perhaps on this occasion she had been using my pencils, but full marks anyway to Mia for creativity. Matching mittens were attached to a string drawn through my new jumper, so that if I took the mittens off, I could never lose them. They hung from my wrists like flippers. The sweaters were so thick that there was no need to wear an overcoat to keep out the chilly winds of winter, spring and autumn, but the coarse wool also made me very itchy.

One winter, Mia knitted a classic Faeroese cardigan for me in the traditional raglan sleeve style, complete with buttons made out of sheep horn. She could not decide which pattern she liked the most, so she used six bands of conflicting styles, making for a rather busy-looking cardigan. In winter, Mia dressed me in so many layers of clothing that I had about as much mobility as if I were wearing a suit of medieval armour. I never felt cold. I was not allowed to. Mia even knitted a cap, which tied under my chin with woollen strings that had pom-poms dangling from them. This I found rather ridiculous and resisted wearing it.

Mia's curious arrangement of layering on underpants was also a real problem for me. Over my normal cotton underpants, Mia would insist that I wear a second pair knitted from thick hairy wool – plain, no designer pattern by Tailor Debes – followed by yet another pair of thick black cotton underpants, or rather overpants. Quite apart from the time needed to put it all on, this garb caused me great discomfort and assured many winters of discontent. I wondered if other children had to endure a similar fate, but was too embarrassed to ask anyone about it, not even Laura.

I did notice, however, that Edny, the girl next door to me in the Flat Iron Building, wore less layers of clothing than I did and she never seemed to get cold.

## Chapter Twelve

*E*DNY WAS OUR neighbour on the other side of Bakkahella 4. She had wavy blonde hair and large blue Viking eyes, a description that could fit almost the entire population of the Faeroe Islands, but her claim to fame was living in a house that was unique. It was shaped like a giant clothes iron standing on its end, the only thing missing being the handle.

Weather permitting, Edny and I played outside in a small vacant area bordering our rhubarb plot and her house, where Mia was able to keep an eye on us from the window of the sitting room. Our rhubarb plot was surrounded by a low wall, which offered feeble protection against the elements. It was quite separate from our garden in the back of the house. A large discarded crate made an ideal ground level cubby house. Even though a tree grew there, we did not know about erecting cubby houses in trees, and in any case, anything up in the boughs would not have stayed up for any length of time given the gale force winds.

I was curious to find out what the inside of Edny's flat iron house looked like and was pleased when one day Edny invited me in. I was surprised to find the rooms so narrow that we had to walk in single file. Upstairs, the bedroom had box beds against the walls with curtains that could be drawn across, reminiscent of the alcove beds in old traditional Viking houses. Edny lived with her mother. Her father did not seem to be around, though he must have been at some stage, as she had an older brother and sister. I only visited

74

Edny's house furtively, being under strict instructions from Mia never to enter anyone's house without first clearing it with her. I don't think that Edny ever came to mine, as the same visitation rules applied to anyone entering our house.

Although Edny was younger than I was by one or two years, she was seemingly more advanced. Edny also attended the Nuns' School and was in a class or two below me. She seemed to know a great deal about the nocturnal habits of grown ups, which she eagerly passed on to me in considerable detail but which were totally lost on me. Only years later did I realise that she was attempting to enlighten me on the facts of life, which she had assembled herself, possibly when her older sister and husband were visiting. Presumably the curtains had not been drawn across the alcove beds at the time. Mia had never broached the subject with me and I would say it was not the practice of her generation to do so. I used to wonder how babies were 'made'. I knew it had to start with a married couple, but after that it was all magic as far as I was concerned. I used to imagine a small patch of flat ground and as I watched this space little feet appeared quite suddenly, then the legs and eventually the rest of the body followed standing upright. I had never had anything to do with babies, so I did not realise that they could not stand up on the first day. I expected babies to be like newborn chicks, with which I was familiar that got up straight away and walked around and occasionally fell on their beaks.

One day Edny and I had a big fight outside her house. Like all fights, I don't remember what it was all about. We had finished playing hopscotch outside my front door, and maybe Edny had made some mention about my origins or the absence of my parents, always a sore point with me. Whatever it was, I got very angry, which was most unusual for me. As Edny was about to enter the Flat Iron house, I threw a spade in her direction, inadvertently hitting her on the temple. She fell down next to her house and lay quite still on the pebbly ground. Immediately I ran, not to her rescue, but to my hiding place in the greenhouse. I told no one what had happened.

Edny did not emerge from her house for several days. I worried terribly that I might have injured her badly, possibly even to the point of death, but I did not share my fears with Mia. If I had had any religious instruction, it had no effect on me as I did not have a conscience about having done something against God's Commandments. Much to my relief, Edny reappeared in our street a few days later, looking alive and well. I approached her with care and offered a small 'hello', but understandably she would not speak to me. Our friendship was over. I was not too disappointed as there were always my books or playtime on the Other Side.

## Chapter Thirteen

*Boats and ships shall guide mankind*
*on the sea of life to the eternal beaches.*

Old Norse proverb

ADHERENCE TO RELIGIOUS service and festivals was a serious matter for the devout Faeroese, who were predominantly Evangelical Lutheran. The weekly high point was the Sunday morning church service. Each Sunday, Mia and I made our way to the nearby Havnar Church, joining the large congregation that always ensured that attendance was high. The faithful could be seen arriving in small groups, their heads bowed against the wind as they clutched their Bible close to their chest.

Religious festivals differed from normal days and provided a pleasant departure from the tedium of the daily routine of the adults. For the children, the festivals were linked to special foods, games and get togethers.

Much hymn singing - at least five - and the inescapable monotonous sermon marked the Sunday service. My eyes would wander to the heavenly white walls and up to the ceiling, from which hung a model of an old Dutch sailing ship, *Norske Løve*, that had sunk off the coast of the island of Eysturoy on New

Year's Eve in 1702. The crew had built the model and given it to the church as a token of thanksgiving for their rescue.

Many churches on the islands had model ships hanging from their ceiling, either donated by the congregation or by the owners of the actual ships. They served as a reminder of the strong connection between man and the sea, but more importantly, boats and ships were a symbol of the voyage across the sea of life to Heaven. In Norse lore, the hull of the ship was seen as the borderline between life and death.

Sunday was also the day of taking the weekly bath and dressing up in our 'Sabbath Best', as no work was performed on this holy day of rest. My bath normally consisted of standing in front of the washbasin in our bedroom, while Mia washed my body in sections with a wash mitten. I was never fully naked and only the necessary parts were exposed at a time. I hated Mia touching me, so there was always a tussle over the wash mitten. Mia never showed her desperation at my behaviour, but I know when I controlled the wash mitten that I didn't do a very good job.

It was normal practice to read the Bible at home, though I never saw Visa or Mia reading it. No one ever worked on Sundays anywhere. The only exception being if a pod of whales was sighted, then even these pious Lutherans would firmly close their Bibles and head for the harbour. The strict evangelical social and work ethics had a profound effect in shaping the lives of the Faeroese. They were diligent, egalitarian, and God-fearing and on the surface a little cheerless, in sharp contrast to my Slavic temperament, dormant though it was. Though anyone who has endured a few stormy Faeroese winters is bound to feel cheerless at the end of them.

Churches were a feature of every town and village, no matter how small. Their simple wooden structures were rather lovely to behold, if only the sermon could be eliminated. There were more churches than pastors on the islands. To address this imbalance, a layman read the Sunday service if the regional pastor was absent.

Churches were also regarded as the 'protected house of the minister's widow' and in the settlement of Miðvágur on the island of Vágar, it was recorded that several widows and their many children simultaneously occupied the minister's house. A testament to the statistic that women outlived men.

The act of baptism and confirmation was regarded as a highly significant rite in the Lutheran religion. In 1953, when I was seven, both Sjúrður and Júst Junior were to receive their confirmation. I think they were around twelve and fourteen years of age. In preparation for this, the boys told me that they had to attend confirmation classes on Saturdays given by the local pastor. They had to learn Martin Luther's Small Catechism off by heart, which was followed by an oral and written test. No one got off lightly.

The day finally arrived when Sjúrður and Júst, together with other children were to be confirmed at the Havnar Church. The boys looked very neat in their shirts and ties; in fact, we were all dressed in our Sunday best. I got bored sitting in the church looking at the backs of the eager worshippers. The minister walked up to the pulpit, which was rather nicely carved and painted. He seemed to talk for hours. I suppose there was a scriptural message or two in there somewhere, but I wasn't listening. The adults looked grim, as though they were obeying a sign outside reading: 'Keep Off the Grass and No Smiling'. The children fidgeted and alternated their gaze between their feet and the ceiling.

The rite of confirmation was finally over and we headed back to Bakkahella to Tulla's kitchen, where lunch, the traditional main meal, was set out in the dining room. Tulla had spent days in the kitchen preparing every imaginable kind of Faeroese and Danish specialty. The chef at the Hotel Hafnia would have cried with envy if he could have seen her remarkable spread. In the afternoon coffee and hot chocolate was served with waffles, freshly made by Tulla's fair hands, and buttery biscuits with raisins in them. As if that wasn't enough, the evening supper featured the Faeroese *pièce de résistance* – *skerpikjøt* – the wind-dried mutton that, like our Danish visitors, I always found to be rather too chewy.

The celebration of Shrovetide, *Fastelavn*, took place three days preceding Ash Wednesday. In earlier times, people were not allowed to eat meat during Lent, and Shrovetide was a feast day, before the observance of 40 days of fast in the same way that Christ observed 40 days of fast in the desert. However, Shrovetide had lost some of its religious significance and had evolved into a celebration of the approach of spring and a new working year.

'Knocking the cat out of the barrel', was one of the games played by children on this day. We would line up and take it in turn to hit with a stick a barrel that had been hung from the ceiling. It contained sweets and a drawing of a black cat. The first child who succeeded in shattering the barrel was named 'Cat-King' for the day and received a paper crown. This habit dates back to a Pagan ceremony, using live cats, when it was believed that cats were servants of the devil.

Later in the day, the children got dressed up in their parents' clothes, costumes, bed sheets and peculiar hats. Some even dared to dressed up as *grýla*, the monster that was used to frighten children, as is evident from this grisly old rhyme which we all knew:

> *Down from the dykes comes the monster*
> *With forty tails and a short sword in its hand*
> *It comes to cut the stomach out of children*
> *Who cry for meat in Lent*

The children went to the houses in the neighbourhood singing and begging for sweets. Mia prepared for this unaccustomed onrush of visitors by buying a large supply of candies. As soon as there was a knock on our door, Mia would open it with me standing behind her. I never participated in this game, as Mia felt it was too risky for my safety – it wasn't, but I really didn't mind, as the idea of knocking on other people's doors had no appeal for me. It was excitement enough for me to see strangely clad children on our doorstep.

The year's most important religious festival was Easter, a period that seemed to mean extra days spent in and out of church. The Faeroese word for Easter is *páskir* and has its roots in the Hebrew *Pesach,* a commemoration of spring when lambs were sacrificed and eaten. The biblical meaning was not as interesting for me as colouring the hardboiled eggs, which I judged to be a wonderful way of filling the time during these high holy days. Forever thoughtful, Mia bought me some decorative transfers, which I had to soak in water and carefully place on the eggs. I made attempts once to decorate the eggs myself, but the results were most disappointing and looked as if I had got the local cat to place her paw marks on them. The highlight occurred on Easter Monday when we rolled the hardboiled eggs down the pebbly hill, past Edny's Flat Iron house. If the shell broke, we had to eat the egg. No egg had a chance of making it to the bottom unbroken, which meant we all had our fill of eggs at Easter time.

On Sundays, Mia made occasional visits to her friends, taking me with her. I remember clearly going to someone's house one evening, or maybe it was during the daytime in winter, which equated to the same thing. It may have been Hedvig whom we visited on this occasion. Hedvig was married to Juul Olsen and they had two children, Súsanne and Knút, both much older than me. Juul was the brother of Laura's grandmother. After a while I became bored, as children do when surrounded by adults talking grown-up stuff and smoking cigars. Yes, Hedvig was also a cigar smoker and while she and Mia jointly filled the room with smoke and drank coffee, I spotted a bookcase and went over to browse through the shelves. I was a prolific reader. I found a large book on World War II and settled myself behind a nearby chair and proceeded to open the pages. When in other people's houses surrounded by adults, I would sometimes choose to sit on the floor behind a chair, rather than on it. This practice would probably make most people a candidate for sessions with a psychiatrist, but for me it had the dual purpose of not making me the centre of attention – I was painfully shy – as well as offering some protection, if needed (though it never was). The book had photographic reproductions showing emaciated Jews leaving the concentration camps after their liberation. There were photos taken not just of numbers tattooed on the arm that I thought bad enough, but as I turned the pages, the photos also showed graphic details of horrendous injuries sustained by the internees. I didn't want to look at them, yet I couldn't stop myself. I kept turning the pages as if an invisible hand was forcing me to do so. I was terrified. I wanted to go home immediately, but said nothing.

In my bed that night, there was no relief. The images I had seen in the book turned into a nightmare...

*I am entering our house. A German soldier has stepped out of the book I was reading with the intention of killing me. I run into a room. For some reason it is completely devoid of furniture and the single naked bulb hanging from the middle of the ceiling gives out very little light. I can barely see the grey windowless walls. I close the door quickly behind me and lock it. Much to my dismay, the door shrinks, rendering the locking useless. I hurry to the door opposite leading to the next room. I close the door behind me and lock it. This door shrinks as well. Rushing to the next door, I lock that one. This time I check to make certain that it is in fact secured. But it too shrinks. I want to run to the next door, but this room is in the middle of the house and only has one door. I am trapped. My assailant catches up with me. I can't see his face, as the light is so poor. He pushes me into a corner of the room. I feel something inside me breaking. I am in the most excruciating pain as my ribs crack.*

As the breath is squeezed out of me I wake up gasping for breath and can hear Mia stirring in her bed.

Even though it was pitch black in the room, I knew that she was turning on her other side. I recognised her nocturnal movements, as I am sure, she did mine. I prayed that she would not come over to My Side. The next morning, I did not discuss with Mia what I had seen in the book or the effect it had had on me. It was not my habit to share my experiences or feelings with her. Had I done so, I am sure she would have comforted me, being the kind person she was, but I did not wish to be comforted.

The next time this nightmare occurred, I found a way of waking up before I got to the painful part. I would close my eyes really tight, and then force them open, crossing from the subconscious to the conscious. It was difficult to perform, but after a few tries I was able to step out of any nightmare or dream. As I became more practiced, I could exit the nightmare as soon as the chase started, even in the first room.

* * *

The annoyance of wearing scratchy layers of woollen clothing through the long winters was somewhat relieved by the celebration of Yuletide. It was a quiet but special celebration in our household and seemed mostly to entail Mia, Visa and me spending time in front of the Christmas tree, which we set up in the formal living room on the Other Side. Christmas trees, of course, had to be imported from Denmark. I loved the smell of the fresh pine. The sturdy branches, densely covered with short needles looked lovely adorned with red candles and our homemade ornaments. On a table we placed the traditional Advent Wreath holding four candles. Mia lit the first candle on the fourth Sunday before Christmas. The lighted candle represented Jesus as the light of the world and the wreath symbolized God's unending love. I wasn't aware of Mia being overly religious – I never saw her read the bible and she didn't give up cigars during Lent, but she observed all the Lutheran festivals and practices. On subsequent Sundays, another candle was lit. It was a solemn ritual that we performed each Sunday. Before Christianity, Pagan mid-winter rituals had also featured a wreath with four candles, representing the elements of earth, wind, fire and water.

Every family fashioned their own Christmas decorations. Mia taught me to make traditional Danish decorations out of coloured paper. The woven paper hearts were unique to Denmark and I loved making them as it was not just challenging, but meant I was allowed to use scissors, normally deemed unsafe, owing to my history of clumsiness. I would take two different coloured pieces of gloss paper, fold them over and cut two identical oblong pieces, about ten centimetres wide, then cut the open side using a glass to form a curve. Next I cut two straight lines into the pieces, making three ribs. The difficult part was braiding the ribs, but once finished, the hearts looked splendid. I had seen in Danish magazines that only the red and white colours of the Danish flag were used, but Mia cut loose and bought every colour available.

Tulla baked enough cakes and butter biscuits for several households and the scent of cinnamon wafted through the cement house. All the house cleaning, baking, Christmas decoration and gift wrapping had to be completed for some unexplained reason by 23 December and there was always a rush to meet the deadline. Under the Christmas tree we placed a nativity scene that Sigrid had bought for me in Italy. The fine plaster of Paris figurines of Mary, Joseph, the baby Jesus and the three wise men were exquisitely made, as only the Italians can do with such things. Even the little lambs were beautifully crafted and looked a sight better than the ones in our outfields.

Nativity sets were very popular, especially at my school, which had enough to supply every Nordic country. Maybe this was not so surprising as the school's patron saint was after all Saint Francis of Assisi, who originated the Christmas crib in his celebration of the Nativity in Creccio, Italy. There he used wooden figures, starting a tradition that continues to this day.

Each year, Mia bought me an Advent calendar depicting a wonderful Christmas scene along with twenty-four little closed window flaps, each with the date printed on it. Every morning leading up to Christmas Eve, I solemnly opened a flap as if my life depended on it. Each flap revealed a biblical scene or, in order to please everyone, a picture of a commercial gift. Mia bought walnuts, which we took care to open up without crushing the shells, so that we could use the half shells for making little boats and baskets to hang on the tree.

It was early in the afternoon one Christmas Eve, and pitch black outside. A thick layer of snow had fallen during the night, making this a truly special Christmas. The church bells pealed louder than usual I thought, announcing the service about to begin. It was only a five-minute walk to the Havnar Church and Mia told me not to worry, that we would not miss the beginning of the service. I wasn't worried; I would have preferred to miss it. Surely the pastor was not going to give his usual droning sermon on this of all festive days. But he did, so I sat there and transported myself into Tulla's sweet-smelling kitchen, where I knew a goose, fresh from our farm, was roasting in the oven having received the final touches of Tulla's imaginative culinary talents. The service was over at last and we all headed straight to Tulla's dining room, where a feast awaited us. After the meal, the candles were lit on the tree and everyone joined hands and sang Christmas carols.

When we got home, Mia, Visa and I went into the living room on the Other Side, where Mia lit for the first time the many red candles on our tree. Then she turned off the electric lights. Oh, it was magical, just like a scene from a Hans Christian Andersen fairy tale, when the Little Match Girl lit one of her precious matches that she had been unable to sell and saw in the flame a Christmas tree glittering with tinsel. The light from the candles rose higher and higher. I looked under the tree, convinced that the Nutcracker King would be standing there; ready to help us crack open the walnuts.

'Why don't you sing some carols in front of the tree,' Mia suggested to me, no doubt encouraged by the earlier carol singing next door. In that instant the magic was dispelled. I felt stupid having to do this and objected strongly, painfully aware that my voice was as flat as the delicious pancakes Tulla made. But Mia insisted. There was nothing wrong with my ears and I was acutely embarrassed hearing my own unmusical voice rising off key above the pine needles. That year, I couldn't wait for Christmas to be over in case I should be asked for a repeat performance, but it never happened. Maybe it had been too awful for Mia as well.

Visa must also have wondered what good my musical exploits with the zither had done me.

On New Year's Eve, bonfires were lit in many places around town. Occasionally, I watched with Mia from a safe distance. The Sivertsen children were not allowed to start any bonfires themselves and the buying of firecrackers was forbidden. However, Sjúrður and Júst got around this restriction by making their own. I had no idea how they made them, as this was boys' stuff. It was all very exciting, although I was a bit concerned that New Year's Eve was the time when dead people emerged from their graves and walked around the earth. Or did they do that at midnight on All Souls' Day in November, the day of remembrance of the dead? I believed everything I was told, especially when it came to spirits. The ghosts of the night were as real to me as flesh and blood people of the day.

Antonia with her porcelain doll on the shore of West Bay, Tinganes, on a calm summer's day. Tórshavn, 1951. This was a photo update sent to her mother in Australia.

Antonia with Per, the dog from next door, overlooking the
harbour of Tórshavn. Summer 1952.

Boats and ships fly their signal flags in Tórshavn Harbour
in celebration of the Feast of St Olav. July 1955.

## Chapter Fourteen


*T*HE MAJOR FESTIVAL of the year was *Ólavsøka,* St Ólav – a national holiday in the Faeroes. People descended on Tórshavn from all the islands during the two days of the festival, which took place each year on 28 and 29 July. Everyone would don their Føroysk *Klæðir,* Faeroese clothes, worn as a symbol of Faeroese identify, but labelled national costume by foreigners.

The feast originated with King Olav Dirge, the son of King Harald - the most famous of all kings in the history of Norway - who also reigned over the Orkneys, Shetland, the Faeroes and Greenland from 1015 to 1030. According to the Sagas he was not very tall and somewhat plump, but strong, hence the nickname Olav the Stout. During a break from raiding, Olav and his men spent a winter in Normandy, where Olav soon became convinced that Christianity was the only true religion. He was baptised and thereafter set about forcing Christianity upon his people. 'Norway should be Christian – or die,' he said, wielding a sword rather than a Bible.

The *Faereyingasaga* (Faeroese Sagas), relate the story of Sigmund, one of the chiefs of the Faeroes, who was commanded by King Olav to ensure that his fellow-islanders also accept the 'yoke of Christ'. Sigmund, himself a pagan until his recent conversion, did not want to take on this challenge, but finally yielded and the King rewarded him with rule over the islands. After some tricky manoeuvres, Sigmund succeeded in having his cousin Thrand and his pagan followers baptised as described in a chapter of the sagas entitled 'Thrand Tricked'. The usual bloody skirmishes followed. I found these stories were fascinating, if not a little bloodthirsty.

Meanwhile, back in Norway, King Olav was having his own problems and had to flee his country. He returned a year later and was stabbed to death at the Battle of Stiklestad near Nidarós on 29 July 1030. A year later, when his body was disinterred, it had not decomposed and his hair, nails and beard had grown as if he were still alive. A lock of King Olav's hair was placed in unhallowed fire. The hair did not burn and then everyone realised that he was indeed a man of God and gave him an honourable burial. Thereafter many miracles took place. His failure as a king was forgotten and his memory immortalised. Olav the Holy was made patron saint of Norway and the island colonies. This commemorative day has survived.

Already the day before *Ólavsøka*, people would start to arrive from every corner of the archipelago. The *Smyril* ferryboats were spilling over with eager passengers. The shops were full of these yearly visitors, buying goods that were unobtainable in smaller villages. Every household soon filled with houseguests, except for ours, though I was always glad of this, given my fear of strangers.

Looking out of my bedroom window on the first morning of St Olav's Day, I think it was in 1955, I noticed after the fog had lifted that all the ships and ferries in the harbour were flying their signal flags. I knew that these were going to be eventful days. There would be boat races, pony races, music, parades and singing. In the evening, the traditional ring dancing would go on until the early hours of the morning. I was at home before the dancing started, but there was talk about it the next day. I had difficulty imagining Mia or Visa dancing, although they may have done so in their youth.

The famous boat race was held on the first day of the festival and I went up to the loft on the Other Side in readiness for the start. Rowing teams that had already competed in lead-up rallies throughout the year were getting ready to contest the championship. I liked to watch the beautifully shaped wooden boats, similar in design to the old Viking boats. High-sided at both bow and stern, today tied with coloured ribbons to distinguish the teams, they were long, but wide of beam. The boat race started out in the fjord and I could tell by their movements that the rowers were eager and the skippers were standing at the bow poised for the starting gun. The boats skimmed over the dark sea. They had been practicing all year for this race. The boats held six, eight or ten rowers plus the skipper. I had absolutely no idea which team won each year; only the spectacle was of interest to me.

Rachel and her sister, Anna Maria had promised to take me with them to watch the parade on the main street, Niels Finsens gøta, named after Niels R. Finsens, who received the Nobel Prize for Medicine in 1903. Arriving far too early next door on the 29th, I found that the girls were still getting ready. Anna Maria was in the bath. I noticed she was wearing her stockings and I asked why she had them on in the bath.

'Both me and my stockings need washing, so I might as well do them at the same time,' she replied, lifting up one stockinged leg and scrubbing it with soap. She said it in such a matter of fact manner as if it was something everyone did. Somehow, I could not imagine that I would be doing that once I started to wear stockings.

I watched as Rachel and Anna Maria put on long gathered woven skirts in dark red with a fine blue line. Over the top they tied lighter coloured aprons. Rachel's had horizontal red and white stripes and Anna Maria's apron had a floral pattern. A black and red knitted bodice was held together in the front with a laced silver chain. The final item was an embroidered cream-coloured shawl with long fringes, draped over their shoulders and held together at the chest by a brooch of Viking design. Anna Maria wore an embroidered cap tied under the chin with a long ribbon, while Rachel went hatless, showing off her stylishly cut blonde hair.

The boys were in jodhpur-type dark pants with black collar-less jackets with silver buttons and red vests underneath. The older generation wore darker ones. 'Danish' shoes, that is, leather shoes with large silver buckles, replaced the usual soft sheepskin ones.

The traditional Faeroese striped cap completed the boys' and men's outfit. Not being Faeroese, I wore regular clothes and I felt certain that this was equivalent to wearing a label on my chest marked 'outsider', even though it was not in the Faeroese character to afford such treatment to anyone.

A bitterly cold wind was blowing and the girls had goosebumps on their bare forearms. Mia had fretted over the coldness of this summer's day and had dressed me in a winter coat. Despite my strong protests, she insisted that I also wear a fake fur bonnet complete with chinstrap. I felt ridiculously over-dressed and much to my embarrassment someone took a photograph of Rachel, Anna Maria and me standing at the back of the rocks of Tinganes. Many prints were made and copies kept creeping up everywhere for years. The wind had picked up considerably and understandably the girls look frozen in the photograph, though brave Rachel has managed a sweet smile. I'm standing between them, looking as if I have stepped right out of a freezing winter's day in Greenland.

We proceeded hand in hand to the centre of town, where it was all happening. The Merkið, the Faeroese flag was fluttering wildly from every government and office building. A choir was singing. It didn't get much more exciting than this. New York had its St Patrick's Day parade and we had our St Olav's Day. The ceremonial procession was about to begin, headed by officials on horseback each carrying a Faeroese flag, which they struggled to hold in the strong wind. The Danish High Commissioner walked immediately behind them dressed in full regalia. At his side was the head of the Faeroese Government followed by senior clergy and politicians walking side by side in a demonstration of church and parliamentary unity. A brass band struck up. I kept looking at the frenzied flapping of the long white feathers on the High Commissioner's head gear, thinking it would really be funny if they all dislodged and blew away.

Everyone was milling about in their Faeroese clothes. They all seemed to know each other well. How was this possible, I wondered, when there were so many people, strangers, from the other islands? I hadn't realised as yet that most Faeroese are related. They were behaving like one big family. Now, I really felt like an outsider, even though I was still holding on to Rachel's hand. At that moment, looking like a Greenlander would have been acceptable, but no, I was overcome by the acute discomfort of appearing like a visitor from another planet. Visa had told me about the other planets and the strange beings that might inhabit them. I had also become aware that my big brown eyes and dark woolly hair put me most definitely in the minority among the blue-eyed flaxen-haired Nordics. Oh, why had I been delivered to these islands, where I stuck out like a Moor at the Chinese court? Where did I really fit in and why wasn't I with my parents? It was all very puzzling, no doubt because Mia's mollycoddling efforts to keep me doll-like and separate always made it that way.

After the church service, the procession returned to the parliament building, a traditional Faeroese building with a tuft roof. Following ancient tradition, the Prime Minister opened the new *Løgting*, marking the beginning of the new parliament year. The Prime Minister delivered an overview of the general state of affairs on the islands. Outside, the brass band played and Parliament went into session. Everywhere was so crowded and noisy. I did not like it one bit. Normally there were more chickens and ducks to be seen in the streets than people.

The pony race was next and we went with the boys to watch it. The races consisted of only two riders per race, mounted on sweet-looking Faeroe ponies of a Celtic breed. Júst – Mia was definitely not interested in sport – explained to me that only two ponies could race at a time, as the track was so narrow. All the races were timed and the participants who had come first and second had to race again to see who would be the winner. For years I thought this was how all horse races were run in other parts of the word as well. In the evening, when I was safely in bed, there was dancing and drinking and much gossip the next day about the drinking - especially that some people had even got drunk. Those who did not drink frowned upon this. There was talk of people drinking up their entire quarterly allowance in one night!

The liquor laws of the Faeroes have always been most peculiar. No liquor shops existed in my time. Liquor could only be obtained privately from Denmark once every quarter and the limit was twelve bottles. There were extra allowances for special birthdays and weddings; needless to say, there were many planned weddings. Yet, even this ration was not granted if a Faeroese resident was not able to produce a revenue certificate stating that his taxes had been paid to date.

It must have come as a shock for visiting sailors to find themselves in a port without a bar, but it wasn't always so. Alcohol imports were allowed up to the nineteenth century, but unfortunately during the trade monopoly unethical storekeepers saw opportunities to acquire farmland for themselves by plying the destitute farmers with potent schnapps. Once inebriated, the poor farmers gave their land away for practically nothing. The *Løgting* put a stop to this unscrupulous practice by banning alcohol all together.

In our dining room, Mia kept a crystal decanter filled with a dark liquid, probably the world famous Cherry Herring, and a bottle of Akvavit Schnapps, which were kept not on top of the sideboard, but hidden inside. When special visitors came, they were offered a glass in a somewhat furtive manner, as though we were doing something wrong. The guest would reverently drink the precious liquid. The decanter was put away, a refill never offered. The Lutherans frowned upon drunkenness. On St Olav's Day, it was rumoured that some men even carried bottles on them, offering a nip to their friends and as the night wore on - even to strangers right there in the street. The more rowdy ones were put in jail for the night. They were never charged, just left to sober up and then released the next day.

The Faeroese are very hospitable and during St Olav's Day, every house had cakes and coffee at the ready for any number of unexpected visitors. Tulla tripled her cake baking production. Mia, who never baked a thing in her life, compensated by buying me gingerbread men. Sigrid also mailed us little delicacies from Italy, such as dates, which we regarded as a luxury food item. The dates came neatly packed in a slim box like a pencil case with the picture of a camel standing under the shade of a palm tree. This in itself was exotic. Inside were two rows of plump smooth dates, perfectly arranged at a slight angle, complete with a little two-pronged plastic fork, carved to look like ivory. One date per day was the allowance for this bounty from the Mediterranean. Sigrid also sent us sugar-glazed almonds; usually five almonds enclosed in a diaphanous white tulle sachet and tied with either a pink or blue ribbon. Sigrid wrote that it was customary in Italy to hand out these *bonbonera* at christenings, Sigrid attending many of these in her line of work.

Another major event in our lives and cause for much celebration was the whale hunt, though unlike the Feast of St Olav, the date was unpredictable.

## Chapter Fifteen

NOT EVEN FESTIVE St Olav's Day could surpass the excitement created when a school of pilot whales surfaced, spouting water high into the air through their blowholes, thus unwittingly announcing their presence.

Pilot whales, also known as caaing whales in Shetland, appear around the islands at all times of the year, especially in late summer when there is an abundance of squid. The whales take several quick breaths and then submerge for a few minutes or longer if it is a feeding dive. They travel in numbers ranging from a few to a thousand or more. These small-toothed, long-finned whales, reaching up to seven metres in length, are called 'pilot' whales because they seem to have adopted the habit of swimming in large schools that follow a chosen leader or pilot. Sometimes the whales rest motionlessly at the surface, allowing boats to approach them slowly. Pilot whales live permanently either offshore or inshore, while others make inshore-to-offshore migrations according to the amount of squid – and the Faeroes have plenty of it. Bottlenose, fin and killer whales also swim around the islands, as well as dolphins and porpoises.

The minute a pod of pilot whales was sighted, either by someone on shore or by a fishing boat, the cry went up, '*Grindaboð!*' – Whales in sight. It spread like wildfire through Tórshavn. In Faeroese, *grind* is a school or pod of whales. *Grind* is also used to describe the meat of the whale. Since the early Norse days, the whale had a long history as a crucial source of food supply, so the sighting of a school always caused great joy. Sometimes I had no idea how or when the alarm was raised, I just knew that the hunt was on. Normally, the fisherman who sighted the whales would raise a makeshift flag from his boat to alert the other fishermen and people on land. At times, someone on shore spotted the whales. There were always some keen Faeromen watching the sea for a group of fins cutting through the water, especially after heavy rains, as this condition was believed to be connected with the whales' arrival. Once the alarm was raised, the elected whaling officials and district sheriff were notified first. In the early days, there was a complex system of smoke signals or white sheets were spread on fields, sending the message from village to village.

Whatever the means of call to the hunt, an electrifying excitement would spread through the community. Everyone stopped what they were doing and made for the shore, as able-bodied men would be needed in some way for the hunt. The first one I remember clearly occurred on a weekday one June. Classes had just started when the news of *Grindabroð* reached our school. When one of the nuns made the announcement, we all jumped excitedly out of our seats, as we knew that this meant no more school for the rest of the day. However, in keeping with the school's disciplinary code we were made to sit down again until the lesson was brought to a quick end. There was no point in continuing as no one was paying any attention. At last we were free to go and watch the hunt. I sprinted home and went straight upstairs to the Other Side. I strained to see as far out into the fjord as I could, as this was where it was all happening. Closer to our place, I watched the men rush into their wooden boats to join the others who had already reached the *grind*. The boats with outboard motors had got there first, while the others rowed like crazy so as not to lag too far behind. The excitement gripped me as well, and I was impatient for the school to be driven into the harbour, so that I could go down to walk among the whales once they had been dragged ashore.

The hunt was always highly organized. Each town or area had an elected *grind* foreman, who supervised the hunt. His boat hoisted the national flag so that he could be easily identified, as the men in the other boats had to take their instructions from him. Regulations stipulated how the whales should be killed and what equipment could be used. Once enough boats reached the school, they formed a wide half circle behind the whales and herded them slowly and at first quietly from the open ocean into our harbour in East Bay. Then on the foreman's signal, the men began to drive the whales further toward the shore by shouting and throwing stones attached to ropes, forcing the whales forward. Sometimes the whales would outsmart the hunters, by breaking up into smaller schools and, depending on the current, making for the open sea. But most of the time, the skill of the hunters prevented them from escaping. The chase was never an easy task, for if the *grind* panicked they could easily smash the wooden boats. At other times, if the school was not close enough to the designated whaling bay, both hunters and hunted would have to rest until the current was right and the tide changed, as the whales could not be driven against the tide. This could require many hours of waiting.

Only men participated in the whale hunt, but there was a story from earlier times, when all the men from a village were away fishing in Iceland and the local women, on sighting some whales, went out in whatever boats were left and successfully drove the whales into the bay.

By late afternoon on this day, the *grind* was entering the harbour and it was time for me to put on my galoshes and go down to the East Bay with Mia to join the rest of the silent crowd lining the quay. The men in the boats were still shouting. I remember the noise was terrible. Before we got there, one of the men in the lead boat, it would have been the foreman, had taken aim with his harpoon at a particular whale, which he managed to spear in the back behind the fin, causing the whale to head at considerable speed for the sandy shore of the bay with blood pouring out of it.

The rest of the whales were blindly following their wounded leader. I wondered how the man knew which whale to choose and how the whales, so much stronger than the men in their wooden boats, allowed themselves to be herded to the point of no return.

As the whales surged towards the shore, following their bleeding pilot, the water became too shallow for them to swim in. Their huge bodies rolled about uncontrollably, tails thrashing, creating waves in every direction. As Mia and I arrived on the scene, men and whales were moving so fast that I couldn't follow what was going on. For a few moments, it looked like chaos, but the Faeroemen had everything under control. The whales continued to swim so fast that they ended high up on the part of shore called *Kongabrúgvin* or King's Bridge. As the whales started to beach in quick succession, the men jumped from their boats into the water, where they stood chest deep. With special long *grind*-knives, which were kept in a belt at their waist, the men killed the whales with two deep, swift strokes to the back of the neck, just about a hand's breadth from the blowhole. The whales went into a violent spasm for a few seconds and then became completely still. I turned away momentarily and buried my face in Mia's coat, allowing her to pat me on the head. I was both excited and frightened.

*Undir Kjallara*, appropriately named Under the Cellars, because of the old warehouses with tall cellars lining the narrow walkway between the bank and the bay, was now crowded with every living soul in Tórshavn. The men, who up to now had been watching silently from the shore, started shouting and jumped noisily in among the whales where they were beaching and helped to kill them as quickly as possible with their own whale knives. Some of the whales did not make it on to the shore and sank in the shallow water. I continued to watch as the men then drove a heavy steel hook attached to a rope into the back of a whale's neck. I covered my eyes with my hands. When I looked again, the men were hauling the whales on to the shore with ropes and some of the bigger schoolboys had joined in. Other whales were winched up by their tails by means of a tall ominous-looking contraption,

98

much like the gallows that I had read about. I noticed that the cold water had turned from grey to red. There was a lot of froth as each whale gave a last shudder before dying.

The King's Bridge – where some of the whales now lay - had been a quay hastily erected for King Christian IX when he first stepped on Faeroese soil back in 1874. It was the inaugural visit by a Danish King, whose ship stopped here on the way back from Iceland, which was celebrating its millennium of settlement. The Faeroese official who gave a welcome speech to the King on this shore, was so overcome with excitement that he dropped dead immediately afterwards, on the very place where many whales had now met an identical fate. King's Bridge was also in my time the place where we children threw out lines to catch small coalfish for the neighbourhood cats. It was a place that served many purposes.

Like the hunt, the whale slaughter, known as *grindadráp,* was carried out in a swift and efficient manner according to regulation. One by one, the whales were sliced open in the abdomen to cool the carcasses so that the meat did not spoil. Mia and I had brought buckets with us, as everyone in the area received a free portion of meat and blubber. The catch was divided into shares according to a complex distribution system unique to each whaling district. The proportioning of the catch was first codified in the thirteenth century in the Sheep Letter legislation. Larger pieces went to the fishermen of the boat that had sighted the school and extra pieces were given to the owners of any damaged boats. The local sheriff supervised this portioning of the meat and blubber. All of us children walked eagerly among the whales as they were being cut up and the more adventurous ones even managed a slippery ride on the whales as they were being hauled up with a rope. The quick ones would pick up a whale tooth or two, which made a prized possession, and I was pleased to note that Júst and Sjúrður had each managed to get one. Like all Faeroese children, I became used to watching the slaughter of animals for our food supplies. We had little experience of going to the butcher to buy pieces of neatly cut meat displayed on metal trays, as I learned to expect in my later life.

As I walked among the rows of dead whales, I used to put out of my mind the slaughter that I'd witnessed and instead imagined myself a mermaid swimming among my giant friends, the whales, with their cute rounded, bulbous foreheads. I temporarily ignored the fact that they were lying dead in a pool of blood at my feet. I truly believed in mermaids, having been brought up on tales of these lovely creatures. I had seen in books, photos of the Mermaid of Copenhagen, sunning herself on a rock in the harbour. Her beautiful human body from head to waist glistening in the sun; her long hair hanging loosely down her bare back. She had no legs and instead wore a smooth form like a seal from the waist down. Local lore contended that mermaids were often responsible for luring fishermen to them and consequently to their certain death. They were also blamed for snapping off hooks from fishermen's lines. There used to be many seals around the Faeroe Islands, especially along the east coast, but sadly only a few remain.

Some of the whale hunts finished late at night, and it was past our suppertime when we received our share of the meat, but I was allowed to stay up late, it being a special occasion. After the hard and cold work of the whale hunt, the exhausted men would head home, their clothes soaked in seawater and blood. If anyone who had helped with the hunt had too far to go, there was never a problem of somewhere to sleep overnight as the Faeroese are very hospitable. Many gathered in the dance hall for the ritual ring dancing and chanting of traditional ballads, or as the expression goes, 'to dance themselves warm', until the wee hours of the morning. There was much drinking and next day people would be standing in the street whispering to each other about men behaving badly, meaning I guessed, that they got drunk. There was hardly ever any fighting, as conflicts were avoided. The Faeroese are not habitual drinkers. The preferred drink is coffee, which is consumed all-day and well into the night, the Faeroese being night owls by nature.

When the whale hunt finished late, the rest of the whale meat was not divided up until the next day and the sheriff would appoint some people to watch the whales during the night. I reasoned that this was not so much because of fear of theft, but in the main due to the threat of Russian rats and Faeroese birds. The sheriff ensured that each whale had a number carved into its head and tail, part of the orderly system of distributing the catch.

The *grind's* thick smooth black skin like wet rubber and its even thicker layer of blubber and whale meat fascinated me. I would watch closely as the men carved out the heart, liver and kidneys. This was my open-air biology class, where I would imagine a teacher announcing, 'Now, children, today in class we will dissect a whale.'

After the slaughter, the water in the bay turned a deep red with the spilled blood of some hundreds of whales, in sharp contrast to its usual pewter-colour. The strong smell of blood and meat did not bother me. Even as a child, I felt an unexplained sense of ancient ritual being played out, from the first sighting of the whales to the eating of them. The Englishman, Kenneth Williamson, who was stationed in the Faeroes during World War II and who married a Faeroese, wrote:

'Should this very remarkable practice ever vanish from the Faeroe scene, then this small nation will have lost an integral part of its nationhood and one of the most significant factors in the curious identity of its life.'

It seemed perfectly natural that the slaughter of the *grind* should take place. It was a very Faeroese thing to do. It was understood that the killing was not done for sport but for food. In the old days, before imported food, a successful whale hunt meant the difference between having food for the long winter or not having any at all. It was not possible to produce fresh meat in sufficient quantities to satisfy the needs of this small population. Though I admit, any foreigners surveying us walking through the crimson blood in our black galoshes would have found this to be a surreal scene. In different ways, all of us participated in this old Viking ritual.

The whale hunt and haymaking were the only times when I truly felt part of the community in which I lived. At other times, I felt as if I was a stranger on an extended visit – which indeed I was. I was included as part of the Sivertsen family, yet I knew I was not their kin. Would my mother ever come to pick me up? I dared not speculate on the answer. As I grew older, I convinced myself that wherever I went, people would look at me and think, 'Ah, yes, there goes the foreigner who has come to live among us'. Had I confided in Mia, she would have no doubt assured me that this was not the case, but I never gave her the opportunity to do so.

Mia and I received our portion of *grind* and *skip* (blubber), which we carried back to our house in a steel bucket. It was heavy and we could hardly lift it off the ground. The boys, Sjúrður and Júst came to our rescue. They were always on hand to help. The whale meat was usually boiled fresh, but some of the meat was also cut into thick strips and hung in the *hjallur* to air-dry in preparation for the meat shortages of winter. The blubber was cut into chunks and placed in salt, where it lasted for years. It was normally cut into thin strips and served with dry fish. It was chewy and I did not like it much. The blubber is full of vitamins, especially vitamin A, which is scarce in the Faeroese diet. Just like the sheep, nothing was wasted. The whale's stomach was tanned and blown up to be used as buoys for fishing nets and parts of the skin and sinews were utilised for ropes and lines. Whalebone was fashioned into rings, pendants and brooches. Many were in the Old Viking style, but some were modern such as my brooch in the smooth shape of a whale. Villagers used the whale skulls for building garden fences.

Once in the kitchen, Mia got the fire roaring in the stove and proceeded to cook, or rather to ruin, the whale meat by boiling it for too long. She was an awful cook and the meat came out salty and dry. She served it with raw blubber, which had an unpleasant leathery consistency. The *grind* was dark red in colour and did not taste like fish, more like rich meat. It was always served with the inevitable peeled boiled potatoes. Boiled shoes would have tasted the same in Mia's kitchen. Meanwhile, next door, Tulla was cooking her family's portion of meat to perfection, which I imagined she served as steaks, covered with delicious brown gravy, accompanied by peeled boiled potatoes.

The next morning, I went down to the East Bay, where tired looking men were portioning off the last of the whales. The ground was strewn with vertebrae and bones and neatly cut up chunks of meat and blubber. The sea was still red and the blood on the ground had turned black.

A whaling station was in operation on our island in vid Áir, between the towns of Hósvik and Hvavík. The station produced mainly train oil for export and great steam vats were used in the boiling down of meat, blubber and bones for the oil.

Occasionally, a sperm whale or a small group of bottlenose whales, usually no more than two or three, would come into a fjord on their own, without being driven. They would probably have become disoriented due to the thick fog and the darkness of the night and have swum onto the beach with the flood tide. When the ebb came, the whales would be lying dead on the beach. This must have been a godsend for the early Vikings, who awakened to find all this food right on their doorstep. Meat of the bottlenose was eaten, but the blubber was inedible, though it is believed to have some excellent medicinal properties.

Unlike the pilot whales, the bottlenose whales were very hard to approach as they were easily frightened by the slightest noise and were therefore difficult to herd.

Bottlenose whales are called *døglingur* in Faeroese. *Døglingur* is derived from an Old Norse word *dòglingur*, which was poetic language for king or prince. Much as the lion is known as the King of Beasts, the bottlenose whale is known in Nordic countries as the Prince of Whales. The ancient belief that the whale has only one eye is thought to be a reference to the one-eyed Norse god, Oðin, who had exchanged one of his eyes for wisdom. *Døglingur* is also a nickname for a one-eyed person as well as a badly made haystack that has blown over in a heavy breeze – such is the diversity of the Faeroese language.

Whales sometimes beached themselves for reasons unknown to us. For centuries, two or three bottlenose whales had been stranding on an almost annual basis on the southern islands of Suðuroy.

A Faeroese folktale explains neatly why bottlenose whales appear mainly on Suðuroy. There was a fight in Pagan times between a troll and a man, who both inhabited the island of Mykines. Trolls were big, strong and ugly – except to themselves of course. Sometimes they had three heads, the extras being of no use to them, and they were deemed stupid and could easily be out-witted by man. Not surprisingly, the troll was defeated. In return for being allowed to stay on the island, this troll offered the man whales and birds that could not be found anywhere else in the Faeroes. The troll made one condition; that no one was allowed to laugh or ridicule the whales. When the first whale stranded on the island, the inhabitants noticed that it had only one eye and fell about laughing. Ever since then, bottlenose whales strand on the island of Suðuroy instead, to avoid any chagrin.

Antonia on the farm outside Tórshavn. In the background is the rocky coastline of Place By the Shore. Summer 1954.

Antonia and her mother in the living room on the Other Side, in a pose set up by the professional photographer called in for the occasion of her mother's visit. Tórshavn, 1954.

Antonia with Anna Maria and Rachel, who are wearing their Faeroese clothes, out on the cliffs at Tórshavn on a chilly St Olav's Day. July 1955.

## Chapter Sixteen


MORE THAN ANYTHING, the sea and fishing dominated almost every aspect of life on the islands. Fishing was the main trade and business was based directly and indirectly on the fishing industry. The main export was klippfisk, dried salt cod. The *toskur*, large cod was enormous, more than half my size and twice my weight. Other species landed were haddock and coalfish, while herrings were netted in the fjords. The deeper waters abounded in blue whiting, redfish, ling, and foreign vessels from Russia, Norway and Britain, as the fishing limit was only three miles off the Faeroese coast. Yet, despite the abundance of fish, the industry was in deep crisis. I was too young to comprehend what was going on, but there was much talk about costs beings higher than the returns from the catch and ship owners going bankrupt. The Faeroese fishing fleet, consisting of second-hand schooners, steam-trawlers and old single-masted sailing boats was desperately in need of modernisation, but money was in short supply. There was an exodus of young people to Denmark, all seeking jobs.

Until the mid-nineteenth century, fishing had been of secondary importance. This might seem strange, but the Faeroemen of the time had only open wooden boats from which they fished by line not far from shore, and the catch was only enough to feed their local community. Wool had been the main export product, so much so that the phrase 'wool is Faeroese gold' was coined. Then, with the abolition of the Danish crown monopoly, the Faeroes bought some antiquated fishing sloops from the British, of which some were still in service in the 1950s.

The first such ship was the famous *Fox*, a 28-year-old wooden sloop purchased from a Grimsby owner. The proud fishermen sailed the *Fox* as far afield as Iceland, where they fished from smaller boats and brought their catch to the *Fox*. Their main catch was cod, which was gutted, cleaned, beheaded, split, salted and dried - and so the production of salting fish began. This *klippfisk* proved to be a successful export to Mediterranean markets, thanks in the main to the Catholic Church's stipulation that fish be eaten on Fridays and certain high holy days. After salting, the fish were placed outside to dry on an area of flat rocks or special drying grounds near the harbour. There was one such area near the Sivertsens' farm. However, drying fish outdoors in a land of rain was a tricky business. At the first sign of rain, the fish had to be taken inside to prevent spoiling. The changeable Faeroese weather meant that in one day, the fish could be brought in and out of doors five or six times. Women and children provided this labour as it was regarded as 'women's work'. It was a popular summer job for the boys and girls from our school. One person was always on guard, to watch for any changes in weather, which there surely was. Maybe it was all that drying *klippfisk* that prompted the traveller, William Morris, to note in his journal on 11 July 1871:

'Tórshavn pleased me very much; certainly there was a smell of fish...'

I could certainly attest to this ever-present odour that seemed hard to escape in some areas, though I did not mind it at all. There was one exception, the pungent smell of cod liver being boiled to extract its valuable oil, the revolting stuff that Mia fed me once a week. The early settlers used cod liver oil to fuel their lamps. The name for this oil in Old Norse was *lysi,* meaning light. In Faeroese lýsi also means both light and whale oil (from liver, whale blubber and the like).

As a child, I was never keen on eating fish, as the bones worried me terribly, especially since an earlier experience of having a bone caught in my throat had sent me into complete panic. Mia had rescued me from the jaws of death, I felt sure, by making me eat a large amount of dry bread. I was truly a fish out of water in the land of fish. Herrings were eaten fresh in summer and even though Mia assured me:

'Don't worry, the bones are soft, so you can eat them.' I preferred the salted herrings, which we ate in winter as to me the bones seemed to have shrunk. There was one fish dish that I really liked and that was boiled cod's head – yes, just as I liked sheep's head, so I also liked cod's head.  No other parts of that fish were used by the Faeroese, since all the cod landed was salted, dried and exported.

The cod heads hung in Júst's *hjallur* for some weeks, where they were air-dried. Mia simmered the heads in water in a big black pot and, for once, she managed to do this without ruining them. The cheeks were delectable, so soft and delicate. Unlike the closed squashed eyelid of the sheep's head, the cod's large jellied eyes stared at me as if alive, daring me to eat them. I took up the challenge and they were scrumptious, but I always made sure to spit out the hard-as-a-pearl cornea.  It was disconcerting to me that, apart from the cod's head, I didn't care to eat the most readily available food source in my small land.

I was pleased that Júst was not a fishermen or ship owner, not so much due to the hardships they were experiencing, but because it meant I didn't have to eat fish all the time. A child's logic thus reigned supreme. I had a sense that life was hard.  I heard stories of men being lost at sea during the horrific North Atlantic storms of winter, though not to the extent of the days of the open fishing boats when sometimes a whole village of men would perish at once. No wonder the North Atlantic was labelled 'the old grey widow-maker'. It was said that people in the countryside living so close to nature had a second sight and a wife would have a dream about her husband, brother and son dying in a shipwreck. When one ship went down, it meant losing all the men folk from one family or a whole hamlet. When a storm raged for a week, fishing activities were brought to a complete standstill and the fishermen had no choice but to go home and sit it out.

In summer, I would watch the young men dive into the cold sea, but it never looked like an inviting prospect and on hearing of disasters at sea, I would have dreams about dying: I would drown because I did not know how to swim. In the dream, my dead body was carried ashore and put on a slab so narrow that it hardly fitted. I saw myself standing close by watching my own corpse. There was a naked light globe suspended above my body. It was the same light as the one in the dream where I am being chased through the shrinking rooms of my house. The light went out and my spirit, in which I was a firm believer, rose and hovered momentarily above my dead body. There were now three of me.

I did not feel sufficiently attached to Mia to tell her about this strange dream, even though as a woman born and bred in the Faeroes she may well have understood its meaning. I would lie in my bed, listening to a storm raging outside. *Thór* was pounding on our iron roof with his strong fists. He shook the wooden walls of our house making them creak and groan so badly that I was convinced they would fall apart plank by plank and bury us; but not before the heavy horizontal rain had smashed in the window at the foot of my bed and sent shards of glass all over me. We would hear news of fishing boats, not just Faeroese but also boats from other nations, being sunk and fishermen drowning. I would silently pull my eiderdown tightly around me, so as to prevent Mia coming to My Side, and sink into an unpleasant dream.

In the 1950s, as many as one hundred fishermen at a time would catch a ride on a cargo ship plying the route to Greenland, where they stayed until the onset of winter, fishing for cod from small land-based boats. Taking their own boats through treacherous waters to distant Greenland proved impractical. The Danish government severely restricted – from the Faeroese point of view – access to settlements in Greenland, but had finally offered the Faeroese harbour facilities in a God-forsaken area in Western Greenland, south of Nuuk. Here the Faeroese lived in primitive dwellings at a place called Føroyingahavn, the harbour of the Faeroemen. Before the war, the fishermen were not allowed to have any contact with the locals, which may not have proved difficult as the place was essentially deserted. I recoiled at the thought of fishermen living there until the onset of winter, being tossed about by the remorseless waves as they wearily cast their lines into the valleys of the ocean. They were away from their families for months at a time, isolated in their quest to make a living.

Our lives were not as harsh as those of the fishermen; I knew that, though we all had to endure the same long dark winters and fierce storms.

## Chapter Seventeen

MY LIFE WAS quiet and secure inside Bakkahella 4 and activities under its roof did not change much with the seasons. Outside it was a different story. Nature was on the move, always giving out obvious signs as to what time of the year it was. No calendar was needed.

The *tjaldur*, oyster catcher, with its black plumage and bright red beak appeared promptly on all the islands each year on 12 March. Its noisy piping call was unmistakable. The *tjaldur* departed just as noisily on 16 September, except for the ones that did not follow the Faeroese calendar.

The start of summer saw our islands become breeding homes to literally millions of seabirds. It was hard for me to comprehend such large numbers inhabiting our small islands.

When eggs from the guillemots were on sale in the shops in Tórshavn, it was early June. Laws were in place limiting the egging season to about nine days, in order to allow the birds to produce another egg, thereby perpetuating the colony. This species nested on precipitous narrow cliff ledges and their eggs, Visa informed me, were top-shaped so that they could not roll off an inclined surface, but instead would roll around in a circle.

Then, a day would come and the birds would disappear. I asked Visa, 'Where do the sea birds go when they leave us?'

'They spend their lives out at sea, never touching land until it's time to breed again,' she told me.

I shuddered at the thought of spending a long winter floating on the icy waters. I had a large collection of feathers and I had tried to make quills out of the longer ones, but without the aid of a razor blade or a very sharp knife, both of which were kept out of reach, I was not successful.

When Júst and the boys went to the farm to slaughter sheep, it was October and the last bit of outdoor activity was done before the onset of winter.

Inside, reading was a year round occupation. I was a prolific reader and had the complete set of Hans Christian Andersen's fairytales. Each tale was printed separately in a miniature book. They fitted into a cardboard bookcase that was supposed to look antique. I loved these fairytales and would never tire of re-reading them. My favourites were *The Ugly Ducking*, since I identified with the ugly one, *The Red Shoe* and the tragic story of *The Little Mermaid* who falls in love with a handsome human prince. She trades in her beautiful voice in order to become fully human in shape, whereupon she attends her prince mutely. Eventually, he leaves her to marry a human princess and the mermaid is left heartbroken. Later, Mia supplied me with any amount of storybooks for young readers. Leading a fairly closeted life, my understanding of the world outside the Faeroes all came from my Danish books.

The Sivertsen children and I were eager readers of Danish comic books and we had a brisk exchange program going. I loved best the Walt Disney characters and developed a particular fondness for Donald Duck, so much so that I spent several weeks one winter making a Donald Duck animated movie. I had never seen movies of any kind but had read about them with great interest. There was no story line, just Donald walking down the street talking to himself. I felt sure that everyone was as besotted with Donald Duck as I was and that just seeing him would be interesting enough. At the end of the movie, Donald stops walking and waves goodbye. First I fashioned my own flipbook of plain white paper. Then, painstakingly, I drew Donald's image on every page, taking care with each fresh page to change the position of his feathered arms, feet and mouth by a few millimetres. To watch the movie I simply put my thumb to the last page and let it quickly flip over the pages and there was Donald moving as if he were alive, with the voice-over lovingly provided by me. The show was all over in a matter of seconds. I never 'released' my movie, as I wanted to keep Donald Duck exclusively for myself, though I did give Mia a sneak preview and was rewarded with several smoke rings from her cigar.

Mia and I used to play card and board games; Mia's repertoire of card games was enormous, but perhaps not so astonishing, since cigars and card games seem to go hand in hand. I think that she may have played bridge with her friends before she was 'tied down with a child'. She taught me many games, which we played together for hours, though my preference was always for solitaire. Someone had procured a Monopoly set from England, where they suffered from equally long winters it seemed, as this game could occupy many dark hours. I was enthralled at being able to buy real estate in London; a capital that Visa said was even bigger than Copenhagen. It was hard to imagine anything big on these small islands.

Sometimes parcels from Mother would arrive from Australia, wrapped in the familiar black and white hound's-tooth paper from the smart department store, David Jones. One of these parcels contained a South American parrot, the plastic kind, perched on a plastic ring and hidden by a curtain of tiny plastic pearls. When I wound up the key at the base of the parrot's feet, the curtain rose up like magic and exposed the parrot. Mia hung it from the ceiling in our sitting room. Unbeknown to my mother, we had our own parrots on the islands: *lundi*, or puffin, nicknamed 'sea-parrot', because of their bright red, yellow and black parrot-like bills. They lived in their thousands on top of the cliffs in grassy areas where they could burrow a metre deep and form their nests on the bottom. They could be easily plucked from their nests by hand.

As cute as these birds looked, they had provided a good food resource since the time of the first Norse settlers and regularly appeared on dinner plates, sometimes boiled or occasionally roasted and stuffed with a sweet tasting pastry containing raisins. Only the chest was served and the puffin and black guillemot were favoured. However, the people in the settlements and hamlets ate the whole bird, including skin and bones, so someone told me. Thankfully, Mia never made any attempts at preparing the birds. She sensibly bought them already cooked from the Hotel Hafnia, the only 'genuine' hotel in town those days.

Mia and I were served fulmars at someone's place once, though I had no idea at the time what kind of bird I was eating. All I knew is that it tasted so oily and fishy that I wanted to spit out the first mouthful, but was stopped from doing so by Mia's cautionary look. Possibly the fulmar's fondness for eating whale blubber contributed to its foul taste. The *tjaldur* was spared the dinner ritual by being the national bird of the Faeroes. It brought bad luck on those who killed it.

Next door to the Hotel Hafnia was a shop also belonging to the hotel owner, Christian Restorff. The hotel and shop were right on the way home from the Telephone Exchange and this was where Mia bought her supply of cigars. She must surely have been seen as *avant-garde* to be smoking cigars, as it was something that very few women did in those days.

In the evenings, Mia turned on the radio. Despite its fierce crackle, it was our main link to the outside world, as we tuned into the Danish news, Luxembourg Radio and the BBC. There was no Faeroese radio station as yet. We listened to broadcasts of the Danish National Orchestra playing classical music, often conducted by King Frederick IX, an accomplished musician. One of Mia's friends had an HMV gramophone with an enormous trumpet that fascinated me. I remember that I was allowed to wind up the machine, reminding me of a little monkey standing on the footpath winding up a music box. I had seen drawings of these poor cute creatures being chained to their music machines by their masters. The needle on that old HMV was the size of a nail. It hit the record with all the gentleness of a sledgehammer and made the record jump so that it always missed the first few bars. The recordings sounded as if they had been made outside in a snowstorm. Added to that, the records scratched easily, no doubt from the nail-sized needle suddenly skimming across the surface. Someone would always state the obvious: 'Oh, there's a scratch on this record.' Still we all listened in rapture. Unlike the radio, it was novel to be able to choose what one listened to.

One evening, Mia asked me to pull down the Holland blind in our sitting room. I noticed that the blind was green on the inside facing me but that the side facing the street had been painted black by hand, evident by the uneven brush strokes.

'Why has this blind been painted black?' I asked.

'Oh, we did that during the war when blackout regulations were put into force by the British troops who occupied our islands,' Mia explained. Visa, forever the teacher, told me that on 9 April 1940, German forces crossed the Schleswig frontier and proceeded with the occupation of the whole of Denmark within a few hours. The Germans broke off all communication between Denmark and the Faeroes, as well as Greenland and Iceland.

'We were completely cut off,' she said. It was not for long as, realising the strategic importance of this rocky outpost in the middle of the North Atlantic, British forces occupied the Faeroes a few days later in what the locals fondly described as a 'friendly occupation'.

The British set up headquarters in the old fort of Skansin. Initially British forces also occupied Iceland; when they withdrew in 1941, the American troops moved in. Later, Greenland allowed the United States to establish air bases to provide air cover for the Atlantic convoys. During the five-year period of isolation from Denmark, the Faeroese, Greenlanders and Icelanders had to set up their own governmental administration, a function normally carried out by Denmark.

The British installed naval guns on the headland facing the approaches to Tórshavn harbour and two of their guns remain in Skansin. On the Sivertsen farm one bunker is still standing. Sjúrður told me the story of a party held by the British troops at the harbour of Skálafjørður on the island of Eysturoy. It appears that everyone got rather inebriated. The local baker was put in charge of looking out over the ocean for the enemy. Air attacks on the Faeroe Islands by the Germans had been limited; however, on this night a German plane flew low over the area and the 'untrained' baker pointed the big gun at the plane and hit it with the first shot.

The British also built a military airport on the island of Vágar on the only strip of flat land they could find in the entire archipelago. It took one year for thousands of men from England and Scotland to finish the airport. By the time the airport was completed it was no longer required. In my time, the airport was not in use.

In 1941, the Faeroese were asked by the British to supply them with much needed fish. The Icelanders were approached first, but sensibly refused to sail to Britain without air escort because of the danger of attack from the air and sea. The British could not agree to this because of the shortage of aircraft. So throughout the war the Faeroese valiantly ferried fish supplies from as far away as Iceland, across the mine-infested Atlantic to Aberdeen. As there was a shortage of food in the UK, the trade yielded an extremely good profit, but Visa told me this resulted in a great sacrifice of Faeroese lives.

The last of the British troops left in May 1945. Relations between the Faeroese population and the British had been very good, so much so that many of the troops took Faeroese wives with them, and the locals were quick to dub this 'the Faeroese invasion of Britain'. The Faeroese also formed a strong bond with the Scots, especially in Aberdeen, which still lasts to this day.

At first, I was fascinated by these stories from the war and would beg Visa to tell me more. But then they triggered off nightmares, so I never asked again.

\* \* \*

I went upstairs to the smaller bedroom where my dolls were kept. Mia had neatly arranged then on the bed the tallest to the smallest.  Here I also kept a sheep's horn and a good collection of pieces of whalebone, including whale teeth – making it an eclectic assemblage of playthings, all intrinsically Faeroese. This room was always so tidy, I am certain it was not my doing.

Mia and Visa kept a clean and tidy house, as was the habit of the Faeroese. I don't believe that I contributed much to the daily chores. Though, when Mia was doing the laundry, an arduous labour-intensive task for womenfolk in those days, I helped her scrub the clothes on a rough washboard before they were placed in a big vat of boiling water.  The washhouse, a wooden shed, was at the end of garden. Mia had to keep stirring the clothes frequently to 'stop them developing yellow spots', she said. Next, there was the tedious task of rinsing the clothes several times, before putting them through a contraption of two rollers to extract the water, a necessary exercise in a damp climate where washing could take days to dry even in the best of windy circumstances.

Playing was definitely the preferred pastime compared to these tedious activities. Mother had sent me two porcelain 'talking' dolls, the likes of which were unobtainable in the Faeroes. When I put them in a horizontal position, their eyelids would close and a 'maaaaa', a familiar Faeroese sheep-like sound, emanated from their stomachs. One doll was pink and blonde, but I preferred the other one with the jaundiced complexion and tough wiry hair just like mine. How I wished I would be allowed to sleep in this bedroom with my dolls, but there was no changing Mia's mind.

117

I was often missing a toy or part of a board puzzle and despite turning things upside down, my search would fail to locate the item.

'It has disappeared – just like that,' I would cry out incredulously. Visa suggested obliquely that *they* might have been responsible. *They* were the *huldufólk* - local people never referred to them by their name – and they had black hair and wore grey clothes, Visa would tell me stories about them, a tiny smile playing on her lips. She was obviously enjoying this. '*They* kept sheep and cattle just like the farmers and even had boats to go out fishing.'

'Tell me more, please Visa.' I was enthralled.

Visa then told me about a farmer who wanted to take his boat out of the boat shed. Try as he might, he could not shift it. He got some men to help him but the boat still could not be moved. One of the men exclaimed, 'Of course, we can't move your boat, because *they* have placed their boat in front of yours.'

The *huldufólk* had the uncanny ability of making themselves and their possessions invisible.

'And in any case,' he continued, 'the weather is not good for fishing today, and *they* would know this, which is why *they* have left their boat inside.'

The *huldufólk* lads and maidens were also known to lure their human counterparts to come away with them for purposes of inter-marriage. Moreover, they were mischievous and would hide things from humans. She assured me though that they lived in the outfields and never spent the night in town. There are many stories recorded about their malicious deeds, including the kidnapping of children who played in the outfields, only to be found later by their distraught parents in another field.

'Well, there is no way I am going to do any wandering in the outfields by myself,' I told Visa.

That night as I was trying to go to sleep, a fierce storm erupted. We had heard about it already on the radio, during one of the frequent storm warnings for shipping. I imagined that the waves were so high that they reached right up to my eiderdown and over

118

my pillow and engulfed me and carried me out to sea. I felt panic-stricken, as I did not know how to swim, but I lay very still as I did not want Mia coming over to My Side. I could hear a faint snoring from Her Side, and it took my mind off my worries of drowning. The snoring stopped and Mia turned on the light; she got out of her bed quickly and went to the basin, where she was violently sick. I watched her from under my eiderdown. She spent some time cleaning up. I did not offer to help her. I was unmoved by her distress. A short time later Mia went to the hospital to have an operation. I don't know what kind of operation it was for as all talk about it stopped the minute my presence was noticed. Visa took care of me and slept in my room. When Mia returned after a week, she asked, 'Did you miss me?'

I did not reply. Though I had been somewhat alarmed that she had to be admitted to hospital. Life was fraught with dangers, it seemed, even inside the protected walls of Bakkahella 4.

## Chapter Eighteen

$S$TORIES OF TRAGEDY at sea were matched by those of courage and survival. I was spellbound by stories of real life adventure and was always eager to listen to anyone's tale.

Guðrun, told me the story of her father, Sofus Dahl Christiansen, Tulla's half brother. An intrepid Faeroese sea rover, the 62-year-old harbour master at Tórshavn survived a fierce storm crossing the Atlantic and the North Sea alone in an open rowing boat, while the sea was still full of wartime mines. A lot of people knew this story, but it had happened before my time, so I listened intently.

In early June 1946, Guðrun and her mother Rosa left on the *S.S. Tjaldur* to visit Guðrun's older sister, who had married before World War II and had moved to Denmark. All contact with her, even letters, had ceased during the five years of the war and Rosa was anxious to catch up with her daughter. Sofus, who was unable to leave his work in time to travel with them, decided to join them later in Denmark. He left Tórshavn on Friday evening, 14 June in his open rowing boat, 11 feet of keel and 18 feet overall, fitted with a small engine in the stern. Tulla went to the harbour with her children to see her brother off. Sofus must not have been superstitious, as most sailors considered it bad luck to weigh anchor on a Friday. However, the weather was calm as he started his journey and this providential circumstance outweighed other superstitions and bad omens.

He set a course for the Lighthouse at Muckle Flugga, a sea stack on the most northerly tip on the island of Unst in Shetland. Nightfall came and a strong wind was blowing in from the southeast. By Saturday afternoon, it had developed into one of those legendary Atlantic gales. The little boat dipped and tossed about in the huge waves and one broke right over it. I imagined that it could have been nine metres high. Sofus bailed the water out as quickly as he could, trying to dodge the rollers and at the same time keeping a look out for mines. The saltwater stung his eyes and it was hard to keep them open.

The storm worsened. As fast as he bailed, the boat filled up again as the waves crashed over her. For the next four hours Sofus sat at the stern, steering with one hand and bailing with the other. The engine stopped. For a while, the boat tossed about uncontrollably. By sheer determination, Sofus managed to get the engine started again. With each big wave the little boat rose up and bumped into the foamy crest, then slid down the long incline and arrived swaying in front of the next wave. At four on Sunday morning, he entered the relatively sheltered Bluemull Sound. To starboard was the peat-covered island of Yell and to port was Unst, the most northerly inhabited island in Shetland. This was home to a string of small settlements mainly on the east and south coast, the landscape unaltered since Viking times. Urging himself on, he surveyed the bleak coastline. By eight in the morning, he finally reached the village of Uyeasound. He noticed a small stretch of beach and made for it. Mooring the boat in the bay, he came ashore, but he was too exhausted to see if there were any people about.

He spotted a nearby stone wall that seemed to provide shelter from the wind. A patchy bit of grass was growing next to it and he dropped down onto it, completely exhausted, and fell into a deep sleep. A few hours later he was found by some local children, who were gripped by fear at the sight of this strange being with a white motley face – the salt had dried on his stubble. The children ran home to tell their parents, who immediately brought Sofus to their house, where he was given dry clothes and filled up with hot coffee and food.

That evening he went to his boat and saw that she had been damaged and had shipped a lot of water. The boat would have to be repaired, as she had split from the stern. Meanwhile a gale was blowing from the northwest and Sofus had to remain in Unst for eleven days until the storm abated.

On the morning of 27 June, Sofus left Uyeasound in fog, but the winds were light from the southeast. However, by evening they had turned into a gale and soon the boat split again from the stern. After driving the boat for fourteen hours, the conditions were so bad that Sofus considered putting out a sea anchor, when he sighted a fishing vessel with its sails up.

With great skill Sofus succeeded in mooring alongside the *Harvid* of Norway. The crew got Sofus and his boat safely on the deck and set a course for Bergen. It was only a few years earlier in World War II that the *Shetland Bus*, a special branch of the British and expatriate Norwegian military forces, had used this same course. They had sailed on the same kind of fishing vessel as the *Harvid* to deliver supplies and information to the resistance movement in Norway to help the Norwegians escape the Nazis. The *Harvid* arrived in Bergen on Sunday, 30 June.

The very next day, unperturbed by his near fatal experience, Sofus and his boat left on the *Aurora*. On Wednesday, the boat was taken off the vessel and at last he had smooth sailing all the way to his destination, Helsingor in Denmark, arriving somewhat later than planned, on Thursday, 4 July. Guðrun and her family were relieved and overjoyed to see Sofus again, as they had feared for his life, especially after hearing the broadcast on the Wick Radio for shipping to watch out for the lone Faeroese sea rover. We all knew about this big radio station located on the north-east coast of Scotland, which transmitted distress communication for those in trouble at sea, even as far as Greenland.

Sofus and his boat caught a ride back home on a Faeroese trawler, which had landed fish in Copenhagen. It had been an unforgettable voyage.

## Chapter Nineteen

*I*T WAS OCTOBER 1954, a month before my ninth birthday, when my mother came to Tórshavn – just like a bolt out of the blue, no, more like a sudden thunderclap from Thór. And then just as quickly, she left. I was totally unprepared for this momentous visit. It seemed as if Mia only told me about it a few days before the ship from Copenhagen was due to arrive.

Initially I was not particularly enthusiastic about Mother's visit, as she was an unknown person in a photograph, whom I had hoped, but never really expected to meet. I did not know what to make of the visit. I was stunned, but not excited which somehow felt wrong. However, once I overcame the initial shock, I did feel stirrings of excitement at my mother's arrival, despite being unsure of what to expect.

I kept opening the album and looking at all the photos of my mother in order to memorise her appearance. It had been five years since I had last seen her and the flesh and blood mental image of her was gone. I was worried that I would not recognise her and she would pass me by when she came ashore. The photo album was kept in the living room on Our Side. The cover was made of dark brown leather, beautifully tooled with a sort of twisted leaf pattern in a medieval style at each corner as well as in the centre. Later, in drawing classes at school, I would often copy this design. In the album were baby photos of me in Italy, some with Sigrid and other nurses, a few with my mother, and some of me on the beach at Forte dei Marmi, taken by a photographer who used the curious business name of *Foto Dell'Innocenti*. There were no photos of my father and me, but there were photos of both my parents in happier times. I used to ponder over their wedding photo. Mother is wearing a striped cotton short-sleeved dress, looking proud and defiant and my father is in a regular double-breasted suit. Her appearance puzzles me, but I only asked Mia: 'Why is Mother not wearing a wedding dress?'

'Probably because they got married during the war,' she offered. I accepted her explanation. I gazed at the photos of their nuptials, taking in every detail. In one, my parents have their right hands joined and are facing the priest, who is clad in vestments of gold brocade, looking elaborately overdressed by comparison. Their hands will remain joined throughout the service as the priest beseeches God to 'unite them in one mind and flesh'. My parents each wear a crown on their head and the photographer would have chosen this climactic moment to take a photo as the bride and groom are set apart as king and queen of a new 'kingdom', which they must rule wisely in preparation for the full responsibilities of marriage and parenthood. The crowns also represent sacrifice and unwavering devotion to each other and to God. There are two men standing directly behind my parents. I didn't know who they were. They are each holding a lit candle, symbolising the spiritual will of the couple to receive Christ, who will bless them through this sacrament. The eternal light of Christ reminds the couple that they must shine in righteousness and purity of good deeds. Of course, I only learned this later as there was no one in Tórshavn to explain to me the symbolism of a Serbian Orthodox marriage ceremony.

On the day of Mother's arrival, I became anxious. What if I could not recognise my own mother? Mia had not met her before and Sigrid, the only person who knew her, was not here. I went once again to the living room and, making certain that Mia was not around, carefully took a photo of Mother out of the album and put it in my pocket. This was not allowed, but I had to take the risk.

The one I chose was of my mother standing on the beach at Forte dei Marmi, looking slim and tall. My plan was to take a look at it every so often on the way to the harbour, hopefully without Mia noticing, just to make sure that I would recognise her. I didn't want Mia to discover that I had forgotten what my mother looked like.

Before leaving the house, I went quickly to the Other Side to the loft bedroom and scanned the horizon for signs of the ship. I saw a moving speck entering the fjord and raced down to fetch Mia, who assured me that we had ample time to reach the dock. At my insistence, we got to the wharf early. The Danish steamship *Dronning Alexandrine*, named after King Frederick IX's mother, came alongside. The 'Dronning' as the locals called her, was a familiar sight, making regular fortnightly sailings to and from Copenhagen. She was a single screw coastal steamer with a black steel hull, a straight stem, counter stern and two masts. The topside comprised two decks, freshly painted in white and a varnished wooden wheelhouse. Her single funnel was painted in three bands of black, white and black. She looked more imposing than our ship, the *Tjaldur*, I thought. Not being anywhere near as big as the ocean liners, she could berth in the East Bay. But today, she took forever, or maybe it was my impatience that made it seem so.

I sneaked a final look at my mother's image, just to make sure. At last, the gangway was let down and passengers started to disembark. Not one of them looked remotely like the photograph in my pocket. Then suddenly a tall, elegant apparition came into sight on the deck, wearing a full-length fur coat, such as no one had ever seen in the islands. Nobody could afford a fur coat. I knew this was my mother. With head held high, she walked confidently down the gangplank in shiny black high-heeled shoes. We exchanged an awkward greeting, consisting of a nervous 'Hello' on my part. Despite my mother being fluent in six languages, we had no language in common. By then, I had forgotten my Italian and knew only a few words of English, which we had started to learn at school. Mother and Mia greeted each other formally, yet I had a sense that they had met before. This

125

puzzled me. They weren't supposed to know each other, so what was going on here? I dared not ask. Júst drove us to the Hotel Hafnia, where Mia had booked a room at Mother's request. Mother's suitcase was being delivered later. A pure silk scarf hung from one of the pockets of Mother's fur. I didn't want her to be so showy in front of all the locals, so I nervously pushed it into the depths of the pocket without her noticing. There was a powerful fragrance around her - some kind of strange scent that I couldn't make out, but it was pleasant nevertheless. It was an entirely new sensation for me, quite different from the uncomplicated smell of fresh fish or freshly cut grass – there at the quayside, I had had my first introduction to perfume.

To capture the moment of this historic visit, Mia had arranged for a professional photographer to come to our house the next day. For the occasion, my mother wore a smart black and white dress of fine wool with thin stripes, designed by the French couturier, Jacques Fath, so she told me. Around her neck she wore a green silk scarf folded to one side and on her shapely legs, silk stockings. Black high-heeled shoes again, I noted and large gold earrings, gold rings and a heavy gold bracelet. Suddenly a world of silk and gold was being introduced to me. Her thick shiny titian-coloured hair was combed up in a fashionable French chignon as she described it to me. She had a fine black line on her eyelids and her eyelashes were thick and curly, but not too curly, which would have been inelegant. Her skin was as smooth as her silk scarf. She did not look old like Mia, yet she did not look like a typical mother either. I didn't dare to touch her. She looked regal and glossy like a royal character from a Hans Christian Andersen fairytale. She made me nervous, but then so did a lot of people. She wore deep red lipstick with matching polish on her long, narrow manicured nails. Her teeth were a dazzling white. She smelled of what I now knew to be perfume. I felt so ugly and plain next to her.

On Mia's instance, I was wearing a much-hated pale yellow knitted short-sleeved top and a pleated tartan-patterned skirt with shoulder braces of the same fabric. The top and skirt did not go well together and all of a sudden I was acutely aware of it. My long woolly hair had been chopped recently by what must surely have been a blind barber. I wore black shoes with beige Bermuda socks, which kept slipping down, as I hadn't put on the little elastic bands that Mia had made for me to keep them up. I wore no item of silk, but around my neck I had a fine gold chain on which hung a medallion of the Madonna and Child that Mother had given me as a baby in Italy.

The photo session took place in the formal living room on the Other Side. I have a photograph of me sitting down on a step looking up at my mother, like a stunned *tierchen* (little animal) caught in one of those dreadful iron traps that hunters place in forests that I had read about. My mother is looking down at me benevolently and the well-meaning photographer has placed my hands unnaturally in her outstretched long elegant ones. I was grateful that I had just got over a recent bout of warts on my hands. They appeared every so often, sometimes four or five at a time, but Mia had the perfect cure: 'Count how many warts you have. Then take a piece of string and for every wart make a knot in the string and carry it on you at all times,' she counselled.

When I didn't have any pockets in the clothes that I was wearing that day, I would put on an apron with pockets, just so I could carry my string. At night I put the string under my pillow. Mia was right; the unsightly warts soon disappeared. Her hocus-pocus remedy worked every time. But at this moment, I would have died rather than tell my elegant mother about this affliction.

Mia invited Mother to have lunch with us in the hardly-ever-used dining room. Mia cooked boiled haddock, with boiled peeled potatoes and carrots, which she served on her precious blue and white Royal Copenhagen porcelain dinner service. This archetype of Danish craftsmanship was used only on rare occasions. The fish was full of bones and I worried that I would choke on them. I had to keep putting my hand to my mouth in order to extract the bones and I noticed Mother watching me disapprovingly. I felt uncomfortable under her sharp gaze. Mother had brought Mia a bottle of cognac. Much fuss was made over it, as alcohol restrictions were still in force and liquor was always a welcome gift in any local household. Mia and Mother each had a shot of the amber-coloured liquid and conversed politely. I didn't say one word. Mother looked too grand to be spoken to. After the meal, Mother smoked a cigarette and Mia broke all rules and had an early cigar.

Every day during her short visit, Mother put on a different dress and jewellery. One day she wore a skirt, made out of 'the finest wool jersey', as she described it. Her knitted sweaters were not the shapeless thick, patterned ones that we wore, but were made of the finest thin wool of a single colour and clung to her graceful body. Everything she wore was offset by gold jewellery. I was very much impressed by her patrician good looks and graceful carriage and would continue to be so for the rest of her life.

Depending on the weather, we went for walks for something to do, Mother comfortable and elegant in her fur coat. I felt sure that she was bored. Without being able to put it into words at the time, I sensed a worldliness about Mother, the likes of which I had not found in anyone belonging to my small domain. I wished we were in Copenhagen instead. Then I would have proudly taken her to the famed Tivoli Gardens, though I had never been there myself. I could not imagine that anything or anybody in Tórshavn would hold any interest for her. If only she would have met someone like the famous William Heinesen, they could have discussed their common love of literature, music and art.

William Heinesen was born on 15 January 1900, in a house named Katrina Christiansen, about three minutes walk from our house. Although there was a cultural proliferation of poets, artists, playwrights and novelists in the Faeroes during the 1920s and 1930s, only a few had gained international recognition; notably William Heinesen and Hans Jacob Jacobsen.

Heinesen's poetry and novels were written in Danish. His father was a sea captain and later a ship owner and merchant and his mother was the daughter of Danish settlers. She insisted that only Danish be spoken at home. She came from a gifted musical family. Two sisters who lived with the family used to sing lullabies to

Heinesen as a child – they sang so beautifully that he remained wide-awake. At sixteen, Heinesen was sent to Copenhagen to study commerce, but this cultural city inspired the writer in him and his first collection of poetry was published when he was just twenty-one. In his early thirties he returned to live permanently in Tórshavn. Some of his works have been translated into English, such as *The Tower at the Edge of the World* about childhood in the Faeroes and *The Lost Musicians*, a tale of a whimsical and amusing cast of characters in Tórshavn at the beginning of the twentieth century. Heinesen's work dealt with contrasts – darkness and light; heaven and earth; the fearful and the idyllic. He was also a musician and an accomplished artist, surely the kind of person, I thought that Mother would associate with in Sydney.

William Heinesen's books were available at the H.N. Jacobsen book store, which I indicated to Mother, as best as I could without words, as the place where Mia bought my books. It also sold stationery. I loved stationery. At the time, I was reading my way through the 'Puk' series of books, written in Danish with little girls in mind. Each had a glossy pink cover and predictably told the story of a girl named Puk. There were no children's books published in the Faeroese language in those days.

I led Mother into the bookshop. Even though she was a prolific reader and lover of literature - she had studied French literature at the Sorbonne - the few Faeroese novels translated into English, telling of lives in the bleak outpost at the edge of the world, held no interest for her. Mother left the bookshop ahead of me, while I was drooling over some coloured pencils. As I came out, much to my dismay, I saw her talking to a man and a complete stranger as far I knew. Without so much as a word, I raced off home, leaving her behind. In my nervous over-imaginative mind, male strangers represented a far greater threat than female ones. I expect the stranger must have been a friend of Mia's, who escorted Mother back to the Hotel Hafnia, which was practically just around the corner.

My mother stayed for one week. The *Dronning,* which had brought her to Tórshavn the previous week, had sailed on to Reykjavik and was now on its return trip to Copenhagen. Mother had made an enormous visual impression on me when she entered my tiny, far-away world. She had also scared me a little. It was her aura of power and strength that I sensed could crush me at will, as easily as squashing a fly. It seemed that the giants of our legends were no match for my mother, and that it was better to stay put in Tórshavn where I would only need to deal with fables, rather than powerful unknown humans.

This sensation I felt about Mother's power was dramatised by a particular incident during her visit. I remember another meal with Mother and Mia, this time at the Hotel Hafnia. My memory as to all the details of that day does not serve me well, but I do clearly recall the atmosphere was strained. During the meal, I was very nervous and often when in this state, one eyelid would start to flutter and I would have to place my index finger over it to make it stop. I dared not do so on this occasion, as I was anxious not to draw further attention to myself. I had problems getting through my stuffed puffin, or whatever bird was being served as the *plat du jour.* In many ways, I felt like the *plat du jour* waiting to be devoured.

After a week, Mother left on the *Dronning Alexandrine* without me. Now that I knew what she was like, or thought I did, it seemed appropriate that she should travel on a ship named 'Queen Alexandrine', rather than an old tub called 'oyster catcher', the name of the Faeroese vessel plying the route to Copenhagen. Whereas the Faeroese owners of the *Tjaldur* had had a chequered history of buying old ships and re-christening them, the *Dronning Alexandrine* had been specifically built in 1927 for the Faeroe Islands–Iceland route by DFDS, a Danish steamship company at the A/S Elsinore Shipyard near Copenhagen. Júst Junior told me the precise technical specifications of the ship. She had a Burmeister & Wain's Mackingbyggeri engine and sailed at 13 knots. She carried 153 passengers and 1,700 tons of cargo. Mother said she had a first class passage booked. I wasn't certain what this meant, except that it sounded as if it was the right thing to do. I don't remember saying goodbye to her or whether I was sad or relieved the day Mother sailed away. I assumed that life would return to normal. I sensed a slight change in Mia - she was more protective of me than usual and it irritated me no end.

## Chapter Twenty

ONE OF THE most distinctive emblems of Faeroese culture was the *dansiringur*, or ring dance, performed with great gusto at weddings and festivals, such as St Olav's Day, and also in villages when celebrating a whale slaughter. This old style of chain dancing was popular in Europe in the Middle Ages and was still performed on a smaller scale in Norway, Sweden and Greece. It remained very popular in the Faeroes.

I never took part in the *dansiringur*, even though young and old participated, but I remember being present at one. I can't recall though if it was at Rachel's wedding, or maybe at a function that Mia took me to in connection with her work.

The year of Rachel's wedding was 1955; I was nine. Rachel and her new husband, Julian, who had recently graduated from the Nautical School, were going to move to Copenhagen straight after their marriage. Everyone said this meant they would have a bright future. The economy was slowly coming out of its crisis and net emigration from the islands had reached dramatic proportions. I was not happy at the thought of Rachel leaving, as it meant losing one more person from my tiny world, but I admired Rachel enormously for organising her life so cleverly. Rachel and Julian were married in the Havnar Church. Rachael looked as lovely as a fairy tale princess.

The *dansiringur* was not accompanied by any musical instruments. Depending on the content and mood of the ballad, the steps would be slower or faster. Dancers linked arms to form a ring and sort of shuffled or stomped with two steps to the left, one to the right, while they sang ancient ballads reaching back to the Viking Age. Some of these ballads contained hundreds, sometimes thousands of verses. In fact, a *kvæði* (heroic ballad) has survived, consisting of 70,000 verses, the stuff that the Guinness Book of Records is made of. The Faeroese ballads have been passed on orally through the centuries; verse by verse from generation to generation. Related to the heroic ballads are the *tættir* (satirical ballads), the most famous of these being the Bird Legend composed in the nineteenth century, depicting the oyster catcher as the hero. Mercifully, this ballad only has 229 verses.

Nora Kershaw in *Stories and Ballads of the Far Past* compares the ballads of the Faeroe Islands to those of the Torres Strait Islanders, where each song is associated with its own special dance and appears to be accompanied by a story.

At the formal reception to which Mia dragged me, the tables were set with white tablecloths and white napkins, so highly starched that when I put mine to use the first time, it caused a tiny split in the corner of my mouth that immediately developed into a sore. Consequently everything on the menu irritated it.

Worse was to come. Being a feast, plain boiled potatoes and carrots were off the menu. Instead, asparagus was served as a side dish to the meat, which I had trouble identifying. The spears were fibrous and needed a lot of chewing, resulting in a ball of string forming in my mouth. I dared not swallow it for fear of choking. I agonised for some time before deciding to discreetly put the dangerously starched napkin to my mouth and spit the offending botany out, all the while certain that a hundred pair of eyes were on me. I placed the napkin back on my lap and fervently hoped that no one would walk up, open my napkin and interrogate me. In any event, the evening was ruined for me and when the dancing started and the guests got up to form a ring, I wanted to go home.

I looked towards Mia, who was enveloped in cigar smoke and realised there was no chance of getting away early. As more and more guests, young and old got up and linked arms, the circle became coiled due to the limited space. They sang continuously and there seemed to be no interval between verse and chorus and the next verse.

There was much shuffling of feet, gradually culminating in heavy stomping and raised voices. Maybe the guests were dancing to the heroic *Ballad of Arngrim's Sons*, recalling ancient times when the Faeroese were allied to other Norse people. Here is the gist of the story and a few excerpts of a total of only one hundred and eleven verses:

Arngrim, a Swedish nobleman, has eleven sons and one bold and beautiful daughter, Hervík. King Örvarodd kills Arngrim and Hervík decides to avenge her father's death and sets sail with her brother Hjalmar. Arriving at their destination, Hervík encounters a huntsman, who makes the big mistake of asking her:

25. O why art thou so sorrowful,
    As a troll had been hunting thee?

This really irritates Hervík and

26. Her good sword out she drew.
    And with it she clove the huntsman
    And him in sunder slew

Hervík arrives at the place where her father is buried and his voice speaks to her:

30. O where are my eleven sons gone,
    Since daughters are visiting me?

Undeterred by his display of chauvinism, Hervík asks for her father's sword and threatens to set fire to his grave if he doesn't comply. He gives over his sword with a poisoned blade. Hervík arrives at the hall of Örvarodd who is feasting with a hundred and five of his knights. After some exchange of pleasantries on his part, not hers, Hervík gets down to business and demands:

40. Stand up and arm thy band!

As his army starts to ride towards her:

43. She blew a blast on her golden horn,
    And struck to left and right.

And, wait for it:

44. So clove to the shoulders every knight
    Who forth against her strode.

The dancers, acting out this ballad, stomped vigorously from left to right and their normally pale Viking faces took on a bright-red hue.

In the end only Örvarodd and two companions are left. The king begs for her sweet mercy – and Hervík's response:

49. And cut him in pieces twain.

Hervík returns home and gives the sword to her brother Angantyr, who has been bemoaning the fact that he doesn't have a girlfriend. His brother Hjalmar opens his big mouth and tells him about Lady Ingibjörg, the fair daughter of the King of Upsala. Everyone ups and leaves for that kingdom. Another bloody adventure ensues, causing the dancers to shuffle more determinedly than ever from side to side.

Finally, pretty much everyone dies, including the Lady Ingibjörg. By this time some of the elderly guests at the reception looked as if they might die as well. They had been dropping out of the ring at varying times. The *skipari,* the lead singer immediately started on the next ballad and the dancing continued uninterrupted; the peaceful loving Faeroese seemingly unperturbed by the gory turn of events.

Another Norse ballad, somewhat shorter, tells the saga of two sisters and a harp. The older sister is an ugly brunette and the younger one a pale beautiful blonde. One day, the ugly one lures her sister down to a deserted beach, where she promptly drowns her. Some time later, the dead body drifts onto the shore and is found by two wanderers. They fashion a harp from one of the arms and use the hair for strings. Now, having rid herself of any competition, the repulsive brunette has found herself a man and is getting married. The wanderers ask if they can play the harp at her wedding. But when they begin to play, the strings accuse the bride of her sister's murder.

Suddenly, blood starts pouring out of the bride's chest and she dies of anger, not remorse, please note. While the moral of this ballad is obvious, the symbolism may not be. In ancient belief, the moon is the corpse of the sun, the harp resembles the moon in its waning phase and the brunette is most likely a symbol of the darkness of the night.

Mia signalled that it was time for us to go home. She had had enough and looked tired. Maybe it was that extra cigar.

There was no more ring dancing for us for the remainder of that year and the time passed in a less bloody fashion. Visa became increasingly weak and spent more and more time in bed.

It was still dark one morning in winter as I went into Visa's bedroom. I wanted to wake her up to let her know that breakfast was ready. She would not open her eyes, even after I had patted her on the arm. I marched down to the kitchen to complain to Mia:

'Visa just won't answer me.'

It was 28 January 1956. Visa had ascended to Valhalla.

## Chapter Twenty-One

*I*T WAS WELL known, that by far the most imposing man-made structure on any of the islands was the ruins of St Magnus Cathedral in the village of Kirkjubøur. In the Middle Ages, Kirkjubøur, which translated as church-infield or church-farm, had been the ecclesiastical and cultural centre of the Faeroe Islands. To reach it required a two-hour walk across a high barren ridge from Tórshavn.

This open-air museum was a popular site for passengers from the ocean liners that sometimes stopped in Tórshavn for a day on their way to Iceland. After a quick tour though our tiny capital and to nearby Kirkjubøur, the passengers were shuttled back to the comfort of their ship. They must have been surprised to find this Gothic cathedral in the middle of such a pastoral setting. It looked strangely out of place architecturally, and yet with time, the ruins had taken on the grey-green colour of the steep rocky hills above, comfortably allowing it to blend into the landscape. The Faeroese called the cathedral *Múrurin* – The Walls.

Luckily, Mia and I did not have to track across the ridge to visit Kirkjubøur as Júst drove us there. Few people were around as Mia and I entered the cathedral through a high doorway with a rounded arch. There was no roof and no glass in the narrow pointed windows at the sides. It was totally empty inside. Mia drew my attention to the soapstone carvings of crosses. The curved crosses were inside a circle; I liked them much better than the simple straight ones that were in the Havnar Church. On one side, a doorway led to a smaller room in which there was a spiral staircase. I had never seen one of these before and wanted to climb it, but was prevented from doing so by the ever-vigilant Mia. This side of the cathedral had sustained considerable damage in the eighteenth century from a great avalanche, Mia informed me.

Right next to the cathedral was a large black farmhouse with bright-red painted windowpanes and doors. It looked much grander than the modest farmhouses I was used to seeing.

'The farm belongs to the Patursson family,' Mia said, 'and the cathedral is on their land.'

When we stepped out of the cathedral, I ran around it several times, ignoring Mia's pleas to stay with her. I loved the feel of the smooth basalt stones of the cathedral walls. Then I ran my fingers over the rough smaller stones that were packed in between and this quickly revealed the contrast. On my second time around the cathedral, I could hear Mia's anxious pleas for me to stop.

I was a rather clumsy child and was always falling over on to sharp stones; never smooth ones. Once I fell flat on my face near the cowshed in Bakkahella, and my face became pocked with tiny pebbles. Doctor Alex Poulson, one of only two doctors in town, took out the embedded little black pebbles with tweezers, only missing one, which stayed faintly visible just under my skin for a few years. He left no scars. Another doctor, Jacob Højgaard, lived near us in *Reyni*, and Mia normally took me to him. His daughter Hjørdis, was in my class at school. I preferred gong to Dr Poulsen because he had built what could only be described as an elegant chicken coop right in the middle of his garden. It was an exact replica in miniature of his two-storeyed house. It was the norm to keep chickens in town so this was not regarded as a sign of eccentricity on the part of the good doctor. On another occasion a sharp rock on which I landed, tore open the flesh on my knee, requiring Dr Højgaard to sew up the enormous gash without local anaesthetic. I imagined that my screams must have reached Dr

Poulsen's chickens and sent them scurrying into the refuge of their elegant house. There were no quiet visits to the doctor for me.

Much to Mia's relief, on this excursion to St Magnus, I managed to circle the ruins a few times without falling over, only stopping occasionally to look up at the nine-metre-high basalt walls, ignorant of the historical significance of the place.

The style of the cathedral was fourteenth century Gothic, Mia continued, taking over from Visa the role of teacher, 'and is supposed to resemble the Gothic choir of the Stavanger Cathedral in Norway.' The sculptures and ornamentation that decorated the cathedral had been of the highest standard. The locals must have been awestruck at first, as they would not have seen the likes of it on any of the islands. Mia said that the church artefacts had been sent to the National Museum in Denmark for safekeeping.

The most celebrated of the Catholic bishops was Erlendur, who resided in Kirkjubøur and he is credited with undertaking the construction of the Gothic cathedral. It was uncertain whether it was ever completed, as it was said that Erlendur's poor parishioners revolted against the high taxes imposed on them to pay for its construction, though there was no proof of this. Bishop Erlendur died in Bergen in 1308; he did not starve to death in his own cathedral, as legend would have it.

A soapstone relief on the choir wall depicted the twisted figure of Christ on the cross. On His left is the Virgin Mary and His right, John the Baptist. I was told that the inscription on the stone relief reveals that relics have come from St Magnus of Orkney and St Torlákur of Iceland and that is why the cathedral was named after Magnus. He was a popular figure in the *Orkneyinga Saga*, where he is described as tall, intelligent, good-looking, generous, eloquent, wise, and much more. All the attributes one would expect to find in a great man. Magnus had a disagreeable cousin named Hakon. After a period of joint rule by the cousins, their power struggle came to a head and Magnus volunteered to be killed in order to bring peace to his people. A cathedral was built in his memory at Kirkwall in the Orkneys. His remains have been found in a wooden casket in that cathedral, missing a bone or two, which seem to have ended up at St Magnus Cathedral in Kirkjubøur.

Mia and I walked from the cathedral to the farmhouse, which was formerly the Bishop's Palace, Mia said, although the bishops on the continent would hardly have called it a palace. Excavations were being carried out at the time and Mia said that it was certain to reveal much more about the area and the lives of the Faeroese in the Middle Ages. Archaeology was new to the Faeroes and the father of archaeology, Sevrri Dahl, had only started excavations a few years earlier.

'This farmhouse belonged to well-to-do farmers,' Mia continued.

Typical farmhouses were much smaller and contained only one room, the *roykstova,* which served as a living room, kitchen and workroom with an open fireplace in the middle and no windows. Ventilation was through a quadrangular opening in the roof, hence the name 'smoke room'. Here the family cooked, worked, slept and told stories. The floor was made of earth. Along the walls were alcove beds where they slept. 'Oh, I've seen those alcove beds in Edny's Flat Iron house,' I piped up, before I realised that I had given away the fact that I had been to Edny's house contrary to Mia's wishes. Mia showed her disappointment in me in her usual quiet manner.

Later, farmhouses would also comprise of a *glasstova,* literally glass room, because it was usually the only room in the house with glass windows. It was not difficult to imagine the austerity that these Faeroese endured cooped up inside a smokey room, sitting on their alcove beds, waiting out a winter storm that might have raged for days. As they moved closer to the warmth of the peat fire, a member of the family, who had a gift for story telling, would start recounting the adventures of their family and local chieftains. He would tell of a battle, an apparition, great deeds and the stories would go on and on. The children especially were enraptured by these ballads and legends and they remembered

140

them well. For additional amusement they were set the task of solving rhyming riddles, until the weather broke and they could finally go outside.

Spending so much time in close quarters spawned all sorts of lore. The early settlers remembered the trees of their homeland and used them as symbols in their ballads and riddles:

> I know of a tree on a mountaintop,
> With thirteen branches,
> Four birds' nests on each branch,
> Six birds in each nest,
> The seventh has golden feathers.

The tree symbolised the year and the branches the months. Birds' nests – four on each branch – represented the weeks. Six birds in each nest symbolised the days of the week and the seventh bird with gold feathers was the Sabbath, the day of rest.

My favourite riddle went as follows:

> I know of a bird with no feathers,
> It perched on a fence, that wasn't a fence,
> A maiden came by,
> Caught it without hands,
> Roasted it without fire
> And ate it without a mouth.

The answer to this riddle is the sun that thaws the newly fallen snow and it no doubt kept many a mind active seeking its solution.

There were two other churches at Kirkjubøur and it is possible that all may have functioned at the same time. One of them was St Olav's church. It was still in use, which was really quite miraculous, as at one time it almost fell into the sea. The church was built on broad flat lowland with ample foreshore, but centuries of strong waves eroded the cliffs and, coupled with the gradual sinking of the island, the sea ended up near the door and the

141

adjacent churchyard. Now, only the northern part was left standing. A bulwark was built in front of the remaining foreshore in 1873, when the church was repaired. It was constructed of rough stone that had been plastered and white washed. The design was typical of cloister churches built in the Nordic countries. I walked around the tombstones in the churchyard, as I liked cemeteries, but only during the day. The dead could not be trusted at night.

As we proceeded further along the shore at Kirkjubøur, we came to a crumbling stone wall, the only remains of a smaller church called Á Líkhúsi, literally, the Dwelling of the Dead, but referred to by the locals as 'The Mortuary'. Some believe this to be part of the oldest church in Kirkjubøur dating back to the end of the eleventh century, but no evidence had been found to support any dating to this period. Except for part of one wall, the remainder, including the entire churchyard, has been washed into the sea. I could still see a stone paved path leading from the church into the sea. It was easy to imagine the dead souls bundling up their bones as they prepared to walk into their final watery graves.

When Mia and I returned home from our visit to Kirkjubøur that day, an airmail letter was waiting for Mia. I recognised the stamps from Australia straightaway. I had started collecting stamps and was anxious to put the newly arrived ones into my album. Mia did not immediately reveal the contents of this letter from my mother, but I was more interested in soaking the stamps off the envelope than knowing its contents. Yet this letter would soon result in a dramatic turn of events in my life. I was unaware that the clock had begun to tick towards my imminent departure from the Faeroes.

## Chapter Twenty-Two

ABOUT A YEAR and a half after my mother's visit, when I was not quite eleven years of age, I developed a strong desire to leave these remote islands. Even though the Sivertsens had accepted me into their family from the beginning, I was not family. More and more, I developed a strong awareness of not belonging. I began to secretly formulate a plan for leaving the Faeroe Islands for good and going to live in Denmark. The economy was still in bad shape and there was a steady flow of young men and women leaving for Denmark to seek employment. While I talked to Laura about my mother returning for me one day, deep in my heart I did not believe that I would ever be reunited with my parents in Australia. I had no sense of belonging to them either. There simply had not been enough contact over the years to establish that expectation.

Nevertheless, I used to fantasise with Laura what it would be like when my mother came to pick me up and take me to the other end of the world, where the sun shone every day and life would be carefree and blessed by kind and loving parents. I imagined that my adventures would be just as exciting as those in the books that we read. Deep down I had my nagging doubts whether this dreamy future would ever become a reality. Still, at no time did I feel that my mother had completely abandoned me. As I understood it, abandonment meant leaving a baby in a basket outside someone's front door, without a note. I never blamed my mother for my circumstances, even though she convinced herself later that this was the case and my protests to persuade her otherwise never changed her mind.

In the 1950s, the Faeroe Islands were still isolated and I felt it acutely. The fortnightly ferry services of the *Tjaldur* and *Dronning Alexandrine* and other ships stopping here on their way to Iceland, Greenland, Norway and Great Britain did not really bring the rest of the word any closer to the Faeroe Islands, or more importantly to me. The shipping movements were just survival stuff, goods coming in, fish going out; other people's relatives coming to and from Denmark, never mine, except on that one fleeting occasion.

Still, our isolation was not so complete that we were not aware of what was going on in the rest of the world. We heard on the news at the end of June 1956 that the Workers' Uprising against communists rule in Poznan, Poland was being crushed by Russian troops. On 26 July 1956, we heard that President Nasser of Egypt had declared the nationalisation of the Suez Canal Company. We also heard about the valiant protest against communism by the Hungarian students in Budapest, which kept Mia tuned into the radio news.

One evening during Mia's cigar ritual, we listened intently as we heard that the Hungarian rebellion had forced the Soviet troops to pull back from Budapest. When the announcement came that Imre Nagy was withdrawing from the Warsaw Pact, there seemed hope for freedom from communism. I had no idea what the Warsaw Pact was, but I knew it was 'bad'. Then on 4 November, a few days before my eleventh birthday, we heard the awful news that that Soviet troops had entered Budapest and savagely reclaimed it. I worried that the Russian ships, which were plying our waters, would come and occupy us as well, remembering only too well the incident of the Russian ship that had berthed in our very own harbour.

'Do you think the communists will come to take us over?' I asked Mia.

I had visions of the islands being infested with rats and communists. But Mia assured me gently that this was all taking place a long way from the islands. Yes, isolation was an advantage sometimes. Collections were organised in Tórshavn for much needed blankets and clothes to be sent to Hungary to keep the victims warm through the coming winter. Mia and I went through our cupboards in search of spare clothes. I spotted the scratchy woollen underpants that caused me such grief each winter and the thought occurred to me to donate them. But, no, I could not do that to those poor Hungarians!

I was thankful not to be living in Budapest, but I was not happy at the prospect of staying in Tórshavn either, for what I now feared could be the rest of my life. In my child's mind, I did not see any positive aspects of life here. I did not fully appreciate the natural beauty, the closeness to nature, and the honourable social traditions of the Faeroese, or their sense of cosmic awareness as expressed through the medium of ballads and particularly the writings of Christian Matras and William Heinesen:

> The snow whirls passionately
> Through the last day.
>
> So your years whirl
> Towards their ending.
> *Night is Coming*

In the same poem, William Heinesen reminds us:

> You yourself were only a fleeting whirling flake
> On its way to extinction.

I was too young to reflect on any sense of the cosmic. All I knew was that I felt like a whirling flake in a tiny far-flung community in a vast stormy ocean, with insurmountable distances to the next country - and I desperately wanted to flee. I did not want to grow old here and die in the bleak embrace of a snowstorm, having my school friends meeting me with the 'friendly eyes and open arms' as described by Heinesen in *Night is Coming*.

My feelings were not the result of any change in the behaviour of those around me, as Mia's care and kindness continued unabated. I toyed with the idea of stowing away on a ship bound for Copenhagen, but quickly dismissed it, as I knew the chances of carrying out such a feat were slim at best. No, I had to leave school as soon as permissible and learn a trade. Hairdressing seemed like a good choice, though I had no real enthusiasm for it. Edny's older sister was a hairdresser, who now worked in Denmark and seemed to be managing well. After my apprenticeship in Tórshavn, I planned to leave for Copenhagen and beg Rachel to let me stay with her and Julian until I got a job. Copenhagen was cosmopolitan by reputation and I felt confident that there would be a diverse mixture of people there; even some that might look similar to me. I told no-one. I wanted to fly away like the seabirds that surrounded me. But flying was out of the question. Air services were still a long way off, though the islands had certainly seen their share of men in flying machines.

Mia had told me that when she and Visa were in their twenties, an Italian adventurer and World War I pilot, Antonio Locatelli and his crew, became the first aviators to land in the Faeroes. His seaplane, a Dornier 'Wal' (Whale) aircraft touched down in Nólsoy Bay in August 1924 and local dentist Arthur Brend rowed out and brought them ashore at Tinganes. The daily newspaper reported that as the aircraft flew low over the island the cows were driven mad with fright and the seagulls flew panic-stricken into the air. Locatelli was attempting a round-the-world flight and the Faeroe Islands suddenly entered into the loop of aviation pioneers. Locatelli and his men were treated like VIPs and were taken to a *pensione* belonging to Frøkun Nicode Mussen. The 'Wal' was roped off and secured for the night. The next morning, under the fascinated, watchful eyes of the entire population of Tórshavn, Locatelli left for Iceland, flying low over Kirkjubøur. Three hours later Locatelli arrived safely in Iceland; however, as he continued onto Greenland, he was forced to crash land and was rescued, this time not by a local dentist, but by the entire crew of the British cruiser *Richmond*.

Charles Lindbergh, the famous American aviator, accompanied by his wife Anne, also stopped in the Faeroes. It was 1933 and Pan American Airways had asked Lindbergh to survey the Newfoundland to Europe route for commercial air transportation. Taking off from Flushing Bay, New York, Lindbergh flew his gleaming metal flying boat – a Lockheed 8 Sirius – to the eastern end of Newfoundland. After turning northwest to explore the coast of Labrador, they flew over water for 1,683 kilometres to Greenland, stopping in Godthaab. There the Eskimos christened the Sirius *Tingmissartoq*, which means 'one who flies like a big bird'. The Lindberghs proceeded to Iceland and then to the Faeroes, landing in the Trongisvágsfjord on 23 August, coming ashore at the village of Tvøroyi on the island of Suðoroy. They stayed for one night at the home of Josefinu Mortensen. The next day the Lindberghs continued to Lerwick.

Normally, I would have been fascinated by the daring exploits of these heroes of aviation, but my juvenile days were now spent in planning my own wingless escape.

## Chapter Twenty-Three

*I* RESIGNED MYSELF to the fact that it would be another four years before I could put my plan into action, and now a more mundane pursuit was in store for me. Mia tried very hard to occupy me and bring me up as best she could, so when I turned eleven, she sent me to dancing classes, which we called *Eingilskdansur*, English dancing, meaning conventional European dancing. This required closer contact with boys, a prospect that did not exactly thrill me, as my past experience with the male species had not been good.

The classes were held in a dance hall and despite several boys and girls from my school attending, it was of no comfort to me, as I did not know most of them. It was winter and even though the classes started in the afternoon, it was almost pitch black outside. Being painfully shy, I disliked the classes from the start. Laura did not come with me as she and her sisters attended special Faeroese dancing classes for children. Laura's father was a founding member of a dance association for chain dancing, so it was only natural that she went there.

From the first day, it was obvious that the classes were not intended to be fun. The rather dour teacher would start off by demonstrating a few steps of the usually light-hearted *Wiener*

*Walt,* Viennese Waltz, in a solemn fashion - it thus became a sort of *dance macabre,* the joy being lost in interpretation.

First we had to practice the new steps on our own, without partners. The wooden floorboards resounded with the thud of circus elephants in a chaotic tap dancing act. Then the time came for us to stand in a line opposite each other, boys on one side, girls on the other. Nervousness mixed with anticipation hung in the air. I surveyed the assembled line of boys and concluded that they were all undesirables as dance partners. There was one boy in particular, who looked most unfortunate and I just knew that he would end up being my partner. Bright pink chubby face, narrow watery eyes, spiky blonde hair. Even worse, he had red protruding ears and matching red lips, as though he were wearing his mother's lipstick. If he were put on stilts, he would have looked like a human lighthouse.

The teacher would call out, 'Choose your partner' – I dreaded this part. The boys seemed to have surveyed the arrangement opposite them and had already made up their minds, moving swiftly across to us. Soon, everyone had a partner except for me; the only girl left standing alone, which in itself was mortifying. I was about to take a seat when the teacher come towards me with, oh no, the odd looking boy.

Unwillingly, Odd-Looking and I took up our dancing position, keeping as great a distance as possible between us. Odd-Looking's hands were clammy. Possibly both our hands were sweaty, though this possibility never crossed my mind. Despite our open stance, I stepped on Odd-Looking's toes several times with my hard black patent leather shoes. Normally, I would have been embarrassed, but on this occasion I was secretly pleased that I had not yet found my dancing feet.

At the dance hall, one of the older girls warned me that I should be careful when going to the toilets, which were located one floor below, as the boys might 'try to do so something'. I had no idea what this meant, but it was enough to set off alarm bells in my head. Once, as I came out of the toilets, some boys approached me. As soon as one of them put his hand on my arm, I kicked him and went into overkill. Their intentions may have been innocent, but I wasn't taking any chances. I shouted in vain for help and when one of them covered my mouth with his hand, I bit him so hard that I drew blood. Poor Mia's attempts at trying to make a respectable young lady of me were not very successful.

Another ladylike activity not to my liking was needlework classes. These were held in a neighbouring house, where a small group of us sat still and silent in a horseshoe arrangement in a small stuffy room, where we sewed little flower designs onto a white cloth using white cotton. We had to use a ridiculously thin needle that I had great difficulty in threading. The kindly woman who instructed us was a perfectionist and the constant unpicking of my awful work meant that I was left with grey stitching rather than the intended white on white finished doily. I was frightfully bored by this colourless activity and equated it with my possible future if I were to remain on these islands forever.

One day I developed a fierce pain in the throat. There was no way I could have managed another white stitch and I was allowed to go home. It turned out to be the mumps and I endured the suffering gladly. On these bedridden occasions, Mia would buy me chocolate on the way home from work. Not any ordinary chocolate, but a large sculpted chocolate piece. A man on a motorbike was the most memorable one I'd ever eaten. It almost made staying in bed worthwhile.

The Christmas school pageant was the theatrical highlight of the year at the Nuns' School and that year in Christmas 1956, I was miscast to reluctantly play the Virgin Mary. There was no escaping this. I was relieved that I was not chosen to play one of the shepherds, as they had to wear dirty old sheep's wool rugs on their backs, and I was certain I would be ridiculed. Parents came to watch our bit of theatre and of course Mia came as well. I looked at them all, hoping that no one would think that Mia was my mother. She had turned 64 that year and I desperately wanted someone younger to be my parental representative. I saw some people of similar age to Mia and felt much better, but only momentarily as, when I checked with one of my friends, I was told that her supporters were her grandparents.

However, I was soon to be rescued from both dancing and needlework by an unexpected event.

## Chapter Twenty-Four

*T*HE DAY THAT I never thought would happen arrived when Mia received a letter from Mother, advising that she was coming back to Tórshavn with the intention to take me to live with her in Australia. Although Mia had received the news in a previous letter, the one that I had steamed the stamps off, she only told me of Mother's impending visit a couple of weeks beforehand.

It was now over two and a half years since her first visit to Tórshavn and I was ready to go. My first thought was, 'Thank goodness, now I don't have to become a hairdresser'. Unfortunately, Mia, out of a sense of misguided kindness, left out a most crucial piece of information contained in that letter. Later it would become one of many factors that would contribute to a disastrous relationship with my mother.

This time when Mother arrived, there was no need to carry a photo of her. I recognised the awesome full-length fur coat the minute she appeared on deck. Our meeting was still awkward, but in my innocence I was confident that this uneasiness would not last. Since her last visit, Júst Junior had been giving me lessons in English and I had acquired a modest collection of English words, which I pronounced with such a strong Danish accent that they bore little resemblance to the intended language.

I was happy as Mia and I packed my suitcase. If Mia felt sad, I was not aware of it, as I was too preoccupied with visions of my bright future. Astonishingly, all my dreams about going to Australia to live with my parents were about to come true. There was not enough time to say goodbye properly to my school friends.

When we left the house of Mia's friends, Hedvig and Juul, their daughter, Súsanna called out to me:

'Tú mást ikki gloyma tað føroyska málið.' (You must not forget the Faeroese language.) I replied, 'Nej tað føri eg ongantíð at gloyma.' (No, I shall never forget it.)

But I did forget my Faeroese in a very short time. Mia kissed and hugged me, while my arms remained limp at my side. I could see tears in her eyes, while mine remained dry as I thought of that sunny land over the far horizon.

It was 23 March 1957, when Mother and I boarded the *Dronning Alexandrine* bound for Copenhagen. I was pleased to be leaving behind me these storm-ravaged islands in the North, and was brimming with expectation of a wonderful life with my real parents, where I belonged.

There was a reasonable swell as Mother and I left the port of Tórshavn on the *Dronning,* but tolerable enough for my stomach. Mother took me to the dining room for lunch. It was set up as for a wedding I thought. Portraits of King Frederik IX and Queen Ingrid in ornate gilt frames hung from mirrored walls. The enormous dining table was cut out in the centre from which rose two shiny columns from floor to ceiling and on a glistening pedestal stood an enormous arrangement of roses and carnations, flowers that I had never seen before. I wanted to get closer and smell them, but didn't dare move. Soon the weather deteriorated and I spent the rest of the voyage in bed unable to keep down any food from the magical-looking restaurant. Mother seemed fine and told me that she and the Captain were the only ones on board who were not seasick.

We stayed a day and a night in Copenhagen, at the Hotel Terminus near the central railway station. I spent the whole day at Rachel and Julian's apartment with Rachel and her newborn son, Bjarni. Mother passed the day at the British Consulate, where she encountered some problems having her stateless child inserted in her passport.

It was my first close encounter with a baby and the novelty wore off by the end of the day. More than anything, though, I loved being with Rachel. She represented everything I wanted to be. She was lovely looking, clever – having after all liberated herself from the Faeroes – she had a nice husband and their apartment was so light and appealing with its blond furniture. Quite different from the serious sombre furniture that I was used to at Bakkahella 4.

Mother and I continued by train to Rotterdam, where we remained for several days until it was time to board our ship bound for Melbourne. We stayed in a modest hotel, situated next to a canal. I felt secure still being near water. The hotel served a wonderful breakfast. In particular, I liked the new taste sensation of smoked cheese.

While in Rotterdam, Mother took me to see my first movie. It was called *High Society* and featured Grace Kelly, the most beautiful woman I had ever seen, except for my mother. Also starring were Bing Crosby, and Frank Sinatra and I couldn't understand why the gorgeous leading lady was not able to find better-looking fellows. They all danced and sang their way through a land of elegant parties and glamorous people. I asked myself, 'Is this what life is like outside the Faeroes?' There was a cinema in Tórshavn, but I had never been to it as it seemed to be mainly for adults. Once though, a few of us from school sneaked in but only got as far as taking a quick peek, before being discovered. A black and white film was playing. I think it was in Italian and the scene we glimpsed was that of rather busty women in low-cut dresses.

The audience seemed to consist entirely of men and they looked much more pleased than they usually did after a good fishing day.

On 2 April 1957, we boarded the new Dutch cargo ship, *MS Giessenkerk*, for our voyage to Australia. The Netherlands *Rivierpolitie* exit-stamped Mother's British Passport, in which the Australian Consulate in Copenhagen had made a notation:

Accompanied by daughter Antonia Pavlovic.
This child has not acquired Australian Citizenship or British Nationality.

I was still a stateless person, yet by virtue of this notation my future had become inextricably linked to my mother.

I was bursting with happiness. However, only a couple of weeks into our long sea voyage around the Cape of Good Hope, in the close quarters of the twelve-passenger cargo ship, I would come to the awful realisation that I was entering the unhappiest phase of my life.

## Chapter Twenty-Five

*T*HE *GIESSENKERK* STOPPED first at Marseilles. It was a brilliant sunny day; the calm water sparkled, as we seemed to glide into this large busy port, so much bigger than the port of Tórshavn. A popular tune, *I found my April dreams in Portugal it seems,* was playing over the ship's loudspeakers as we entered the harbour. The many fishing trawlers and cargo ships made the place seem less foreign to me. Mother took me to a little restaurant where we sat outside and consumed the local specialty *bouillabaisse.* 'A bit rough,' said my mother, but she meant the clientele, not the soup.

At Marseille, a French family joined our ship with their son, Pierre, who was about my age and rather cute I thought. We were to be the only two children on the ship. Sadly, we were both painfully shy, and spent most of the voyage avoiding each other. There was no entertainment of any kind. Being a cargo ship, deck space was limited and there was basically nothing for anyone – adult and child alike – to do. The only provision for entertainment was shuffleboard, which one can only play so often on a six-week-long voyage. The adults amused themselves with card games and drank a lot. One man in particular succeeded without fail in getting blind drunk every evening. Unwittingly he provided much needed entertainment, by having us guess at the end of each day, if he would need one or two people to assist him to his cabin.

Fortunately, he was not the captain, but he was a relative of the owner of the shipping line, or so he kept telling us.

The cabins were roomy. Mother referred to them as 'state cabins'. But very soon into the voyage, I would feel its uncomfortable proximity. Two normal sized single beds were separated by a large writing desk, with a lid that lifted up to convert into a dressing table, complete with mirror. Each cabin had its own bathroom, which impressed me greatly. Mother's sea trunk impressed me even more. It was fitted with drawers and hangers that contained exquisite clothes. I could hardly believe that I was the daughter of someone so elegant.

The next port of call was Genoa, the place of my birth. Sigrid was still working in the hospital, but for some inexplicable reason, we did not see her, so I can only presume she must have been away at the time. It was somewhat puzzling, but I held back quizzing my mother on Sigrid's whereabouts. From Genoa, we were going to sail via the Suez Canal, stopping at Port Said, Aden, and Colombo, Singapore and then on to Australia. The canal had been closed for more than six months because of damage and blockage caused by sunken ships from the Suez Canal crisis. The United Nations emergency forces helped to clear the canal and completed it ahead of schedule on 10 April. The *Giessenkerk* was to be one of the first ships to pass through the canal. It was the talk of the deck. However, the situation in Egypt was still tense so we were delayed for several days in Genoa, while deliberations went on at the ship owner's headquarters in the Netherlands.

To fill the time, Mother took me to see my second movie, a black and white film set during the Roman Empire. The hero was dark haired and very good looking, but towards the end of the film he was killed and I was sad for him; in my ignorance I thought that if the script called for a character to die, the deed was actually done.

Mother and I also walked through the *cargo*, the tangled alleyways, in the old town of Genoa, unchanged since the Middle Ages, It was dark and gloomy and it reminded me of Tórshavn. I wanted Mother to show me where we had lived, but did not yet feel comfortable enough with her to ask her. A few days later, a decision was made to abandon passage via the Suez Canal and to alter our course to sail via South Africa.

On the day we were to leave Genoa, Mother and I had an argument – the first of many. I had finally worked up enough courage to ask her about Sigrid and somehow I mishandled it. Mother accused me of being insolent, but after that I did not understand a single word she said. I had never engaged in a serious argument with anyone before this, and I was so shocked by the altercation, that I decided to take myself off the ship without any plan of where to go. I did not get very far as the sailors from the ship soon caught up with me. I was hauled before my mother, who was positively steaming with fury, more out of embarrassment than worry, I assumed. When necessary, Mia had always been firm but gentle with me, but the consequence of my action that day in Genoa was something I had never experienced. It was to be far reaching and the course was set for anything but a loving mother and daughter relationship. My fantasies of a perfect mother were shattered. For her part, Mother accused me of 'growing up wild in the Faeroes', though I was really shy and retiring and totally unexposed to any such wild deeds. Perhaps she regretted taking me back with her to live in Australia, I wondered. I stood on the deck and looked across the vast blue ocean with no sign of land. Even the threatening Sea Voice would have been of comfort to me now.

The next port of call was Las Palmas in the Canary Islands. It was my first experience of hot weather and I loved it. The sun shone all day and there was not a cloud in the sky. I thought this a miracle in itself. But when we went ashore I saw people begging. I had never seen any beggars in Tórshavn, but soon spotted a man on crutches, making his way quickly towards me. He was very bony and had a cigarette hanging out of his mouth. I wanted to hide behind my mother, but dared not do so. One side of his trousers was pinned up near his waist and then I noticed that he had only one leg. I was quite overwhelmed by how this could happen to anyone.

Vendors had set up their stalls on the quay where our ship was berthed. Some were selling the biggest dolls I had ever seen. Even though I had outgrown playing with dolls, I eyed them with keen interest, as they had been my very good companions for a long time. Mother thought I was hinting to her to buy me one. She scolded me severely for wanting to have more of what I had already. Her harsh words took me aback. Mia had never got angry or shouted at me. It was not the Faeroese way. Mia and I had communicated well without words. It soon became obvious that I had to condition myself to this new parental authority.

Between Las Palmas and Cape Town, Mother told me that she was to be remarried as soon as we arrived in Melbourne. I was bewildered. How could she do this, when she was already married to my father? 'Didn't Mia tell you that I divorced your father some years ago? I wrote and told her,' my mother demanded in a highly irritated tone of voice. 'No, she didn't,' I replied feebly, worried that this might cause another scene. Out of nervousness, I started to fiddle with my hair

'And don't fiddle with your hair. It's very unbecoming.'

No doubt Mia had felt that I should be spared the news about Mother's divorce and had left it out when translating Mother's letter to me. I was most disturbed by the prospect of not being reunited with my real father and having to adjust to a stranger, who was going to take his place. Had I managed to take a look inside Mother's passport, I would have seen that she had officially reverted to her maiden name of Putnik. But Mother always kept her passport and the personal details of her life well hidden from me.

Mother explained that Stephen, my stepfather-to-be, was twenty-two years her senior. He was Hungarian and had an impeccable pedigree, Mother stressed. Stephen had been born in the city of Novi Sad, which had then been part of Hungary, but was now in Yugoslavia. After graduating as an industrial chemist, Stephen had emigrated to Australia in 1925, where he had built up a very successful business manufacturing face and body creams. None of this interested me, as I continued to be deeply concerned at suddenly being told that I was not going to live with both my parents. At this stage, my mother had not yet enlightened me to the fact that my real father had no interest in me whatsoever. While, my English had improved rapidly on this voyage, no doubt out of necessity, if I wanted to be sure that she understood a phrase, I would also say it in Danish, which Mother comprehended because of her German. We had obviously got off to a bad start and I tried hard to communicate more clearly to avoid misunderstandings. Despite this, we would continue to misread each other's signals throughout our lives.

To while away the time at sea, Mother told me a little about her six months stay on the Continent, before coming to pick me up. For most of the time she stayed in Vienna with a long-time family friend named Milla Metzner. Milla was the proud owner of a parakeet called Koko Metzner. He was a cheeky little bird, but could be most polite when he felt like it, charming the older generation with his formal Austro-Hungarian greeting of 'Küss die Hand' - I kiss your hand. A lengthy article about Koko's idiosyncratic ways appeared in the newspaper. Koko had the uncanny knack of saying the right thing to the wrong person and vice versa. Once, at a blessing of animals, Koko had come out with, 'Kiss me on the...' just as the priest was leaning over him to bestow his benediction. I laughed for the first time in weeks.

Although Mother was anxious to visit her family in Belgrade, she was not in a hurry to enter 'Communist Yugoslavia'. She told me that she would never again refer to her former country simply as Yugoslavia. The celebrated split with Stalin in 1948 meant that Yugoslavia had developed outside the Soviet bloc and as such, life was a little more open and better than in the Soviet bloc countries. However, with Stalin's death in 1953, Khrushchev and Tito began to normalise relations. Remarkably, Mother's brother, Radomir, called Papi, was part of a delegation that Tito sent to Russia to negotiate the resumption of diplomatic representation and trade agreements. Uncle Papi was not a member of any socialist or communist group; one could only presume that there must have been some business opportunities for him on this visit.

Mother waited until December to go to Belgrade. 'Imagine,' said my mother indignantly, 'I had to apply for a visa to enter my country of birth.' She stayed with her brother Djordje and his wife Zorica in their apartment in the city and visited her ailing father, who was still living around the corner in the family home on Francuska Street, though he was only permitted to occupy a small section of that grand family house. After Tito came to power, Mother explained, several families appropriated the rest of the house. Uncle Djordje, Mother's favourite brother, had become a pulmonary specialist and professor of medicine at the University of Belgrade. Radomir, along with his wife Vera, had absconded to the French Riviera, jet setting between Amalfi and Nice and on occasion driving in the Formula One racing circuit. Mother's sister Sofija, and her husband Milutin, who was a doctor, were also living in Belgrade but were hoping to get a transfer to a hospital in West Germany. Mother's eldest brother, Uncle Bogdan and his wife Mira would always remain in Belgrade, Mother reckoned. Since the death of his wife in 1945, while Mother was pregnant with me, Grandpa Dušan spent his summers at the large country residence of Milutin's family in Vrnjacka Banja. Fortunately, Aunt Pepa had, in a fit of unusual practicality, Mother told me rolling her eyes, let out the first floor to some nuns, thus saving the house from being divided up by the State. After a few weeks in Belgrade, Mother went back to Vienna.

The *Giessenkerk* stopped in Cape Town for a day. Mother and I went to a park; I think it was the gardens around the parliament. Mother bought a packet of something I had never seen before, peanuts in their shells, which I fed to the squirrels. I watched them with fascination, as they quickly took off the shell with their dear little paws. I saw for the first time dark-skinned people. In the Faeroe Islands, everyone was of fair complexion. I asked my mother about them. She explained something to me that I did not understand. I was not to know that it was already the eighth year of the apartheid regime.

After crossing the Indian Ocean, the *Giessenkerk* stopped first in Australia at Fremantle and then at Adelaide, where my father still lived. Mother asked if I wished to see him, but I declined, having read somewhere that divorced couples hated each other to such an extent that they were likely to kill each other on sight. I did not want this to happen.

The *Giessenkerk* docked in Melbourne on 22 May 1957. My stepfather-to-be was waiting for us. Stephen was well built, but shorter than Mother I noted. He looked elegant and wore a beautifully fitting dark grey suit. He hugged and kissed Mother and gave me a silver charm bracelet. For his trouble, I kicked him in the shins! No doubt, he too regarded me as an untamed child.

Mother and Stephen were married the next day at the Wesley Chapel. Mother wore a smart red suit with an orchid spray on her lapel and I noticed she had put on flat shoes. She had a fur stole draped over one shoulder. I did not attend the marriage ceremony and I do not recall actually being invited. In any case, I preferred to sulk in my hotel room. Nothing had turned out as I had expected. This had indeed been a voyage of discovery. I had left behind my world of turbulent weather and inner domestic calm. I was entering a new world, where everything was in reverse. My life was to be turned inside out.

## Chapter Twenty-Six

LIKE A FAEROESE boat tossing about in a cruel storm, was how I felt when I arrived in Sydney. Much like Sofus, Guðrun's father, on his lonely voyage across the treacherous North Sea; I had to look out for mines in my new surroundings. I was not equipped with the same seafaring skills as Sofus. I searched for a fjord in which to shelter, but here the calm bays were unwelcoming and did not offer the refuge I needed. I was still recovering from the revelations of the rocky voyage to Australia, when I was plunged into a cultural collision. Everyone and everything was different from what I imagined. I searched for comforting similarities, but found none.

The sky was always bright blue and there were few overcast days. The sun would shine all day every day, which I found quite astonishing. People wore sunglasses. Trees grew everywhere. When it rained for a few days in a row, everyone complained:

'Terrible weather, isn't it?'

If rain were to be the source of grievance in the Faeroes, we would have complained every single day. A 'southerly' change followed by a storm, was to my mind a mere change of wind direction, not a real storm as we so often experienced in the Faeroe Islands.

In my first summer, Mother's new husband, Stephen, drove us to a place called Church Point, where he owned a piece of land. No houses were to be seen and the bay was a deep green. It was all forest. 'It's called the bush,' Mother corrected me. When we got out of the car, we were surrounded by a deafening sound. It was my first encounter with cicadas, immediately followed by a greeting of a million blowflies. I opened my mouth to ask about the cicadas and a fly flew into it, which I inadvertently swallowed. Ah, I had moved from the Island of Birds to the Land of Flies.

At first, we lived in the Sydney suburb of Elizabeth Bay. Up the road from us the nuns of the Order of the Sacred Heart ran a private girls' school, and I was sent there with my mother's confirmation that it was 'one of the best schools in Australia'. It was 'exclusive', she said, which was completely meaningless to me. The pupils were predominantly from Anglo-Saxon and Anglo-Celtic stock and it soon became apparent to me that once again I was to be an outsider. Most of the girls had long straight blonde hair, whereas mine was dark, curly and very Afro. I felt awkward and uncomfortable in their company. They called me 'Antonio'.

'I'm not a boy,' I told them, but they looked at me blankly. Some suggested that I should be called Tonie, but I objected and refused to answer to such a peculiar sounding short name. Though my English was improving rapidly, I spoke 'funny', I overheard a girl say, but she wasn't laughing. Some of the girls were sleek and judgmental and I gathered from their gossip that they led very smart lives outside of school, well in advance of their years. They knew that I led a dull life and never went anywhere. I was stuck in my 'reffo' status, a word coined in post-war Australia to identify refugees. Though not tolerated by the nuns, this label was heard often enough outside of school. I knew that I was labelled as one of them.

When I told the girls in my class that I had spent my childhood in the Faeroe Islands, just below the Arctic Circle, and once they had established that the Faeroes had nothing to do with the Pharaohs of Egypt, the response was always the same:

'It must have been absolutely freezing over there.'

'No it wasn't,' I replied. 'The islands are visited by a main tract of the Gulf Stream, a surface current that brings warm water northwards, raising the temperatures considerably.' I continued full of confidence: 'The harbour never freezes over in winter. The summers are cool, but the winter temperatures only drop below freezing point for a few days at a time.'

By now, I had lost their interest, I could tell. I also wanted to tell them that this sounds pleasant enough, but that it is not the case as the islands are constantly battered by the furious storms of the Atlantic, even more so than Iceland, such as one would never experience in Sydney.

Mistaking the Faeroes for the Pharaohs, as some people still do if they have not seen the name in print, may not be so ridiculous after all. Nelson Annandale wrote that there was a curious belief held in Scandinavia, linking the seals, which abounded in the caves of the islands, with the soldiers of Pharaoh, who were lost in the Red Sea. The soldiers were not drowned, but turned into seals, which swam away to the North Seas. Annandale's book, *The Faroes and Iceland: Studies in Island Life*, is full of little gems, not least of which is his encounter with an elderly Faeroese villager, who had travelled the world, working at various trades and had even made it to far-off Australia, where he was an assistant to a blacksmith in the state of New South Wales. Unfortunately, the place where he lived is not given. On his way back to the Faeroes, the villager stopped in London, where he was so terrified by its size that he hardly ever left his room. However, his feelings for the English were so sympathetic that he was nicknamed the 'English Consul' by the village priest on his return home.

The large school had commanding views of the harbour and extensive grounds leading right down to the water's edge, though this did not make the school more attractive to me. Inside, strong disinfectant smells rose from the polished floorboards. It permeated our clothes, our skin, everything. Mother would demand that I take my uniform off the minute I stepped through the front door and I understood why perfectly. It was even worse than the smell of cod liver boiling. The nuns also had a peculiar smell emanating from their mediaeval habits, as if the garments had not been washed for centuries. It was rumoured that they wore clothes handed down from dead nuns and I developed my own theory that these clothes were not washed from one dead nun to the next. I was grateful that we had to wear a school uniform, as otherwise I would have stuck out even more. I was quite certain of that. After a time, I made some friends, but we never met out of school. Oh, how I despaired at being here, yet I did not want to go back to Tórshavn either. I was stuck. There was no escape.

The modus operandi of the nuns was bizarre at times. When a whole class of girls had to walk from one area of the school to another, it was always in single or double file. This part was no different from my school in Tórshavn; however, the nuns' mode of communication, namely unseen castanets, was. To stop or start walking, the castanets, which seemed to live inside each nun's many-layered black skirt, were clicked once or twice indicating either stop or start. No verbal command was given. It made me want to laugh, as I was sure this was how Donald Duck would have sounded if he had clicked his tongue.

At home as at school, I was a fish out of water. My mother and her new husband were suddenly plunged into the role of unwilling parents. Stephen had no children from his previous marriage and, being in his late fifties, had little patience for them. Day to day parenthood didn't suit them. I cramped their style. I did not fit into their lives.

'We send you to the best school; buy you the best clothes; feed you well. You live in a lovely place, and this is how you repay us,' Mother would exclaim, exasperated by something I had said. I exasperated my mother rather a lot. I did not understand about the

166

repayment. Did the smart girls at my school repay their parents? And if so, how did they do it?

Mother and I remained uncomfortable with each other. My romantic illusion of mothers being gentle, cuddly and soft had already been crushed on the voyage to Australia. Whereas earlier in my life I had accepted my parentless situation, I was now deeply hurt that my mother had bundled me up like a package and posted me to a far away place marked 'Do not return to sender'. Mother's frustration with me reinforced this. The hurt led to resentfulness and just as I had emotionally withdrawn myself from Mia, I now did the same from my mother.

The very thought of opening my heart to Mother sent shivers down my spine. I was certain that she would be frightfully angry with me if she realised that my unhappiness was caused by her actions. Mother was always in the right and I had witnessed many a friend of hers who had dared to stand up to her never to be heard of or seen again. I did not want this to happen to me. What if she threw me out of the house? Where would I go? I had no other family living in Australia. I resigned myself to the obvious, that it was to be a matter of surviving my adolescence, not enjoying it.

My mother's sharpness of tongue, overbearing personality and physical strength scared me. Though finely boned, she was powerfully built, statuesque with large flashing eyes and a larger than life aura about her. She was a matriarch among matriarchs. She made me very nervous. 'How many times have I told you to stop fiddling with your hair?' I would often say or do the wrong thing, because I was too tense to think straight, only making matters worse for both of us. The punishments were severe. A thorough hiding was the norm for most offences, leaving me very sore and wondering if my mother possessed superhuman strength.

Both my mother and stepfather had fierce tempers and almighty mood swings, such as I had never experienced as a child in the Faeroes, where such behaviour was never displayed. When they were in a good mood, however, they were most entertaining and I would laugh at their antics. They were totally unpredictable in their behaviour. I never knew how the day would shape up. One day, I would come home from school to find Hungarian gypsy music playing. Mother and Stephen would be drinking French champagne for no apparent reason and dancing the *Czárda* - all was well with our world. The next day, I was greeted with sullen looks and ordered to stay in my bedroom. Arguments seemed to be the order of the day. Many times I was hauled out of my bed in the middle of the night to answer for my perceived bad attitude towards my parents and my 'insolence'. I was the cause of all their troubles, they said. I was deemed a troublemaker. I found this perplexing, as, apart from going to school, I never ventured out of home, so there was no opportunity to 'play up'. Movies, parties and visiting girlfriends in their homes were out of bounds. I couldn't understand why Stephen and Mother had such terrible arguments or why they often dragged me into them. It was obvious that Stephen adored my mother and showered her with affection and jewellery. He told me that he had fallen in love with her at first sight. I could well believe it. I was in awe of Mother's lovely looks and intelligence and could easily understand why a man would fall for her.

I felt unlovely and unloved. I was also painfully thin when we arrived in Australia. Mother took me to the family doctor who pronounced me to be undernourished.

'No wonder,' scoffed my mother, 'Mia probably fed you on nothing else but sardines on toast.' I didn't dare to disagree. The doctor's diagnosis spurred my mother into cooking extra treats for me, such as Austrian-style pastries, Hungarian *dobos torte*, chocolate éclairs, and Danish apricot pastries, which I consumed without gaining weight.

To add to Mother's troubles, I was left-handed. My mother decided that I should learn to write with my right hand without delay. I wanted to retort that no one had minded my left-handedness in Tórshavn, but stopped myself in time.

'What will it look like when you sign the church register at your wedding with your left hand?' my mother exclaimed. She pushed back an imaginary bridal veil from her face as she bent down

168

towards an imaginary register. She picked up a pen and made an exaggerated display of signing with her left hand, twisting it to such an extent that I thought she must be double-jointed. I tried to suppress a giggle.

'See,' said my mother, 'you'll be the laughing stock at your own wedding.'

During the changeover period, my head and my right hand felt unnatural as if they did not belong to my body, but someone else's. Much to my distress, I started to stutter. This was especially noticeable when I tried to speak French, in particular when starting a sentence with 'I': 'Je...je...je...je...'

'Good God, child, you'll never amount to anything,' sighed Mother.

Eventually, I stopped stuttering and I managed to write very nicely with my right hand. However, I still could draw, paint and use scissors only with my left hand. Mother did not seem to be troubled by this, as presumably I would not be engaged in these activities on my wedding day.

No sooner had I come out of my undernourished state and my unsightly left-handedness, than my mother was quick to inform me one fine day that I was an unwanted child.

'I never wanted to have children. By the time I realised I was pregnant, it was too late to have an abortion.' I looked at her, unable to speak, she continued bluntly: 'I kept having my period after I became pregnant and was already four months gone, and the doctor said it was too dangerous for an abortion.'

I found Mother's revelation quite unbearable and I cried myself to sleep for many nights afterwards. This had a profound effect on my feeling towards my mother. Whereas I loved her, I felt that I could never be devoted to her after this. I no longer thought of her as 'my mum' but as a disinclined mother. We were both trapped in a situation from which there was no escape. I realised that other families might be caught in similar situations, but this brought me no comfort. With maturity, however, I would come to understand that not all females have maternal instincts and that this was likely

169

the main reason why my mother had not wanted to take me with her to Australia when she and my father emigrated from Europe. I did not accept her once-only fleeting explanation that it was due to the uncertainties of her marriage in the setting of a new country. After all, I reasoned, they were not migrating to a war zone.

My relationship with Stephen did not get off to a good start, when one day I threatened him with an iron. I don't recall what provoked this incident, except that whatever he said, offended me deeply. I was ironing my clothes at the time, thinking about the heavy cast iron that Mia had used. Stephen and I would spend weeks without speaking to each other, usually brought on by something innocent that I had said to which he took personal umbrage - the slightest thing could set him off. Mother was always quick to take his side, even when it was clear that I was the innocent party. I would look at her pleadingly while Stephen was having one of his tantrums, but she never agreed with me on any matter involving him.

'This will not end until you apologise,' my mother would tell me. Sometimes I dared to stand my ground and would reply that I had done nothing wrong, therefore an apology was unwarranted. Eventually, after a week or more, I would have to give in. I could not understand why Mother had to choose between Stephen and me. I sensed that she had to humour him, even at my expense. I was amazed that such a strong woman would give in to him, but I supposed it was a way of keeping the peace between them.

However, with time, Stephen grew very fond of me and we would laugh when people said to us: 'You look more like your father than your mother.' Certainly, I did not look anything like my mother and I wondered sometimes when she would grumble:

'They must have switched babies at the hospital,' if in Italy, as in the Faeroes, there also lived trolls, who were known to steal an infant from its mother and leave their own infant, a *changeling,* in exchange. *Changelings* did not fit in with humans very well and they were also slow-witted. This part worried me greatly as my mother would often tell me that I was stupid.

It was obvious to anyone that my mother and I did not share similar physical features. We were both tall with big brown eyes, but there the similarities ended. Mother had a lovely aristocratic looking face, hooded eyelids and a fine nose. I had a democratic face, I declared, which did not amuse Mother one bit. I might as well be adopted, I thought, we didn't even have similar traits. Then one day I noticed in a photograph of Grandmother Denise that she and I had the same eyelids. Finally I had found a family resemblance. I pointed this out to Mother, who agreed, but nevertheless gave me a pitiful look.

'My mother was such a gentle person,' Mother informed me as she caressed the photograph, 'and Papa Dušan gave her a hard time.' I was sorry that my grandmother's gentleness had not been transferred to my mother. We both knew that she had more of her father's nature.

However, there was another face to my mother, which I enjoyed enormously and that was her humour and social repartee. She was a great *raconteuse* and her beautifully crafted stories would keep our guests in rapture the whole evening. Mother could have competed with Oscar Wilde for witticism any day. Always the centre of attention, men would flock around Mother as she drank and traded jokes with the best of them. She was the very picture of a man's woman.

## Chapter Twenty-Seven

SOME MONTHS AFTER my arrival in Sydney, we moved from Stephen's flat in Elizabeth Bay to a large house in Northbridge on the North Shore, right by the water in Sailor's Bay. Our three-storey white house had expansive terraces and a large garden of hibiscus and exotic plants. Outdoor entertainment and swimming were to be the norm here, 'outdoors' being a peculiar world to my Faeroese mind. Northbridge epitomised all the positive qualities of the 'lucky country' of Australia, especially for people from Europe.

The living room on the top floor overlooked the entire bay. Persian rugs covered large black and white tiles. The coffee tables had marble tops, something I had never seen. The marble felt icy cold to the touch, not warm like the stone slabs of my childhood. The wall opposite the windows was mirrored, to capture the light and reflect the magnificent view of the bay. The black satin-finished furniture and specially made sofas in an off-white raw silk fabric came from an interior decorating shop called Cabana. I could not imagine that a shop would be devoted entirely to interior decorating. It was all very exotic, if not a little overwhelming. Everything was highly polished and new, except for the antique pieces which Mother said 'were in mint condition'. Gone from my life were the warm hues of faded brown and black timber and wallpaper from which one could conjure up a myriad tales.

The swimming pool was built in the sea and surrounded by wire netting. The overhanging branches from a large willow tree touched the water at high tide. The colour of the bay changed from green to blue, about as different as one could get from the bleak sea colours of the North Atlantic. Next to the pool was a little boat shed. On sighting it for the first time, I experienced a rare touch of nostalgia for the Faeroe Islands.

Our large house provided the perfect venue for big parties, which were held on a regular basis. Mother was a superb cook, far surpassing Tulla, I soon realised. Complicated French dishes with rich sauces and desserts such as soufflé *au Grand Marnier* were prepared effortlessly. In summer, weekend barbecues for twenty guests, sitting down at beautifully laid tables on the wide terrace, were regarded as casual entertaining. Mother grilled Serbian meat specialties, such as *ražnijici, cevapcici* and *pljeskavica*, which Stephen called French hamburgers. I had never seen anyone in Tórshavn using a barbecue. In true form, Mother trained our gardener, Giuseppe, to help attend to the guests at these outdoor luncheons.

Mother was at her best when she was not playing the role of mother. At these parties, I loved standing behind a pillar, out of sight, listening to her funny tales. The guests were mesmerized, I could tell. Some of her true stories I had heard before, but with each retelling she changed the facts, so that they were like a new story. At times, when I mixed with the guests, I made the mistake of correcting Mother on a point of her story, which I knew was not accurate, as I had witnessed the particular incident she described. It was not that I wanted to correct her in front of others, I just thought she might have forgotten how it happened and I was there to help her remember it correctly. This did not go down well with her and I soon learned to keep my mouth shut.

Mother created an aura of good breeding, privilege and exclusivity around her. By comparison, everything 'Australian' on the outside was, well, ordinary, unrefined and oafish. I remember that a friend of hers had bought a genuine Pucci silk dress in Italy with the distinctive geometric colourful pattern; however, according to Mother, it looked like a copy from a department store. Other people's diamonds looked like glass. Even when Mother consented that someone's jewellery was genuine, she would comment: 'It looks fake, so it might as well be fake.' Mother's jewellery was big and showy; one could spot it across a crowded room. Other people's *bijoux* were so small that 'you have to go over their neck and hands with a magnifying glass in order to find it!'

I had noticed during my first summer in Sydney that swimming was a popular sport. Mother was a superb swimmer and diver. As I did not know how to swim, I would sit by the side of the pool and dangle my toes in the water, watching my mother's strong graceful strokes. After a few weeks of my reluctance in getting wet, Mother decided to teach me to swim, which she did with uncharacteristic patience. I still, however, preferred to sit on our jetty - familiar territory - where I would catch yellowtail fish for our Siamese cat. It reminded me a little of the fishing I had done with hand lines in the harbour in Tórshavn, though I was now using a finely made French fishing rod. Stephen had the best fishing tackle, the best hunting guns and all sorts of other top quality gadgets and equipment.

When we first went out in Stephen's motor cruiser, I expected huge swells as soon as we left our bay, but throughout the other bays in the winding Middle Harbour, the sea remained as still as the water in a wash basin. Even in this small boat, I couldn't feel the currents. Everyone on the water seemed to be just cruising around. Nobody was fishing, so what were they doing out? Stephen warned me about man-eating sharks. I had been used to such creatures, but in the Faeroes we ate them, they didn't eat us. It was all very odd here in Australia.

One day after a southerly change, a young kookaburra fell from his nest into our garden. He had a damaged leg and wing and Mother showed great talent as a veterinarian. She made a temporary home for the bird in a storage room underneath the garage and gave him the name of Kookie. Mother taught me how to feed Kookie by pushing food down his throat, wearing thick rubber gloves as protection against his sharp beak. When we were entertaining outdoors, I would get Kookie, who was not yet fledged, to hop on my hand and show him off to our guests. My hands were covered with Band Aids and the guests thought that the bird had bitten me, but they were covering the scars from my warts that had been burned off by the dermatologist. The string with knots that had been so effective in Tórshavn for getting rid of warts, did not work in Sydney. More and more, I noticed nothing was the same.

Moving to Northbridge meant that I had to become a weekly boarder at school, due to the distance. Sleeping in a dormitory was completely alien to me, as it must have been for the other girls as well. I suspected that the austerity of the narrow iron bed, the plain night table and wooden cross above the bed head were meant to inspire us to become nuns. I recoiled at the thought and began to think that sharing a bedroom with Mia was almost preferable. I couldn't make up my mind what I disliked more, boarding school or weekends at home. I found in favour of home because of the delicious food and my dog. Mother and Stephen had bought a daschund, which they named Waldi, short for Waldemar, after one of Stephen's hunting dogs in his native Hungary. I understood this was my dog and was thrilled to bits to have a companion, until my mother told me that it was really her dog, because he loved her more. Waldi however, was unaware of this change in ownership and chose to follow me everywhere. Sometimes I kept him secretly in my bed at night, where I would cry into his fur. He never objected to being made wet and even snuggled closer to me.

At boarding school, mass was held every morning before breakfast in the chapel, where we spent a lot of time on our knees, feeling hungry and faint. Now I realised how good I had had it in Tórshavn, only having to attend a single Sunday church service.

At mass, we had to cover our heads with black lace mantillas. Together with the castanets, the routine seemed all very Spanish, I thought, and odd for a French order. But this was Australia and everything was peculiar.

Unlike the Nuns' School in Tórshavn, religious instruction, or Doctrine, as it was called, was a significant subject. I became somewhat concerned about the possibility of not being baptised and still living in Original Sin with the prospect of burning in Hell forever when I died. There was much talk about this fate during sermons, I noted, on those odd occasions when I bothered to listen. The nuns were alarmed that I might still be unbaptised and have lived up to the age of thirteen in Original Sin. I convinced my mother to let me be christened, as she had no idea if this sacrament had ever been performed on me in Italy. The nuns thought it was best that I should be confirmed at the same time. Afterwards, they were so thrilled that my soul had been saved that afternoon tea was served in the inner sanctum - the nuns' parlour. Nice walnut table, I noticed. Little did I know what I was letting myself in for, as there was now the tricky matter of the confessional to deal with. I tried it a few times and did not like it. Consequently I stopped going. When questioned by the nuns, I simply told them that living in this school, there was absolutely no opportunity to sin, therefore I had nothing to confess. 'At home, I never go anywhere either, so again, I can't sin,' I explained.

'Ah, but maybe you have had impure thoughts,' was their response. Well, this really got to me and I decided to boycott the confessional. Anyhow, I felt uncomfortable having to whisper my perceived sins to a priest, a mere man after all.

'He represents God,' the nuns explained.

'I'll deal directly with God,' I replied.

Mother would have been proud of this feisty response and especially that I planned to go straight to the top.

'Always insist on speaking to the managing director,' Mother counselled.

Among her many talents was sewing and Mother could whip up an evening dress from a Christian Dior pattern in a matter of days without any telltale signs of it being made at home. As I had loved watching Tulla, I now enjoyed watching my mother sewing and cooking, though I never felt completely at ease in her company. Mother and Stephen attended many parties. Stephen had all his clothes, including his shoes, custom made. Mother also had many of her clothes made by a fine Serbian dressmaker. In the Faeroes, people knitted and made their own clothes and dresses, even for Sabbath Best, but this Australian life style seemed to require a far more extensive wardrobe. People dressed casually on Sundays and neither Mother nor Stephen or any of their friends went to church, except to attend weddings and funerals. I went by myself to our local church, a much longer walk than to the Havnar Church in Tórshavn. The nuns had put the fear of God into me and promised eternal damnation if I did not attend Sunday mass. My earthly needs were greater. More than anything, I needed the Sunday mass to get away from Mother and Stephen's company.

Mother looked terribly glamorous in her wonderful gowns, many with a low *décolletage* that showed off her satin-smooth neck and shoulders and her favourite three-stranded South Sea Islands pearls. I loved watching her while she was putting on her makeup and getting dressed. I always had to help her pull up the zipper on the back of her dress, so that she would not ruin her long freshly painted nails. I thought she looked like a movie star and I no longer minded that I felt ugly by comparison. When one day in a rare moment of unfamiliar confidentiality, I ventured to tell Mother this, she kept tactfully silent, which I took to mean that it was in fact so.

Even worse, when I looked in the mirror one morning, I gasped at the awful sight of the many pimples that seemed to have erupted overnight. Each was topped with a white centre, much like snow-capped Mount Fuji. 'I hate these pimples. They make me so ugly,' I said in a depressed adolescent tone. 'When I was your age, I had such perfect skin,' replied my mother.

177

'Oh, terrific,' I thought, 'now I feel so much better.' I did not dare express this out loud. I was starting to be sarcastic about myself as a way of coping with the typical trials of my teenage years.

A few days later, Mother took me to the hairdresser in the dreary Northbridge shopping centre, where a person with scissors, for she could not be called a hairdresser, proceeded to take fistfuls of my hair and quickly cut it off close to my scalp. My hair looked as if it had come out of a bush fire. I looked towards my mother for consolation: 'Oh, you're always full of *tzores*,' meaning woes, she shot back.

Evidently, it was more important for grown ups to look their best. Mother and Stephen made such an elegant couple, I thought, as I watched them smoking and sipping a scotch and soda, or three, before going out. The next day I would ask:

'How was the party?' The standard reply from Mother would be, 'They all adored me.' And I could well believe it.

'Elephants shouldn't catch flies,' said my mother, lighting another cigarette and indicating for me to sit down. She was about to embark on one of her lively post-mortem descriptions of a party she had attended the evening before. Mother could outwit and outsmart most people. She was of course the elephant, and the flies the unsuspecting guests, some of whom might be spared Mother's sharp wit due to their insignificant stature and inability to defend themselves. In many ways, this metaphor applied to my relationship with Mother. Like the elephant she was a matriarch, no one challenged her. She demanded respect. Nothing stood in her way. She was a social creature with a long memory. And I was an insect. I could be tossed about, trampled on and squashed at will. I would never be able to defend myself, due to my small stature. I would never grow to be the size of my mother. Whereas I buzzed nervously around her, trying to please, I knew that I often irritated her and I sometimes experienced the powerful smack of her trunk.

Like all good entertainers, Mother loved an audience and would require little encouragement to perform. She always had pet hatreds that lasted for a time until replaced by a new, more entertaining one. One of these was marching girls, or drum majorettes, as they were known in Australia. We would see them in parades or on television, before football matches. Mother thought the concept of uniformed marching girls was the most comical thing imaginable and at the slightest provocation, she could be encouraged to do her 'Marching Girls' act up and down the living room, lifting her knees high and wielding a silver serving spoon for a baton. We would fall about laughing, much to Mother's pleasure, who would then grace us with a repeat performance. Despite Stephen having lived in Australia for decades and very much considering himself a successful Australian, Mother always brought their European-ness into sharp focus and managed in her mind to stay 'one-up' on the folk beyond the battlements of our home. They both had 'background'; few around them shared this quality she believed. Mother spoke 'King's English', as she called it, with an accent, whose origin could not be determined. We all spoke with an accent. I had to practice the 'how now, brown cow' drill before Mother, so that my vowels would not sound flat 'like an Aussie', Mother often told me pulling a face. However, she very much liked the Australian sense of humour.

Mother and Stephen had an interesting mixture of friends, including many Australians and some impoverished and not so impoverished titled and untitled middle Europeans, as well as members of the diplomatic corps. I learned how to curtsey and greet diplomats and other dignitaries in several languages. In between this glamorous lifestyle, which came as a shock to the system after the somewhat austere life in the Faeroes, there was the unpleasant reality of living day to day with my mother and stepfather. I seemed to offend them without even trying. After a good spell, I would experience some stirrings of affection for both of them, but their next argument, which they inevitably embroiled me in, would soon put an end to that.

As I became more emotionally withdrawn from my mother, she in turn became more exasperated by my perceived ingratitude and lack of appreciation for my comfortable situation, private schooling and privileged lifestyle. We did not understand each other at all. Our relationship was doomed to be tainted by our separation in my early life. I had a growing sense of being alone. I longed to have a sister or a cousin in whom I could confide, or a close girlfriend, but given my closeted life, I had neither. I did not think about my father, who was still living in Adelaide. We didn't exchange greetings for our birthdays and Christmas. I realised, with some guilt that I did not even know the date of his birth, but I did not feel sufficiently at ease with Mother to ask her.

One night I dreamt that something sinister, I wasn't sure exactly what, had happened to my father. It was strange that I should suddenly have a dream about him, but I thought no more about it. A few days later, Mother received a telegram announcing my father's death. I was thirteen at the time. Despite not knowing my father and never giving him much thought, I cried into the night and regretted terribly not visiting him when the ship had stopped in Adelaide. My father left his estate to his lady friend, among which were two portraits in oil by Stanislav Rapotec. Mother was not pleased that I was not left anything in his will, though it made perfect sense to me, since my father had not acknowledged me as his daughter. For years afterwards, she would occasionally lament:

'He could at least have left you those paintings by Rapotec.'

Gradually, I came to accept the fact that my father had not cared for me one bit. My feeling of rejection increased and I became more withdrawn. Yet, I was only so in Mother's company. When I was at school, away from her sphere of influence, I knew I acted as if I were a different person. I felt free, and I even found that I too could be funny. It was as if I had two personalities.

To my mother, I was an ungrateful, sullen and obstinate child.

'You don't love anyone except yourself and you'll suffer for it later in life. You'll see.'

180

I loved my mother, but I did not like her much as a person, and she was too clever not to sense that. On occasion, my mother could be affectionate, but mostly I never seemed to get it right. Whatever I did or said would often result in punishment. I developed low self-esteem and kept apologizing to everyone for my existence. Saying 'I'm sorry' for everything was a habit I found hard to break, even as an adult.

I tried to find an explanation for Mother's rejection of me. How much like my father was I, I wondered. Did I act like him? Was I a constant reminder of the man who had been unfaithful to her and dared to adore other women as well? Her earlier words, 'you were an unwanted child' kept ringing I my ears. I wanted to leave home - just walk out - but not having money or anyone to go to, I knew this was a futile wish

Some consolation came to me from Stephen's sister, Tante Nini, who lived in a flat in Elizabeth Bay with their elderly mother, whom we all called Mutti. Stephen had brought them out from Hungary several years before my arrival in Australia. When I visited them, Tante Nini would take me for walks through Potts Point and Kings Cross, which in those days was the cosmopolitan centre of Sydney and was full of 'Continentals' like us; not drug pushers and other seedy types as there are now. Tante Nini, who was vivacious and warm-hearted, told me I was nice looking and allowed me to put on lipstick. We always joked and giggled a lot. On rare occasions, I stayed with her overnight and slept on the divan in her little sitting room. I would have gladly slept on the floor just to be with her. She was so easy going and relaxed, unlike her brother. When Mutti died, Tante Nini came to live with us at Northbridge and Mother and Stephen took advantage of this and went off on an extended world trip. I was in seventh heaven being able to experience such peaceful living in the company of just Tante Nini, the maid, the gardener and dear Waldi.

Unfortunately for me, Tante Nini had a boyfriend and a daughter back home in Hungary, and decided to return to live in Budapest. I was devastated, not least because she chose to return to live among communists, remembering the close encounter I had had with them and their rats in the harbour of Tórshavn. It meant losing my one and only friend and protector. Being sweet and gentle, Tante Nini was not able to defend me all that well during the horrendous arguments in which her fiery brother and my excitable mother embroiled us. Poor Tante Nini would fight back the tears and retreat to her room, leaving me defenceless against my parents. Like me, Tante Nini was always getting into trouble. She must have been glad to get away from the domestic maelstrom at Northbridge.

I remember one evening when we were giving a dinner party and Tante Nini was put in charge of watching Mother's delicately prepared potato *croquettes*, which were frying in hot oil. Mother repaired to join Stephen and her guests in sipping vodka martinis with a twist. But Tante Nini was more interested in reading the latest copy of the *Women's Weekly* magazine and the *croquettes* went far beyond the required fine, golden colour. For once I was blameless, having been put in charge of opening up several bottles of wine, which I did quite expertly by placing the bottle between my thin legs and, with the old corkscrew, pulling the cork out with all my might. Stephen had earlier given me a list of the wines he wanted me to fetch from the cellar. I was always receiving mixed messages from both of them; I was alternately treated as an idiot child and then was given an adult task to perform. Tante Nini never lived down the misdeed of burning the *croquettes* and after Mother's initial upset at this culinary disaster, was teased by her about it for weeks afterwards.

Mother's talents were not confined to home duties. Recognising this, Stephen tutored Mother in the ways of his business and she became the public relations and advertising manager of his company. My mother easily managed the transition from Baudelaire and Nietzsche to entrepreneur. She loved being one of the few women in a world of business that was very much dominated by men in those days.

I admired my mother enormously for her many talents and quickly figured out that she was different from the average mum. There were many times I wished she had shown more interest in me as a person, yet I also soon realised this was not going to be the case and I would have to steer myself emotionally through to adulthood.

It was a troubling prospect.

## Chapter Twenty-Eight

*M*Y LIFE IN the white house in Sydney was much more controlled than it had been in the black house with Mia and Visa in Tórshavn. Strict codes of behaviour and modes of speech were in place, none of which I seemed to follow very well. The circumference of my world in Sydney was as small and lonely as it had been in the Faeroes. It was like being on a roller coaster, with Mother and Stephen taking turns in controlling the ride. I sat in the back and as we went down the dip, I cried with fear and then laughed when we came up to the crest, but no one could hear me.

My mother and Stephen were a close-knit couple. He adored her and she loved being adored. Everything was geared around their interests alone. There was no room for me. Not that I wanted to be the centre of their attention. In fact, whenever this happened during one of their frequent fights, it resulted in dire consequences for me. All I wanted was to be let into their lives a little. I concluded that I would remain an outsider in my own home until such time as I reached adulthood and could move out. I walked in the shadow of my mother, though I did not resemble her in looks or character. I felt that I had no identity of my own whatsoever. I was merely some kind of living organism that occupied space in the house and that needed to be fed and clothed.

Outside of school adults surrounded me. I never visited girlfriends' houses or attended parties, but this did not trouble me, as I had grown used to my own company. Mother and Stephen's friends were kind and included me in their invitations, though none of them seemed to have children anywhere near my age.

Mother had the habit of nicknaming almost everyone she knew. Whereas some of the names were endearing, others posed a problem, as they could only be used *en famille*, never to the persons themselves for fear of offending them. There was the *Zigeuner Baron* or Gypsy Baron, the Sausage Maker (a manufacturer of industrial equipment, not small goods), the Innkeeper, Birdie, Tricky Dicky (pre-Nixon), Pudding Face, Rabbity Bones and many more. This was all very amusing until we were faced with one of them and could not think of their real name. Mother would remember, but refused to help Stephen and me out.

It was bound to happen, and yes, after a while, I was also given a nickname. 'Snooky', later changed to 'Snoozie'. I was told that this had been the name of one of Stephen's dogs in Hungary and it was about the worst thing for someone suffering from low self-esteem as I was, to be named after an animal, even though I loved dogs. I much preferred 'Gugghi', Sigrid's nickname for me, though as a teenager, I naturally felt that I had outgrown it.

Mia wrote to me regularly, but I never answered her letters. Her correspondence irritated me. I wanted to wipe out her memory and that of the Faeroe Islands completely. Having one mother was now more than I could handle. I did not know how to manage the transition from Mia and Sigrid as mothers to becoming my pen pals of sorts. Mia had packed in my suitcase a framed photograph of herself in a polished wooden oval frame. When I arrived in Sydney, I removed Mia's image and threw it out. I know she wanted me not to forget her and I knew I wouldn't, but I also could not feel any fondness for her despite my disappointment at how things had turned out with my mother.

I kept the frame for a long time afterwards but never replaced it with another photo. Mother sent Mia some photos of me and of our house in Northbridge and I wrote a few words on the back of them.

One day the Danish Consul telephoned my mother to enquire after my well being, on the urgent request of Mia. When Mother questioned me as to why I had not answered any of Mia's letters, I told her that I did not want to have anything to do with Mia or my previous life in the Faeroes. Surprisingly, Mother respected my wish. Even during the many years of living with Mia, I had never formed a strong attachment to her; hence there was no emotional pull to motivate me to keep in contact with her. It was evident that she missed me, but I did not miss her.

After I had been living in Sydney for some years, Knút, the son of Hedvig and Juul Olsen, friends of Mia's in Tórshavn, came to visit us. Knút was working in the merchant marine and I got quite a shock when he suddenly appeared for lunch at Mother's invitation. He seemed much taller than my memory of him in Tórshavn and I hardly spoke one word to him, as if doing so would entrap me in my previous life in the Faeroes. As a result, he would have had scant news to report about me when he got back.

As in the Faeroes, my time was spent reading. I fell in love with the English classics and re-read them many times over. I identified with the orphans and the poor children of Dickens and the tragic heroines of the Brontë sisters, though I fervently hoped that my life would not turn out to be as gloomy.

In my mid-teens, I started on the Russian classics and I recognised certain dark moods as being similar to those of Stephen and Mother. Thankfully, they had shown no interest in Russian roulette or in throwing themselves in front of trains, though their behaviour was certainly erratic. I came to realise that Mother was a complex person and that no characters in the novels I read, not even the Russian ones, came close to capturing her mercurial ways.

When Alexander, a Russian friend, whose life was typically full of tragedies *à la russe,* came to visit, the clicking of vodka glasses could be heard well into the night. On one occasion, Mother had told Alexander about a venison dish by Escoffier that she liked to prepare. A few days later Alexander appeared on our doorstep with a complete deer. We never dared to ask him where he got it from as we strongly suspected it came from the zoo.

Stephen and Alexander sometimes went hunting together and I remember them bringing back a bag full of quail, which Mother prepared à la Dauphine, served on a purée of fresh peas.

'Have they been stuffed?' I asked my mother, remembering the stuffed puffins of the Faeroes. 'No,' my mother said coldly. I could tell she had read my mind and knew I was thinking of that Unmentionable Place.

'I know what you're thinking,' Mother would often say to me. On this occasion she was right, but often she was wrong and then I got into a lot of trouble, as she insisted on being right every time. As she served the roasted quail, she warned: 'Chew gently and watch out for pellets.' I didn't understand at first what she meant. It had never occurred to me that people shot birds. I had presumed that they caught them with their hands or with a net as was done in the Faeroe Islands.

Mother and I fell into a tactical habit of avoiding Faeroes' Child. Whenever I would comment: 'That reminds me of the Faeroe Islands,' even when said in a positive manner, Mother would give me a dark look and I took care not to refer again to that Unmentionable Place in front of her. None of her friends in Sydney knew where I had been living as a young child, not even her closest ones. I don't know what stories she told them, but it was as if I had been living in a vacuum. No one ever questioned me about it and I didn't dare tell anyone. In later years, some of her friends found out that I had spent a great deal of my childhood in the Faeroes and they were quite shocked, though they in turn never let on to Mother that they knew.

For years I continued to feel like a foreigner in Australia and I confessed to my mother that I did not like how everyone always asked me, 'Where do you come from originally?' in a oh-you-poor-thing sort of voice, as though I had just emerged from the bilge of a migrant ship. Should I say, 'I was born in Italy, but I lived in the Faeroes (...where?) but my parents are Serbian.'

'Don't bother to say any of that,' my mother replied, just say: 'I come originally from Elizabeth Bay.' After all, my mother explained, that is where you first lived when you came to Australia. I tried this the next time and found it was like the kiss of death for any conversation. The person questioning me would promptly turn around and walk away often much to my relief.

Dinner parties in our house required days of meticulous planning and Mother, the maid and I would be busy with preparations. Mother liked to cook a variety of European dishes, which often required obtaining ingredients from all over the city. Before the advent of commercial filo pastry, the only place to buy it was in a Greek shop in Crown Street on 'the other side of the bridge' from where we lived. Mother would order the pastry by phone and send me in a taxi to pick it up. The taxi driver always complained that he would never be able to find this shop among the many small shops and restaurants along Crown Street.

I'd say, 'Don't worry, they always play their bouzouki music really loud, so you just have to follow the sound.'

The drivers, usually Australian, were unimpressed, though I noticed they always slowed down on hearing the music. While the taxi waited, I would race past the group of unshaven men outside the shop, all smoking furiously, and into the Greek shop, where the bouzouki music was blaring. I would collect the filo pastry, shout a hurried *kalimera* and *efkharisto,* for they spoke absolutely no English, and be back in the taxi within minutes. I suffered badly from car-sickness, but always made certain to place the pastry well away from me on the back seat. I would need the rest of the afternoon to recuperate from the motion sickness, but it was worth it just to eat Mother's sweet cream cheese or sour cherry *pita* as it was called in Serbian. Tulla quickly fell from being the number one on my chart of great cooks although she lived on in my memory.

When I was about sixteen, there was much talk about Mother needing a serious operation. I was not told what kind of operation and had to wait until the Sister in the hospital helpfully explained that Mother had had a hysterectomy. It sounded terrible, but when I went to Mother's room, she was half sitting up in bed despite the pain, her titian hair bouncing off her pillow, red lipstick on and doused in perfume. She complained to Stephen and me about the bad service and food as if the hospital were a luxury resort.

It was decided that I should accompany Mother to the Blue Mountains for a week of recuperation. On reflection, this would have been the ideal opportunity for us to form a close attachment, but it never happened. Even though it was winter, the hotel room had no heating and I felt too cold to hold a conversation. Didn't Australians believe in heating? In the mornings, I would always be the first to take a shower, so that the steam would heat up the bathroom for my mother. To stay warm at night, I slept with my mother's fur coat thrown over my blanket and that is about as close as I got to her.

The coat smelled strongly of her perfume, but this gave me no comfort. I had come to the conclusion that the sole reason I was sent to the Faeroe Islands was because my mother did not want to have me around her, and from what my mother had told me my father felt the same way. Yet, I forgave them, as a good Catholic girl should. Still, I was resentful for what they had done and I battled with feelings of guilt. I had never experienced guilt in the Faeroes; it was only when I started to receive religious instructions at school in Sydney that a new world of guilt in all its Catholic manifestation was instilled in me. I worried that in experiencing negative feelings towards my mother I was committing a mortal sin and would surely burn in Hell for eternity.

I had no idea how other mothers behaved, as I never went to my girlfriends' houses and I couldn't bring myself to ask anyone at school:

'How does your mother behave towards you? And how do you feel about her?' I realised that my situation was far better than that of many other children and Mother never failed to remind me of my material comforts. Instead, I knew I should be grateful for my comfortable situation. Instead, I felt more guilt.

I loved the Blue Mountains. Even though they were wooded, they reminded me of the bald Faeroes' Mountains because of their primitiveness. I asked about wood spirits. There weren't any on the Faeroe Islands I said, but I knew that Norway was full of them. I was told not be ridiculous as I was far too old to believe in such nonsense, and perhaps I was. However, when I looked at the old gum trees with their grey white twisted branches like arms, I knew they contained spirits that needed little encouragement to be released.

In the hotel dining room Mother made me laugh with her comments about the other diners. The woman sitting near us was a *debelka* (fatty in Serbian) and the waitress who kept dropping the cutlery was a *budala* (Serbian for silly). One woman, who seemed out of place in her Transylvanian style dress, caught my mother's eye: 'Look, she is dressed for a night at the opera in Baghdad.'

All these comments were made in a loud stage whisper, which worried me, but I thought it very daring. At parties, Mother would imitate film stars and local celebrities, with appropriate accents, much to the delight of our guests. She had the uncanny ability to look just like the person she was impersonating. She was always the star of the show, and there could be only one star. I was an inexperienced stagehand and not very good at my job. Sometimes I enjoyed the plays, but often I did not and each year I wondered how I would survive the season.

While Mother was still in hospital, our maid left us. We had a series of live-in maids - they never lasted for more than a few months. A replacement had to be found before Mother came home, so Stephen and I interviewed several women. I was thrilled to be asked to sit on the interview panel as I was normally deemed to be too stupid for any such activity. We settled on a sweet young Lebanese woman. However, I thought she looked pregnant. Stephen felt certain this was not the case as, 'All women from that country have lovely well-rounded figures,' he explained. On returning home, Mother took one look at her and promptly nicknamed her The Belly Dancer. A few months later, The Belly Dancer left us, heavily pregnant. Her brother, with whom she spent her days off, turned out to be her husband.

Next came Mrs. O'Neill, of a certain age, but highly recommended. Mrs. O'Neill hated Stephen and me, but loved my mother and would always say to her most sweetly:

'Oh, me poor darling,' while looking daggers at Stephen and me.

St Patrick's Day came and Mrs O'Neill was given the day off. That night in my bed, I was awakened at a very late hour by a light shining through the venetian blinds in my room. I peeked through the blinds and saw Mrs O'Neill swaying dangerously on the steps of our garden. I rushed out to her aid. She shone her flashlight right into my face and as I gave her a big grin, the light from the torch illuminated the braces on my teeth.

'Oh me God, it's the devil for sure,' she exclaimed and promptly fainted. Mother and Stephen dined out on this story for many weeks and I enjoyed enormously the notoriety of being the subject of such a droll tale.

Mother was particular about me behaving in a well-bred manner, so everything I did had to be *comme il faut*. I learned quickly what was *de rigueur,* though much to her despair, I would make the occasional *faux pas* at social gatherings.

'Mia brought you up wild,' Mother would often exclaim as she tried to instill some *noblesse oblige* into me. I defended my past Faeroese behaviour by explaining that I had only bitten a few school children and then only in self-defence.

'Bodje moje,' (My God) she exclaimed. Mother was a walking dictionary of foreign terms and phrases. Even though her English was fluent, she would lapse into another language momentarily, and then come back to English. Stephen, who liked to have the last word, but rarely got it, would join in with one of his many Latin phrases such as *gustibus non est disputandum*.

Mother was also a firm believer in the separation of 'Upstairs' and 'Downstairs', something that was unheard of among the egalitarian Lutherans in the Faeroes and most people in Australia. Though she treated Downstairs very well – 'Remember, Antonia, maids and trades people should know their place,' Mother would say firmly - our maids, who were mainly from Middle Europe and hardly spoke a word of English, were all trained to say: 'Yes Madam,' in their best British accent. This was required at dinner parties when Mother would use an antique sterling silver bell to summon the maid to come to the dining room to serve the next course or take dishes away. How very complex life was in Australia, I thought.

I had just turned seventeen when the Consulate General for Italy was invited to our house for a formal dinner, bringing with him his guest, an Italian prince of the Borghese family. Mother was anxious that I should meet him. I mused that maybe she thought if he kissed me I would turn beautiful. Being painfully shy still, I stayed in my room until Mother called for me. I advanced towards the prince with great caution and then stopped too far away for any kind of proper greeting. Mother could see this and gave me a nudge in my back to encourage me to move closer. This caused me to fall flat on my face; my forehead landing on top of the prince's highly polished shoes.

That same year, 1962, I received my Australian citizenship and was no longer officially stateless. Still, I did not feel like an Australian and I had no particular attachment for my new country. My sense of not belonging to anyone or any country continued. This has since become a positive sentiment, as I feel at home in most countries and never get homesick.

## Chapter Twenty-Nine

WHEN I FINISHED high school in 1963, I was sent, much to my relief to West Germany, where I first attended a girl's finishing school in Bavaria, which I disliked intensely. It was not my sort of place. Later, I went to live with my Aunt Pepa and Uncle Milutin in a gritty industrial town in the Ruhr, where I studied commerce - again not my sort of thing. Stephen, who had gone to university in Berlin, wanted me to become fluent in another language. I would have preferred French, but was voted down, even though my grandmother came from France. My study was to be in German - that was that. I would have dearly loved to attend art school in Sydney, but the thought of enduring a few more years of living under the same roof with Mother and Stephen was more than I could bear. Maybe my departure from Sydney was a relief for them as well.

As with everything connected with Mother and Stephen, there was a catch. Even though my educational needs in West Germany were taken care of, I was given no pocket money. While not a great tragedy, it meant that I could not pay for even a cup of tea. A part time job was out of the question.

'I'm not having a daughter of mine working,' was Mother's final word on the subject.

When Mother came to pick me up, we travelled back to Sydney via some wonderful cities, but on the trip she informed me that she had engaged the services of a private investigator to follow me around for a time and that he had taken photos of me in a nightclub in Munich. Mother suspected me of sleeping around and being on drugs. I was deeply hurt as neither was true. I was too petrified at the dire consequences of sleeping with anyone or taking drugs. Mother's lack of trust in me and her invasion of my privacy hurt me deeply and widened the rift between us.

While in Europe, I did not see Mia or Sigrid again, as I had neither the means nor the desire to visit them. Mia continued to work at the Telephone Exchange. She finally retired after 50 years of service, earning herself a medal from King Frederick IX. Mia died on 5 November 1967, just after I had returned to Sydney. She was 78. Sigrid continued her work in Genoa, though she moved to another hospital, the *Clinic Montallegi.* Her niece, Anna Maria had come to live in Genoa while Sigrid was still there. Sigrid returned to Tórshavn for her retirement, where she died in 1980, at the age of 89.

One might wonder whether I may have had regrets about not keeping in touch with my mothers. There was no family or emotional bond that tied me to them. In adulthood, I came to appreciate the tender care they bestowed on me, but even with the passage of time I could still not muster any feeling of affection towards them.

Having cut off contact with everyone in the Faeroes, it was not difficult for me to drop any references to it or entertain any thoughts of returning. Mother must have been pleased. I got on with my life. It was best not to dwell on the past. I had enough problems trying to cope with my domineering mother.

When I returned from Europe, nothing had changed. Even after I moved out, I had to toe the line and agree with everything. I got a job with an international airline, which suited my *wanderlust.* Still, Mother held me in an iron grip. When I was with her and

Stephen, I felt that I had no personality whatsoever. Mother's continued control over me was all encompassing. When someone asked me a question, Mother would quickly respond, before I had the chance to answer. On the other hand, when I didn't bother to reply, expecting my mother to do so, she would put me on the spot: 'Cat got your tongue? Answer the question,' and I would be ill prepared and mumble something incoherently.

Sometimes I felt as if my relationship with Mother was like a boxing match and I had been knocked out so many times that I had lost the ability or will to stand up again and leave the ring. But stand up I did, and, once I left home, happily got on with my own life, while my relationship with my mother deteriorated.

When I was 24, I married Roger. While he came from an early landed family, was well travelled internationally and sophisticated, his double Achilles heel was that he was Australian and had no money. Mother and Stephen had entirely different plans for my marriage partner; a crusty old aristocrat or doctor of Middle European background perhaps. A title too would have done nicely, and it went without saying that he would be moneyed. They resisted my choice right up to the ride to the church in the bridal limousine, when Stephen made his final plea. Four years later, our son, Andrew was born.

For the first year of our marriage, Mother would not speak to us. When we returned from our honeymoon, Mother's dressmaker informed me that she was holding the rest of my belongings, which my mother had placed in a cardboard box for me to collect. During this time, Mother communicated with us by means of her handyman, who delivered the odd gift or tiding.

From the moment we met at the introduction of a mutual friend, Roger reminded me of Peter Sellers and made me laugh. My husband was probably the only person who could match Mother's wit and, once Mother resumed speaking to us, they made a highly amusing pair.

The rapprochement happened on Mother's Day, 1971. I had phoned her up a week earlier to invite her and Stephen to our place for lunch. Predicting a negative response from her, I quickly said:

'I know you are not busy on Mother's Day, as you don't have any other children.'

They came, like a small royal visit, no doubt curious about our domestic circumstances as we lived in a suburb that was not on the dress-circle list. We had a pleasant meal and the ice was broken. But ever after it was like the Titanic having a near miss - there was always that killer iceberg lurking in the dark April seas.

After my year off from Mother, I was once again engaged unwillingly in hand-to-hand combat, but at least I had Roger to support me. He always said, 'If you can deal with your mother and Stephen you can deal with anyone.' Roger, with the rest of us, would fall in and out of favour, a situation beyond our control, as it seemed entirely dependent on Mother's capricious nature. Stephen usually toed the party line, but he was sometimes the quiet voice of reason. Interestingly, after that first year, only one of us was ever *persona non grata* at a time. My parents needed players in their game and it was no fun not to have anyone to talk to.

Despite being re-united for so many years in Australia, my relationship with my mother remained taut, and at times was so tightly stretched that only a sense of responsibility kept the relationship going, however tenuously. Sadly, Mother would remain convinced until the end of her life, that I held a deep grudge against her for having sent me to the Faeroe Islands. I told her that it was not in my nature to entertain ill will against anyone. Our philosophy of life was vastly different. And we had very little, if anything in common. However, there was no way that the time I had spent in the Faeroe Islands could be reversed.

Still, we enjoyed some good times together since I appreciated her wit and humour, her great intellect, her perceptive observations of human peculiarities and, not least, her eccentric behaviour, which landed us in some hilarious situations. I continued to admire her great looks, which she never lost. I loved how every social invitation entailed the preparations of an Opening Night: the showy jewellery, the Oscar de la Renta silk caftan, the great care taken with hair and makeup. When she made an entrance at a party, it was as if the star of the show had stepped onto the stage to great acclaim. Every performance ended in a standing ovation. I joined in the applause because she was indisputably a master of her game.

At parties, male admirers surrounded Mother, much to the despair of poor Stephen, an intensely jealous man. When I was with them, he cleverly took me by the hand and as we made our way towards Mother, he would call out: 'Oh, Mummy, Mummy, there you are!' 'Mummy' would glower, but continue circulating.

In the 1970s Stephen bought a condominium in Honolulu, where he and Mother installed themselves in great style overlooking Waikiki Beach. They spent nine months of the year there. I entertained the thought that Mother might become more lenient with me due to her relaxed lifestyle, but I was mistaken. Sometimes I would visit them; never certain if the trip would be pleasant or unpleasant. One took pot luck as to how it would turn out. On one enjoyable occasion, I went with them to a cocktail party given by a rear admiral and his wife - the sort of people Mother liked to mix with, when the kind hostess remarked:

'Antonia, you look lovely.'

Before I had an opportunity to thank her, Mother had stepped out in front, completely obscuring me. She threw her arms out wide - she was dressed in a voluminous silk creation by an American designer - and quickly retorted: 'Of course she does. She is my daughter after all,' with the emphasis on *my*. I treasured this incident and must have told it a thousand times around Sydney.

A friend once remarked: 'Antonia, the only suitable thing you have ever done right as far as your mother is concerned is to produce a grandson - not a granddaughter.' He was referring to Mother's well-known preference for men. The same friend once told Mother to her face that she had 'balls'. I held my breath, fearing an explosive response, but Mother took it as a compliment;

in her eyes, unlike most women, she had guts and was not afraid of making big decisions. She was always in control and feared no one.

True to character, at first Mother showed no interest in her grandson.

'All children are brats,' said Mother, pulling a face of disgust. 'Children should be neither seen nor heard.'

Babysitting was out of the question. When Andrew, our son, was about four years old, Roger and I divorced, and even though Mother was not the babysitting type, I would dearly have loved her occasional help. But once Andrew reached puberty and became 'more interesting' as she put it, she enjoyed his company enormously and showered him with love and affection. She also showered him with her foul temper, which she displayed only too often, and which would last for days. We were all subjected to this and never knew when it was coming.

Mother had a healthy respect for money. She was rather good at making it. When Stephen died of cancer in Honolulu, Mother took over the management of his properties and share portfolio. She loved it. She also loved the power that money gave her and used it to the fullest extent.

'I'm off to a board meeting,' she would announce imperiously.

I exasperated Mother by my lack of enthusiasm for money making and all the trappings that came with it. Not that I didn't appreciate drinking Château Mouton Rothschild out of Waterford crystal glasses, or using Jeorg Jensen sterling silver cutlery, personally monogrammed with Mother's initials, to cut my chateaubriand.

'You're always sharing and giving away clothes and jewellery - things that I have given you and paid taxes on,' said Mother, glaring at me cigarette in one hand, a glass of Moët et Chandon - 'Darlings, is there any other kind?' - in the other.

In my mother's eyes, I had no respect for money or belongings. I liked nice things, but I did not share my mother's attachment to possessions. I thought capitalism to be an unjust system. This immediately earned me the titles of socialist and 'Commie', even though I was neither. To Mother, I was no better than the hated communists of her former country.

'I am a *Woman of Property*,' my mother would announce proudly. The feminine version of Soames Forsyth. But I was never to be Fleur.

'Without me, you would be destitute.'

I was happily living with my son in a nice rented flat, which I paid for out of my salary, as I was not really impoverished, when Mother insisted that we move into one of her properties, a lovely apartment. This I did reluctantly, knowing Mother's ledger of payback would be extracted in blood and tears. I lived to regret the move, being constantly reminded that Andrew and I resided there *by her grace and favour*, like discarded courtiers at Hampton Court, a fact Roger - we had remained friends - jokingly picked up on by calling Andrew and me *Grace* and *Favour*. There were perpetual threats of disinheritance and dislodgment. Yet, despite the manipulation and all her conditions, I realised she loved me in an odd sort of way, a sentiment which had not been in much evidence when it was most needed.

Shopping expeditions with Mother, on the other hand, were most entertaining, complete with typical theatrics. They would start off by my mother casting her beady eye over my attire from head to foot and announcing:

'There is no way I'm going to be seen with you dressed like that!' Looking horrified, she would continue: 'You look like Orphan Annie. What will people think of *me*?'

Mother squiring me around some fashionable shops, where I was smartly outfitted at her expense, quickly remedied this situation. Soon my friends all wanted to go shopping with Mother. Andrew in later years was afforded similar treatment and sported a small but top-notch wardrobe for a young man, all carefully chosen by Mother.

When she turned seventy, Mother decided to move back to Sydney permanently. For a decade she had spent most of the year five thousand miles away in Hawaii. I had grave misgivings about this turn of events, as, selfishly, I was thinking of the difficulties that would lie ahead for Andrew and me for years to come. Roger was working overseas and luckily was spared most of this new life with Mother close at hand. Even though Mother's eccentricities kept us in stitches, the Slavic black moods would often take over and my son and I had to bear the brunt of them. It was truly sad, as her highly irritable disposition caused us much unhappiness, herself included.

Despite Mother's positive attributes, the vicious outbursts that she directed at me managed to kill any real affection that I might have had for her. Her malice was not simply mischievous; it was a life-long game and was more often cruel and menacing than playful. I loved her because she was my mother, and admired some aspects of her character, but underneath it all, my relationship with her remained that of a frightened little girl from the Faeroes. We grew further apart.

Mother perfected the art of playing games, but eventually I realised it takes two people to play. So when my mother would start a Parent-Child Game, I took care not to become the little child that Mother could push around. A favourite pastime of hers was trying to play my son and I off against each other and she would have succeeded, had it not been for the fact that Andrew and I communicated well with each other. My son and I had a close and loving relationship, which seemed to irritate my mother to no end:

'Really, Antonia, it's terrible the way you adore your son,' said by Mother in the same tone of voice as if she were saying, 'it's terrible the way you mistreat your son.' I believe in the end, Mother was sorry that we did not have a close relationship. She wanted my blanket adoration, as she had received from her friends and admirers throughout her life. I felt sorry for her that I could not comply. God, how she would have hated to know that, as she would have regarded it as pity.

'I've always been a very nervous person,' Mother once declared proudly, in the same manner as one would say, 'I've always been a very talented person.' I suspected that beneath that remark was perhaps a telling clue of unresolved issues.

Over the years, Mother developed a Shit List, a mental list, aptly named by Roger, Andrew and I. It contained friends and family who were out of favour with Mother, a frequent occurrence. This also required the creation of a Good List, where Mother's secretary of her company, her accountant and lawyer, held permanent membership, similar to the United Nations. Roger, Andrew and I were mostly on the Shit List, but occasionally rotated to the Good List, where we had the equivalent status of the republic of Yemen. Annoying incidents occurred when Mother would run into people who, unbeknown to themselves, were on the Shit List and Mother would have to be polite to them, as they were being charming and complimentary to her. Even though we joked about it, being on the Shit List was not fun. On the contrary, it made life a misery for us. Mother defended the Shit List, by stating that it saved her going to a psychiatrist.

One day, Mother showed me her extensive collection of fabulous jewellery and asked if there was a particular piece or pieces that I liked. Frankly, there was not. I just couldn't justify owning or wearing an ornament that cost as much as, or more than, a luxury car. Mother was bitterly disappointed. She could not comprehend my lack of interest. Jewels suited my mother, she wore them proudly. To add further insult to my disregard for possessions, my mother's fears of my 'socialist leanings', even if said in half jest, seemed to come true, when I got a job in a peace centre at a university.

'I suppose you will be happy,' Mother said, taking a large swig of her Stolichnaya, then carefully adding, 'now that you'll be working among Reconstructed Marxists.'

This caused great amusement among my colleagues, or should I write comrades.

## Chapter Thirty

*O*VER THE YEARS, I had recounted to my son and close friends stories of my Faeroese childhood. They seemed to find them entertaining; perhaps like my mother I was a good storyteller, without the embellishment, which was her wont. The truth was entertaining enough. Often people suggested that I write a book about my story on these islands that few had ever heard of. Only in the last couple of years did I consider writing down the memories of that large part of my early life.

Roger was very encouraging, knowing my childhood past only too well. There is a great deal of difference between the act of telling a story and the writing of it, which requires discipline, introspection and research, and so the decision was made to travel to the Faeroes. I also hoped to fill in the blanks of my life in Italy with my parents, as given our fragmented relationship, I could never ask my mother. To her, the past was water under the bridge, but it was a different matter for me. Although, I wasn't at all sure what I would find when I got to Tórshavn, I had no fear of addressing my childhood and set out on my inward journey with a great deal of expectation. I also wanted to view my childhood and the Faeroese people with adult eyes. My childhood memories, I knew, were based on good and bad, and all or nothing perceptions.

Before departing Sydney, I discussed with Andrew and Roger whether or not to tell my ailing mother that I was making the trip back to the Faeroe Islands. We came to the same conclusion; it would be best not to mention anything to her. Painful experiences over the years concerning such matters had inured us all to broaching this chapter of the past to my mother in any great detail, if at all, and this time was no exception. Originally, Andrew was going to accompany me, but we felt that one of us had to be here for Mother. I told her that I was going to visit friends in Denmark, which was technically correct, since the Faeroe Islands are part of the Kingdom of Denmark and I was stopping in Copenhagen for a couple of nights. Mother was used to my frequent overseas trips, so I was confident that this journey would not arouse her suspicions.

It had been two years since I had initially made the decision to revisit the Faeroe Islands before I found myself outside the airport terminal on the island of Vágar. I had been disappointed to see a parking lot, as I had expected to find sheep grazing, not parked cars. Yet, as soon as the bus left the airport, nearly everything seemed as I remembered it. Colourful isolated villages and hamlets, clung to small coastal lowlands, closely surrounded by emerald green mountains. We passed through multihued fields; their small plots at various stages of harvesting. And boulders lay everywhere - home to the *huldufólk*. Looking out from the bus window, I felt as if I were viewing a film of a previous life, so long ago had it been since I had lived here.

Surprisingly, it took only two hours to travel from the airport to the capital. First by bus, then the car-ferry crossing between Vágar and Stemroy islands, and again by bus. In my childhood such a journey would have taken three times as long. When making the crossing, I could really feel the pull of the strong current between the islands.

It was late afternoon when the airport bus finally reached the terminus at the little harbour. The passengers, all locals, got off and quickly dispersed. Suddenly, I was the only one left standing there with my small bag by my side. I had a momentary sense of panic until the comforting smell of salt air calmed me. It felt strange to be arriving here alone and have no one to meet me but, due to my ambivalent feelings about this visit, I had not arranged that. The weather was overcast as usual, but not windy for a change. The fishing boats were neatly moored on the still, pewter-coloured water. There was no movement in the port. Not a single sound came from anywhere, creating an eerie atmosphere of emptiness and abandonment. It was a chilly but pleasant summer's day for this part of the world. I looked anxiously around me, at the blue building opposite, at the red-brown buildings on the peninsula. I heard the sound of kittiwakes in the distance, but could not see them. Turning around, I searched for familiar landmarks among the dreary post-war buildings, interspersed with much older wooden ones separated by narrow lanes. They must have been there in my time, yet I recognised nothing at all. When I had planned this trip, I had realised that my memory of this place was fragmented, having long buried its images, but now at the harbour, once so familiar, I drew a blank. I used to walk around this area every day some forty years ago. I had known every house and crooked lane, every stone. A surge of consternation swept over me. I had arrived back without my memory. I had lost my way home.

The driver was walking away from the empty bus and it occurred to me that I had better ask him for directions to my hotel. I spoke to him in English having long forgotten my Faeroese tongue. God, it felt weird not being able to speak the language any more. The hotel was only a short walking distance away he assured me. I started to walk away from the harbour, my eyes scanning left, then right for something, anything, to bring back a spark of memory. I longed for a glimmer of recognition, but did not get it. Then I noticed a lane next to the blue building and I stopped. Wasn't that the short cut to my house? I could not be sure. Every deserted street remained unfamiliar. This was getting depressing. Before long, I spotted a sign for Hotel Tórshavn on top of a building. I had chosen the hotel only for its name; I knew it had not existed in my time, of this I at least was certain. I turned left by a building of basalt stone, which I sensed I should know, but didn't. Proceeding down a small hill, I came to what I presumed to be a hotel entrance. The sombre building of a few storeys seemed to date from my time. A man was standing outside the main door. I asked if this was the Hotel Tórshavn, there being no signage anywhere at this level.

'Nei' was the not so welcoming answer. Undaunted, I went in and proceeded through another door leading further into the building and came to a small reception area. 'Is this the Hotel Tórshavn?'

'Ja, ja,' was the sweet answer from the girl at the reception desk.

'We have been expecting you. We know all about you.'

What a relief that was, even though I failed to see how the receptionist could know all about me. Had my fax requesting a room revealed that much? I was tempted to ask her for directions to my house, but decided against it.

How strange it was to be checking into a hotel instead of my home, I thought, climbing the stairs to my floor. As I turned the key in the door to my room, I hoped that I was also unlocking a door to my past. As is my habit, I went straight to the window to examine the view, which showed another part of the harbour, but there was still no recognition. Dejected, I started to unpack. Before leaving Australia, I had scrutinised a map of Tórshavn, but it had only shown the main roads, so I had been unable to locate the small street where I had lived.

Then it came to me, just like that. Suddenly the way to my home was clearly mapped in my mind. Dropping my things on the bed, I ran like a child out of the hotel, past the startled receptionist. I continued running up the hill, past the Havnar Church on my left, past the straight row of houses on the right until I reached the flat iron building, where I turned left and sprinted further up the next hill. And there - in my excited state, I was panting a little more from excitement than the run - there on my right was Bakkahella 4, the black house of my childhood. It was completely unchanged. I took a deep breath and immediately the familiar smell of painted tar on wood invaded my nostrils. The front half of the house looked freshly tarred, giving it a dense shiny blackness, in marked contrast to the stark white window frames. The Other Side of the house had not seen a paintbrush for some time and had faded into shades of grey, giving it the appearance of two separate houses glued together.

I couldn't believe that my house appeared exactly as my memory of it, yet the lanes leading off Bakkahella seemed shorter and narrower. The neighbouring houses were closer together than I had remembered, as if during my absence a giant had squeezed everything together with its massive hands. My house looked deserted; after all everyone who had lived there was now dead, except for me.

I peered through the windows of the living room that led off the kitchen, nervous that the ghost of Mia or Sigrid would jump out at me. On a wicker table lay a novel, *Memoirs of a Geisha,* in English. It was open in the middle as though someone had been reading it. Next to it was a strange looking chair, with a peculiar footrest higher than the seat that had not been there in my time. Is this where the ghosts of my past now rested while they brushed up on their English? The solitary tree opposite the house was gone, possibly grown weary of fighting against the endless strong winds. Its branches had once reached up to my bedroom window on the first floor where I would watch the leaves change with the seasons. In autumn they never stood a chance to dry and wrinkle up, for no sooner had they fallen to the ground than the rains came and turned them slimy and slippery, right here where I now stood.

Turning to my right, I was pleased to see that the rhubarb patch was still here, bringing back memories of years spent eating rhubarb stew, rhubarb compŏte, rhubarb preserve, all served with fresh cream. But now there was only a solitary plant or two struggling for dominance among the weeds.

Moving down the lane at the side of the house that I knew led to the garden, I thought of climbing the fence in order to take a closer look, as there seemed to be no one around. Sadly there was no fence to climb and no garden to look at, just weeds. The greenhouse where I used to hide was also gone and so was the wash shed at the bottom of the garden. How could I have expected everything to remain the same after four decades? I searched among the tall weeds for the currant bushes that had borne such delicious red berries, the few fruits that reached full maturity in the short growing season on the islands. The bushes were also locked in a useless struggle against the weeds. I reached out for one or two berries, which were still hanging forlornly on scraggy branches. What beautiful jam they had made. But wait; there was something terribly wrong here. Where was the unpainted cement house next door? Surely not gone as well? However, it had indeed disappeared and in its place was an uneven grassy strip. Some children were playing there, the first sign of life. I lifted my hand in greeting, but they ignored me and quickly scurried into one of the neighbouring houses. The turf on the roofs of the adjacent houses looked dry and withered. It used to be so green. What had happened? I had always been proud that our house had a corrugated iron roof, even though it was noisy when it rained.

Before long, I had made the full circle of the house and was back at the front door that led straight off the street. It looked freshly painted in the usual brown colour. An arrangement of large stones was still in place on either side of the door, in a half-hearted attempt at landscape designing. What would I say if the door was suddenly opened?

'Oh, you don't know me, but I used to live here as a child a long time ago,' sounded feeble. I had no idea if the house still belonged to the Sivertsen family. I felt many pairs of eyes watching me from behind the curtains of the houses opposite, but the streets remained empty of people. Suddenly I felt very cold and alone. In my excitement, I had not noticed that the temperature had dropped considerably as evening was approaching, or that I had hardly spoken a word to anyone since my arrival. However, I was happy to realise that I was not suffering from total memory loss after all, and I silently prayed that I would be able to see the inside of the black house, the vault of my secrets from childhood.

I stood still and observed the silent house. I was elated at finally taking the first step back into my childhood, but it still felt unreal.

## Chapter Thirty-One

As SOON AS I woke up the next day I looked out of my hotel window to reaffirm that I was back in Tórshavn and it was not just a dream. The fog was so dense this morning that I could not see anything. Still, I felt ready to go about my task of discovery in earnest, and I was determined to throw off the mantle of amnesia that had covered me so completely on my first day. My excitement at being back was dampened though, for once I had stepped outside into the cold summer's day, a melancholy mood had crept upon me and I realised that the enveloping fog had triggered an emotional state from long ago - a feeling of perplexity as to where I belonged. Ethnically and physically Slavic, I remembered how I had felt very much out of place amongst the fair-haired and fair-skinned Faeroese. My early years in Italy had provided me with a Mediterranean temperament and while I had been too young to reflect on this, at least there I had fitted in.

I was especially nervous about contacting Sjúrður - even though he was expecting my call - having effectively cut off all contact with the Sivertsen family when I left the Faeroes. I was certain it was just as amazing to Sjúrður as it was to me that I was back in Tórshavn. I decided to delay phoning him until after I had taken another walk up to the black house.

Pulling my jacket tightly around me, I set out for the place that until a couple of years ago, I had never intended to see again. On my left was the Havnar Church, where I had attended Sunday services. It was still painted white with gilded yellow trimming. An enchanting little garden of lovely shrubs surrounded the church in which stood a few trees - possibly sustained by divine protection. The straight row of houses on the right above the pier now housed a travel agency and the Atlantic Airways office. Instead of heading straight for Bakkahella, I turned left and meandered through my old neighbourhood. I had the curious sensation of both familiarity and discovery; I knew it, but didn't know it. There was a complete absence of people. I never once caught sight of anyone coming or going from any of the houses, but I always had the feeling that someone was silently watching me from behind the freshly washed curtains.

I passed old houses erected on top of tall cellars with foundations constructed of local rough stone, painted white. I was delighted that this area had remained unchanged, as it kept my childhood memories intact, but was a little disappointed to see that cars had replaced the chickens and ducks. Every household seemed to have a new car parked outside their old house, there still being an absence of garages in our domain, although I noticed that a few households still kept chickens. As I was about to enter Bakkahella from a narrow passageway, a front door swung open and a woman stepped out with her dog. We both pulled back with a start - perhaps shocked at seeing someone in that quiet quarter - then smiled apologetically at each other and went our separate ways.

A few steps later, I came to the black house, which today looked grey due to the thick fog. I could barely make out the peculiar flat iron building and wondered if my childhood friend, Edny, was still living there. I stopped in front of the familiar brown-painted door through which Sigrid and I had entered when I first arrived here as a three year old, then turned and headed back to the harbour, East Bay side, confidently making my way through the murky alleyways and down the steps, where I came out next to the blue building that I had not recognised the previous day. It

209

housed The Faeroe Islands Tourist Board, and now I remembered that it had been a bank in my time and painted light grey.

A couple of cars were driving away from the harbour and one solitary figure with a duffle bag was standing still, lighting a cigarette. I noticed that the harbour had been built up and the quay extended. A small modern ferry had docked at the quay, but in its place I saw in my mind's eye the old steamer that Sigrid and I had arrived on. It surprised me just how easy it was to conjure up that long journey as a small child back in 1949 and the very place where I had first stepped onto Faeroese soil.

I decided to make that much postponed but all-important call to Sjúrður from the tourist office, being a little apprehensive about what language we would communicate in. I had forgotten my Faeroese and though I could still understand Danish, I was uncertain how we would manage. Sjúrður beat me to it. While I was in the office he called - up to now, the Tourist Board had acted as our go-between - and thankfully, Birita, one of the friendly staff there took the call.

'He wants to talk to you,' she said.

Nervously, I picked up the receiver, but Sjúrður's voice was welcoming. We spoke haltingly, his English was limited and we had no other languages in common. He would introduce me to his wife, Eyðhild, their children and eleven grandchildren. One of them - he told me the name, but I promptly forgot it - had a birthday and there would be a celebration that evening, to which I was invited. I had a feeling that there were to be some revelations in store for me about the first years of my life, things I would never have found out about had I not returned to Tórshavn

It was strange in a way meeting Sjúrður again after forty-odd years. We had both changed in appearance rather drastically. From that thin little boy, Sjúrður was now tall and well built and his straight blonde hair had lost its colour. I was also thin with big melancholy brown eyes and curly brown hair, which has retained its colour only thanks to my hairdresser. He now sported a moustache, though I'm pleased to say I didn't! He hadn't even started shaving whcn I left. Even as a child, Sjúrður had a responsible, kind look about him. I had just known he would turn out to be a good and reliable person.

'Your eyes remind me of your father's,' I said on meeting him. 'The aquamarine blue of the Faeroese seas on a clear summer's day.'

The minute the words were out of my mouth, I realised that I had made a forward and un-Faeroese comment. But in his typically self-effacing way, Sjúrður assured me that his brother had their father's eyes. He introduced me to his wife Eyðhild. They told me that Rachel and her family still lived in Denmark and that the younger sister, Anna Maria, was living in Genoa.

We arrived at the house of his son and daughter-in-law, Jógvan and Guðrið, (pronounced goo-rear) and took off our shoes in the hallway. I had forgotten about this custom and wondered how it originated, but no one seemed to know.

We sat around the dining table, which had an impressive display of high-cholesterol desserts and cakes, beautifully garnished with full cream. Before long I was shown photos of members of the Sivertsen family whom I would have known from my childhood. The most wonderful photo was of the four Sivertsen children, dressed in their Sunday best. It had appeared in the local newspaper about fifty years ago, shortly after my arrival in Tórshavn, I was told. No one knew the exact year or story line, if indeed there was one. But wait; as I looked again at the photo, there were five children, not four. In the middle, as if part of the family, sat a brown-eyed, dark-haired *bambina* wearing a lovely Italian dress, no doubt bought by my mother, who was always fashionably dressed.

It was then that Ann Mari, one of Sjúrður's daughters-in-law, dropped a bombshell, 'You know, of course, that you never lived with your parents in Genoa. You lived with Sigrid in her room at the hospital. It was not permitted, but she got away with it.'

I made a conscious effort not to let my mouth drop open.

'It was only when you got older, and naturally wanted to wander around by yourself, that it became a problem,' she revealed to my amazement.

211

I was somewhat taken aback, but hid it well. I couldn't wait to get back to my hotel to phone up my son, Andrew, in Sydney and tell him about this revelation, since I would never have heard of it from my mother.

'It's amazing,' I told him, 'to think that for my entire life, I believed that I lived with my parents in Genoa. Instead I now find out that I lived at the hospital with Sigrid.'

My son was equally flabbergasted, but we both agreed that it should come as no surprise, knowing Mother as we did.

I said to Andrew: 'Now it makes sense why my baby photos always showed me in the company of uniformed nurses. I used to look at the photos and wonder why they were always taken in a hospital, when to the best of my knowledge, I was not suffering from any sickness.'

My memories of the dogs Bim and Boom must have been from when Sigrid and I visited my parents in their house. I have a faint memory of a tiled terrace and a large garden – not my parent's house I now realised, but the *Ospidale Evangelico Internazionale* that was actually my home in Genoa. The photos showing my mother and me on this same terrace were probably taken on her visits to my home in the hospital.

Mia would have known about this arrangement, but kept it to herself in order to protect me. Had she told me, my fairytale image of my perfect mother would certainly have been shattered. Mia's position was somewhat precarious; she would not have wished to poison me against my mother and also would have been concerned as to the effect it might have on my psyche. It would have been too great a risk to take. Mia was not to know that my mother would keep this significant fact to herself, as she did many others. I think Mia would have presumed that Mother would tell me the truth when I was older and better equipped to handle it.

My early years obviously required a lot of re-arranging and I prepared myself for further revisions. I suspected that more discoveries about my childhood past were in store for me. I didn't press the Sivertsens for further details that evening. What I had learned was astonishing enough for one day.

212

## Chapter Thirty-Two

*T*RY AS I MIGHT, I could not at first recall what Guðrun, Tulla's niece had looked liked when I lived here. Guðrun's father, Sofus, was Tulla's half-brother and Guðrun's mother, Rosa and Sigrid, had been best friends, so we had met on several occasions despite the difference in age. I was also struggling to remember how my childhood friend Laura looked, and this would be the case with everyone from my past.

Guðrun and I met in the foyer of the Hotel Hafnia. Guðrun is still very good looking and a smart dresser and she defies her age whatever it is. She recognised me immediately. 'My memory for places is better than for people,' I admitted over coffee at her house. The only explanation I could come up with was that living under the roof of Bakkahella with Mia had been the sole focus of my existence. Guðrun still remembered my first arrival in Tórshavn quite vividly: 'We all thought that you looked like a porcelain doll and you wore the most beautiful clothes we'd ever seen.' Most people in the Faeroes were rather poor at the time so I must have stood out. Just as well I was too young to realise it.

Guðrun has an excellent memory and she became one of my most constant sources of knowledge about the family and local lore. She remembered the rumours that went flying around Tórshavn when I first arrived about my parents being refugees and in hiding from the Italian authorities.

213

'Yes, they were war refugees and stateless after the war, but the Italians would hardly have had the time or the inclination to chase after millions of refugees that filled Europe after the war,' I assured her. I told Guðrun that my parents appeared to live in favourable circumstances, openly travelling to France and other parts of Italy, renting villas on the Italian Riviera. Recently, I had found my father's business card, giving an address in Torino, not Genoa, and a photograph of my parents - again in Torino - in happier times. Not surprisingly, Mother never mentioned that my father, or both of them, had lived in that city, but I was starting to realise that anything about their past - and even mine was possible.

Then Guðrun surprised me by handing me my old autograph book, which her sister, Helena, had found. In it were inscriptions from my *skolekammerate*, schoolmates, dating back to 1956 and '57. However, this was not merely a book containing signatures. Each friend had taken up two pages, one of which had a drawing, or a picture and on the other page was an ode, or a fond message. Without fail, every one was noted with the anagram 'lev vel', live well. Later when I met my school friend, Jórun Arge, she showed me what I had written, in her book, a rhyme in Danish, which translated reads:

> *Know my name I don't*
> *As I was plunged into the font*
> *The priest got the hiccups*
> *My name I didn't pick up.*

Guðrun showed me her English translation of her father's logbook from his lone journey across the ocean in an open rowing boat. She told me that when her father was in Bergen, being interviewed by a journalist about his epic voyage, he was asked what his thoughts were when the waves were breaking over the boat continuing to fill it with water. The journalist expected an answer such as, 'I thought of my wife and children.' But no, all Sofus thought about was that he must carry on bailing as fast as he could. Guðrun felt this was a good answer, as her father never

214

believed for a moment that the boat would sink and he with it. Hearing this story again brought me giddily back to my Faeroese past - a past inhabited by strong and silent seafarers and supportive families bound into a community challenged by the vicissitudes of unpredictable seas and events. I reflected that some of this had rubbed off on me and was now part of my character.

As we were leaving to go to Laura's house, I spotted Tailor Debes' famous knitting book, *Bindingarmynstur*, which Guðrun's mother had fashioned half a century ago into a hardcover, ensuring its survival to this day. It stood as new among the books in Guðrun's library ready to guide any modern knitter.

I asked Guðrun about Lisa and Ulla undir Kletti and the origin of their surname. 'Why would anyone change their name to Beneath Rocky Ground?' I questioned her.

'Because,' Guðrun offered reasonably, 'their house is situated beneath a huge boulder and their name now steadfastly associates them with that place.' As a child, I would never have given a second thought to a surname such as Beneath Rocky Ground; I had taken it for granted that names were associated with local lore and topography.

Guðrun had the answer for taking off ones shoes in the hallway, before entering a room. She thought this custom probably dated back to the time of the *glasstova,* the glass room. In those days, everyone wore sheepskin shoes, the same as the ones Júst used to wear. Soap was not commonly in use and sand was used to clean the wooden floor. In order to protect the floor and to save the precious sand, shoes were taken off.

As we walked to Laura's house, I was grateful she had sent me a recent photo of herself, so I didn't have to go through the agony of trying to remember how she looked. Like Guðrun, Laura's remembrance of finer details would also be of invaluable help. We had not seen each other since we were eleven years old, yet I felt confident that we would bridge that gap in a short time. We had corresponded at length before my arrival and had restored as much as possible the remembrances of those years as school friends, terminated by my abrupt departure. Laura had sent me

215

photographs taken of our class, on which she had painstakingly written the name of every child, but sadly, short of submitting myself to hypnotherapy, only the names of one or two *skolekammerat* raised a glimmer of recognition. I knew that I was going to meet two other friends from the Nuns' School. I still felt like a victim of amnesia and felt uncomfortable that this would be apparent to them

As a child, Laura had been spirited and lively and now meeting her again, it came as no surprise to find she had developed into a bubbly personality. Laura had been instrumental in starting up a professional theatre company, housed in the old dairy, and also acted in many plays, though now she is mainly involved in theatrical direction and promotion in between helping her husband on their farm on Sandoy, Sand Island.

When I confided to Laura that I had thrown the spade at Edny, she offered that I must have displayed the 'southern element' of my nature, though this side of me had never been evident to her. Faeroese will speak of 'northern temperaments', meaning a reserved non-confrontational nature, while 'southern temperaments' indicate an excitable 'un-Faeroese' manner of behaviour. Forced 'mingling' of a small portion of inhabitants with pirates from Algeria or Spain had caused some of them to have what could be perceived as an excitable nature, the same Mediterranean disposition it would seem as mine. Edny now lived in Denmark so I could not offer long overdue apologies.

Laura reminded me: 'When we played together it was always pre-arranged between Mia and my mother and, Mia always came to fetch you at a set hour. I can't remember that you ever took part in the usual games with the children of our neighbourhood.'

Laura considered Mia's over-protectiveness of me to be understandable; I was 'on loan', she said, and indeed, I remember feeling as if I were borrowed and overdue for return. I did not want an extension. I wished that someone, anyone, would pay the overdue fine, and return me. But where to? I remembered always being uncertain about this part.

The next day, Sjúrður was taking me to see the inside of Bakkahella 4, my home for nine years. I still felt strangely shy toward Sjúrður and the other members of the Sivertsen family, though there was no reason for this, as they were unfailingly hospitable and all went out of their way to make me feel welcome.

Sjúrður recommended that I contact his sister Rachel who lived in Denmark and ask her to help me out with details of my early years in Tórshavn. He assured me that Rachel, with her excellent memory, would remember much more than he could. He was absolutely right. Rachel said that she had some old photographs and other information that she would mail to me. Who could these photos be of and what was this 'other information'? While I had already found out something new about my past, I knew there was more and could hardly wait to receive her letter.

Mia in the living room on Our Side, next to the Italian lamp with a painted scene of Venice. Tórshavn, 1960s.

The black house on Bakkahella today, unchanged except for the
house next door that has been pulled down. Tórshavn, 2000.

## Chapter Thirty-Three

*T*HE MUCH-ANTICIPATED day arrived when I would revisit the black house that had been so central to my early life. I was excited, but did not show it, deciding instead to adopt the Faeroese demeanour of calm composure as Sjúrður and his daughter-in-law, Ann Mari, arrived to accompany me. Sjúrður had not yet been able to organise access to Our Side. Instead we were going to see the Other Side, my vast indoor playground where my dolls and I had spent many entertaining hours. I told Sjúrður that I had always believed the Other Side had been intended for Mia and her fiancé. He was highly amused, as the Other Side had been built for Visa, not Mia, who had never been engaged, but somehow Visa never got around to making the move.

The Other Side had a separate entrance opposite the rhubarb patch. Members of the younger generation of the Sivertsen family were temporarily living in the Other Side and I was grateful that they allowed me access. We were welcomed into the small hallway, where the ghost of Mia's betrothed used to hover. At least he had in my imagination.

We were first shown the kitchen and eating area; my disappointment was immense. It looked cramped and no longer held for me the strong feeling of newness and spaciousness. As we entered the living room, my distress was immediate. It was nothing like I had remembered. The entranceway connecting the living room on Our Side had been sealed off as surely as the imaginary games of my childhood. The forest flower wallpaper was replaced by flat white paint. None of the original furniture remained and the room itself seemed so much smaller than I had remembered. I remained silent for fear of offending the occupants. I was disappointed that it had been modernised. This had resulted for me in the loss of its character, so important to my mental image of that intimate place. The magic of my private childhood retreat was no longer there.

I hoped that Our Side would not be so drastically changed. That was somehow important to me. While the Other Side had been my refuge, my escape from Mia's continuously watchful eyes, I knew that I was more emotionally attached to the old family quarters that had formed Our Side. I prayed that when the time came to see it again, I would not be overwhelmed by the disappointment that had swept over me today.

Sjúrður then informed me that he had been told I cried hysterically when it was time for me to leave Tórshavn, so much so that it was decided Mother would have to leave without me. I don't remember this at all. He thought this was when Mother first came to visit me when I was nine. However, Mother's old passport and Stephen's correspondence to her, strongly point to there being no intention to collect me at that time. If it happened at all, why was this crying incident so deeply submerged in my psyche, that to this day I cannot recall it? While I can easily recollect many other notable incidents - even unpleasant ones - this potentially important memory still eludes me.

Back at my hotel, I noticed that a fisherman had returned to port and was displaying his catch on a metal tray on the quay at *Undir Bryggjubakka* - Under the Pier Cliffs. I recognised it as being herring, having retained a good knowledge of fish species from childhood. Locals were clustered around the catch, buying fish by the bag-full. I could not believe what I saw. Here in the pure unpolluted Faeroe Islands, plastic bags were being used. I was disappointed that this nasty modern practice had reached these pristine islands.

In my time, buying one fish meant simply putting one's finger through the gill and carrying it home; for several fish, the fisherman would draw a piece of string through the gills. Modern packaging seemed to have replaced the former natural ways, adding to the accumulation of waste and this left me with a bitter taste of the price of progress.

The material promised by Rachel soon arrived in a large thick envelope. I was tingling with anticipation and opened it at once. In it were more fragments of my past. First came photographs of me in Genoa and these were particularly revealing. They were taken outside of what I now knew to be my home in the Ospedale Evangelico Internazionale. I am posing with Sigrid, who is in her nurses' uniform, along with other nurses on a wide *terrazzo* with lovely terracotta tiles in a cream-colour I ventured to imagine. In the background were traditional Mediterranean wooden louvre shutters. I took out a photo of my mother and me. It was dated January 1948, Genoa, when I was two years and two months old. My mother, looking glamorous as always, was wearing a fur coat and gorgeous suede shoes, low cut in the front with double ankle straps. We are standing on that same terrace and it looks like she is going somewhere. Now, newly aware of the fact of our separate Genovese domiciles, I could acknowledge for the first time that I would not have been going with her and that she was only visiting me. Fortunately, I took these facts in my stride, having long since grown used to the direction Mother charted for herself.

In the envelope were also photocopies of Sigrid's old Danish passport. These were even more revealing and I was confronted with yet another puzzle. In Sigrid's passport, I could see a photograph of myself affixed next to hers and my name had been added as if I were her child. Knud Linder, Secretary of the Royal Danish Consulate in Genoa, had signed this endorsement. The date was 16 September 1947, which surprised me greatly, as it was one and a half years earlier than my supposed departure in 1949 from Genoa for Tórshavn. Why was this? Surely, the plan to send me to the Faeroe Islands had not been formulated more than a year in advance. I felt that there must be some other explanation, but I would have to wait patiently until Rachel could enlighten me further.

## Chapter Thirty-Four

*T*OURISM IS NOW the second largest industry after fishing for the Faeroes. This came as a surprise since, in my time, life on the Faeroe Islands seemed to be taken up by hardships brought on by wrestling the mighty waves and ceaseless wind on barren islands that could only grow rhubarb and potatoes, and barley in small patches, as well as sustain some hardy sheep. Following old Viking customs was the only way to survive. I would have agreed with Leon Hansen, who wrote in an article in the National Geographic magazine in 1930, that the islanders 'have little time for the tourist and his money'.

Need brings change, however, and happily the Faeroese people have more than survived. They now have a thriving tourist industry, except of course in winter, when nothing thrives. Even though the economy could boom or bust – and had done so, being dependent on the fluctuation of fish supplies and market prices – these enterprising people have embraced modern technology and combined it with old Norse ways to turn it to their advantage. The English businessman who sat next to me on the flight to the Faeroes had been invited to Tórshavn for talks on a deal still in its infancy. 'Typically Faeroese,' he said. 'The minute one makes a business proposal, the enterprising Faeroese want to hear more straight away.' He was right; the Faeroese always keep a sharp ear out for new ventures.

Now, with my adult eyes, the gloom being dispelled long ago, I could appreciate that the stark beauty of this remote archipelago would not just be an attraction to the weary tourist on his way to Iceland, but a tourist destination in its own right. I was told that the majority of visitors who now came for longer stays were from the Nordic countries, principally Denmark. This was a far cry from my time, when ocean liners called at Tórshavn for just a day on their way to other places.

On my way to the Tourist Board to enquire about the possibility of a sailing trip - Mia was no longer around to fret about its dangers - I retraced the route that we used to take decades ago. Now, I almost skipped along the narrow familiar lanes, peering at the little houses on the way, all so remarkably unchanged and becoming familiar again. I stopped outside Lisa Beneath Rocky Ground's house and checked on that particular boulder which seemed to be firmly in place - unlike the rocking boulders in Oyndarfjørður. Just beyond the shore of the quiet village on Oyndarfjørður is the mysterious setting of the two *Rikuskusteinar* - Rocking Stones. No one knows how they got into the sea, but they have been lying there for centuries, rocking to and fro with the movement of the tides. They are never still. It is said that these are the obdurate remnants of two pirate ships that threatened the village and were promptly turned into stone by the obliging local witch.

Birita from the Tourist Board recommended that I go on a jazz cruise to the island of Hestur. It was one of the best tours available, she assured me. Back in the 1950s, this would have been about as ridiculous as recommending an inter-galactic cruise. Unfortunately, the Faeroese weather was misbehaving - actually, behaving as usual - which meant that one minute the cruise was off and the next minute it was on again. There was a steady light drizzle, quite normal for any time of the year, but angry clouds were closing in. Consultations were held with the skipper over a three-hour period. Finally, at about one o'clock in the afternoon it was decided that bad weather should not be a hindrance - after all, in the Faeroes, one could wait for weeks for good weather. In summer a number of music festivals were held, I was told, and this cruise promised to be special as it featured visiting jazz players from Denmark. With my newly found memory, especially in relation to the wet weather, I decided to buy a pair of galoshes to wear on the boat. The shop near my hotel, belonging to Guðrið's family, sold black ones in every size, but I settled for a turquoise pair at only half the price. Perfect, considering that I intended to leave them behind anyway. Never mind that they were one size too large, as a pair of wonderfully thick Faeroese socks fixed that.

It was raining steadily as we sailed beyond the harbour in a lovingly cared for blue schooner named *Norðlýsi,* Northern Lights. Many of these lovely wooden boats were used for fishing in my time and I was pleased to still see a few of them in the harbour, even though they were currently only used for catching tourists.

It continued to rain; it actually started to pour down as we left the harbour. No, rain in the Faeroes does not pour down, it comes at you horizontally – no vertical showers here! As I was becoming drenched and we were still a long way from the cave where we would be serenaded by the jazz quartet, I asked if there were any wet suits available. 'Wet suits below deck. Help yourself,' I was gruffly told. The suits were wedged between the musicians who were down below drinking and generally having a good time, something heightened further by my attempts to extract the suit without interaction with them. The wet suit, which was not intended to be a fashion statement, was so thickly padded with eiderdown that I could have survived a long Arctic winter in it. Unfortunately, it was already wet on the inside when I put it on and it also leaked rather badly. In no time, there was enough water trapped inside my suit to fill a bathtub. However, due to the thickness of the padding, the water heated up from the warmth of my body and I didn't feel the cold at all.

Finally, after just over two hours, we arrived at the island of Hestur, Horse, and dropped anchor at the mouth of a cave.

*There was a legend associated with this Horse Island concerning Magnus, a young Viking from the neighbouring island of Koltur,Colt, who had fallen in love with a maiden on the island of Hestur. Magnus would swim a very long distance on the ebb tide every night to visit his beloved in secret - since her father opposed the match - returning some hours later on the flood tide. However, one night as he staggered ashore on Hestur, Daddy was waiting for him with nothing less than an axe. 'An honest visitor would come in daylight', said he, 'but you come like a thief after dark. Swim back or face my axe', he challenged. Magnus chose to turn back. He dived into the sea, never to surface again. This legend adds credence to the belief that, to this day, the current between the islands of Koltur and Hestur is the fiercest and the waves stronger than anywhere else in the archipelago.*

We were transferred - there were about ten of us tourists - with some difficulty from the *Norðlýsi* to motorised rubber dinghies, which were to take us inside the grotto where the jazz performance was being held. For some unexplained reason, I was asked to transfer from one dinghy to the next. However, after one look at the choppy waters, I decided not to cooperate - I stayed put in the one I was in, and it did not seem to matter as no one else was asked to move. Once inside the grotto, it was perfectly calm. We had entered the mouth of the Sea Voice, but not a sound emanated from its throat, as if cowed by our presence. The setting was dramatic. The wet walls glistened as if lit by cleverly hidden spotlights. The acoustics promised to be as good as at La Scala. The talented musicians were remarkably nimble climbers and had positioned themselves strategically on the narrow slippery ledges around the cave walls. We sat in our dinghies on the still, ink-black water mesmerised by the setting and the sound of the music, while at the same time we could hear the roaring of the Atlantic at the mouth of the cave. The tide rose rapidly, while the musicians continued to play yet another classical jazz piece. The experience would have been even more enjoyable had it not been for the tepid bath water trapped between my body and the dreadful wet suit. I found myself in an Alice in Faeroeland Adventure.

On the return trip, the Atlantic decided to show its full fury. We sailed past impressive sheer basalt cliffs on which nested thousands of birds, giving the appearance of overcrowded tenements. Wrapping myself around a mast in order to take some photos, which I knew from experience would not turn out well on my normal 35m camera, I braved the rough seas in order to take a valiant shot.

The number of sea birds inhabiting the many sheer vertical cliffs of the Faeroe Islands can reach three and a half million at certain times of the year, especially on the western and northern coasts. Some birds are residents but most are visitors, spending their lives out at sea and coming ashore to seek out the best real estate for breeding - overhanging rock-balconies all with magnificent uninterrupted views of the ocean. During the breeding season over two hundred different species jostle for space, a Nirvana for ornithologists and something promoted by the tourist board as a *must see* bird-watching experience.

Following the ways of their Viking ancestors, fowlers can still be seen swaying precariously from the end of a rope in order to reach the underside of the slippery rock ledges, more than three hundred metres above the sea. It is a hazardous occupation, requiring great skill and courage as well as knowledge of the behaviour of the different species. Besides wearing a safety rope, the use of earplugs would also seem to be a necessary fowling accoutrement, as the noise of millions of birds screeching at once is quite deafening. There is hardly room for the fowler's feet on the narrow shelves of the cliff as he nets the birds in flight. The birds are netted with a peculiar looking instrument called a *fleyg*, a large triangular net at the end of a long pole. The *fleyg* seems to have been around for a long time and probably dates back to the Viking times. There is quite a knack to catching birds this way and only one bird can be caught at a time, but an experienced fowler can catch hundreds of birds in one day. When caught, the bird's neck is twisted and hung around the fowler's belt.

The evening before, Laura had reminded me that her grandfather, who came from Mykines, held the record for a time by catching the most puffins in one day - precisely 999. However, puffins with fish in their beaks – usually sea eels, which are their favourite food – are never killed, for this indicates that they are feeding their young.

The bird colonies leave behind a terrible mess on the cliffs. Yet, this is taken care of by the mighty waves of winter that clean them up in readiness for the next summer's invasion, perpetuating the endless cycle of renewal that I came to understand during my nine years living so close to nature. Eating cute looking birds and whales was part of our normal diet.

Our boat did not need cleaning, but the unrelenting waves were doing just that. I decided to let go of the mast for a few minutes and went below for a cup of tea. The jazz players were by now having a very good time. I clutched onto the table, as it was impossible to stand without being thrown from one end of the cabin to the other and I certainly did not want to risk landing on one of the musicians' lap – an uninviting prospect given their overly cheerful state. As I reached for the boiling kettle, I felt my stomach rise up to my throat. I hurried back on deck and embraced the waves with great joy as they crashed over me. My stomach settled immediately - once again, a true child of the Faeroes. I thought of my mother and her trusted *Russian Remedy for Everything*: a shot of icy vodka. But, absent that remedy and foregoing the tea, fresh air was my only restorative.

That evening, I spent some time drying off in my hotel room. This was an habitual Faeroese chore and I remembered as a child being caught in a sudden downpour without a raincoat. I didn't run for cover, I just kept going like the rest of the Faeroese inhabitants and got rather wet. Strong winds meant putting my head down as I struggled to make headway, or putting my brakes on if there was a tail wind. Arriving home from school drenched, Visa quickly dried me off, knowing that Mia would have fainted if she had seen me like that.

These memories made me both curious and eager to see the inside of Our Side. Would I be disappointed as I had been with the Other Side? Would Our Side have changed beyond recognition? And, more intriguingly, would my childhood recollections need reconstruction as a result of seeing it once more?

## Chapter Thirty-Five

*T*HE LONG AWAITED day finally arrived when I would re-enter Our Side. So many poignant memories were associated with this side of the black house. Sjúrður and I made the short trip from my hotel to Bakkahella 4 and arrived outside the brown front door. By force of habit, I wanted to reach up and fetch the key, which was kept on the ledge above the door, but instead I let Sjúrður knock. I took a deep breath, remembering Sigrid holding my hand as I crossed that same threshold for the first time so many years before.

The door opened and I half expected Mia to be standing there. Instead a young woman with short blonde hair and the Sivertsens' blue eyes greeted us. Was this how Mia had looked in her youth. But, no, it was her great-niece, Elin, Rachel's daughter, who was staying in the house. Rachel's four children were born and raised in Denmark and Elin, who is a doctor, enjoyed coming to Tórshavn for her summer vacation, much of which she spent working in one of the hospitals. I could see a definite resemblance to her lovely mother and I thought, or maybe I imagined, that there was a slight family resemblance to Mia as well.

Inside, the first thing I noticed was the tall chest of drawers still standing in the far left-hand corner of the entrance hall with the same little table lamp on top. And then I cast my eyes over the walls. Oh no, they were not brown, as I had so distinctly remembered. Rather, they were a Dijon mustard colour, the kind of colour that looks awful on a cement wall, but works fine on wood. The skirting boards and ceiling were trimmed in green.

'Oh, you painted over the brown,' I said. 'No, not at all. This is the original colour from when you lived here,' Elin replied, seemingly surprised that my recollection was so far off the mark.

We entered the kitchen to the right off the hallway. It was also not anywhere near as dark as I had remembered and again there was the absence of brown. What tricks one's memory can play. It occurred to me then that the colour brown may have reflected my regular gloom at the prospect of being stuck on these islands forever. I never felt I belonged here, I sensed it most acutely and not just on the odd occasion when I was being teased, 'Go back where you came from', to which I would respond unhappily, 'But I don't know where I come from'.

Now, not being on an extended visit, I quickly reconciled myself to the real colour scheme that was actually warm and inviting in an old-fashioned way. The kitchen was little changed. The same wooden table and two chairs stood next to the window, which was dressed with a starched white curtain with lace trimming. A slightly more modern one had replaced the old black coal-burning stove. I had a flash of Mia reluctantly placing her hands over the stove to check the 'temperature' before cooking an infrequent awful meal. The three of us, Elin, Sjúrður and I now sat down for coffee at the same wooden table where the three of us – Mia, Visa and I – had eaten all our meals. The only modern addition was a small refrigerator, which seemed out of place in this almost unchanged kitchen.

'I wonder if the tiffin carrier is still here,' I said to Elin. It had become an important test of my memories from childhood, since I had been so badly mistaken about the colour scheme of the house. Elin offered to look for it, but I stopped her. I went straight into the larder and quickly found it, after over 40 years; in the same place we had kept it. I checked the shelf where the dreaded bottle of cod liver oil was kept, but there was nothing there. When I mentioned this to Elin, she told me that Mia had done a good thing by giving

231

me cod liver oil, as it contains vitamin A and D and so would have rewarded me with a healthy heart.

I walked up the narrow stairs leading to the bedrooms. The bedroom I had once unwillingly shared with Mia was now painted white, the wallpaper long gone and the old beds replaced by new ones. The negative energy was thankfully gone and the room was cheerful and fresh looking, the very opposite of how it had appeared in my time.

The washbasin on Her Side was still there. As I looked at it now, I had a flashback of Mia putting some treatment into my hair when I came home from school one day with my woolly hair full of lice.

*I held my head over the basin, which Mia filled with a milky solution that she kept pouring over my hair.*

*'Keep your eyes closed. Don't look in the basin,' she warned, when she had finished. Of course I looked, only to find hundreds of dead lice floating in the liquid. I let out a scream.*

A modern poster now hung over what used to be Mia's bed, which brought on a little smile. It was hard to imagine Mia and modernity. Thinking back, I recalled how keenly I had felt Mia's oppressive presence in our bedroom, causing me to mentally divide our room into 'Her Side' and 'My Side'. I came up with this domestic nomenclature for my private usage, hence also the use of Our Side, Other Side. Although I did refer to the downstairs rooms as such on occasion when speaking to Mia and Visa, I never divulged to Mia my names for the division of the bedroom we shared. As an adult, I realised that Mia had been very fond of me and it must have been upsetting not to have her affection reciprocated. I appreciated too late the tender loving care that Mia and Sigrid had bestowed on me.

Looking out the window on My Side, I had forgotten what a lovely view it has of the harbour. Most houses in Tórshavn have a harbour view and it does not cost any extra. Wherever one looks, one is always in close proximity to the sea and the mountains, which is one reason why the Faeroese believe themselves to be part of nature, just as nature is very much a part of them.

I looked down on the sad rhubarb plot, now a weed patch, and the play area, now a place for the neighbour's car. But I was not as disappointed as I had been when I revisited the Other Side of the house a few days earlier. Our Side still had the feel of my childhood and thus better preserved its memories. As I left our bedroom, I recalled the great sense of release I experienced when I walked out of it for the last time so many years ago.

Making our way downstairs again, we entered the little sitting room off the kitchen, the same room that I had caught a glimpse of from the outside on my first day back. Memories flooded back, of many short damp winter days and long warm evenings spent here with Mia, during what seemed like an endless dark season. The few hours of daylight were often made even shorter by the wild storms that raged non-stop for days. Sometimes the midnight sky would be lit up by the spectacular Aurora Borealis - Northern Lights. I imagined Mia in the V-necked dress, sitting in her usual chair lighting up her evening cigar, penknife at the ready, blowing out spectacular smoke rings.

Walking with Sjúrður and Elin through the black house, I was certain that I had entered a time warp, so unchanged were the surroundings. There was no rush of emotion, even though Bakkahella had been the centre of my being. After all, this was the place from which I had wanted to flee, even though under its corrugated iron roof I had only known care and kindness. I was comforted that the kitchen and sitting room had changed so little and I hoped that this would be the case with the other rooms as well. As Elin opened the door leading into the dining room, I suddenly felt compelled to turn around and take a final look at the sitting room where Mia and I had spent so much time. I easily conjured up a vision of smoke rings rising to the ceiling. The dining room, which we hardly ever used - Mia did not entertain much - was considerably changed. It was painted white and fitted with a couch, which seemed out of place in a dining room, but the original sideboard was still there. I resisted the temptation to check if it still held bottles of Cherry Herring or Akvavit.

The living room was just as dark as my memory of it, the brown-toned wallpaper from my time having only just made it through to the new millennium. It was coming loose in several places where there had been recent water damage. Gone was the table lamp with the unusual oblong shade on which was painted a scene of Venice that Sigrid had brought back from Italy. Sigrid had always brought interesting gifts for us. I looked sadly at the place where the entrance had been that led to the living room on the Other Side. The former archway had been closed off and was now wallpapered over. I was sorry that I could no longer take the two steps down to the Other Side. Laura had told me the previous day that she remembered well those couple of steps leading down to the 'posh living room', as she described it. Every room on Our Side was exactly the same size as I had remembered. No perceived shrinkage had taken place, thus preserving the original dimensions held in my memory.

I felt elated after my latest visit to Bakkahella 4 in a 'mission accomplished' sort of way. Yet it had been strange walking through it. Once it had been 'my' house. I had felt comfortable in it. I had had the run of the whole home and knew every nook and cranny. And now it was as if I had intruded on a stranger's house. I hadn't asked Sjúrður or Elin enough questions, especially about Mia and Sigrid. I believed that I had no right to seek answers after having shown no interest in their wellbeing during these many intervening years.

When we left, Sjúrður had another treat in store for me: the family farm, the place that brought back the sweetest memories of carefree summers and long bright days.

We drove along *Yviri við Strond* and the sea glistened, just like it used to. When we reached the farm, I noticed that it was much rockier than I had remembered. Mistakenly, I had kept a vision of smooth, velvety pastures and had forgotten that it was studded with boulders. The little house and sheds were unchanged. The two British bunkers were still standing and I was glad that some vestiges of the old days remained.

Sjúrður 's older brother, Júst, now lives permanently on the farm; lucky man, I thought. Júst's brilliant technical mind had flourished in that placid location. Now in his mid-sixties, his deep-set intelligent eyes look as lively as ever and his memory is also just as keen. He is one of those people who, instead of buying a television, would build it himself. Or better still, would buy a television, dismantle it and rebuild it into a rocket. Nowadays, Júst potters around with his ham radio and television. He does not care that the little farmhouse is as primitive as it was in my time, and still has no modern conveniences. As a concession to modern times, he has installed a satellite disk. As a young man Júst had been a Visiting Fellow at the Mechanical Engineering Department at Sheffield University. When I met him this time, he unnecessarily apologised for his English, in absolutely perfect English. I wanted to ask him if I could take a walk around the farm, but I was overcome by my old childish shyness. I looked over to where Visa's garden had been, her pride and joy. It was fenced off and as children we dared not enter it. 'After Visa died, someone left the gate open and the sheep came and ate up everything,' said Júst.

Looking back on my nine childhood years in the Faeroe Islands, I would not on the whole have termed them a happy time of my life, though there were particular happy occasions, such as visiting the farm. It was difficult sharing a house with a substitute mother that I didn't love, even though I felt secure with her. Had I remained with Sigrid in Genoa, I'm sure that I would have continued to love her, as I had for my first years in Italy. I remembered longing to be with my real mother, and my rejection of a substitute elderly spinster twice my mother's age, no matter how kind, overshadowed my time in the Faeroes. I don't know how Mia felt about the situation. I can only venture to think that she must have found herself in a challenging role, entrusted with the absolute care of another person's child whom she had to bring up as if she were her own daughter, yet mindful that this child belonged to someone else. In a way, we were both doomed to an unfulfilled relationship that could satisfy neither of us.

## Chapter Thirty-Six

AFTER DECADES OF hardly giving the Faeroe Islands a passing thought, I found myself devouring every history book and other reference works about the islands. Many sources were used to gain details about the lives of first Norse settlers and one of these were the sagas. The Old Norse word *saga* cognates with the verb segja 'to say' and originally meant, 'what is said', but had come to be used for narratives 'to tell'. Historian Magnus Magnusson calls the sagas 'historical novels'. The plot is often complex, the heroic adventures of the chieftains and their families intriguing, if not exaggerated. Affairs of life and death are told in a matter of fact manner. Genealogical data abounds, a sort of 'Who's Who' of the Nordic world.

My own saga, though not as swashbuckling, was continuing to unfold. One unsuspecting evening over coffee, I found out from the Sivertsens that the reason I ended up in Tórshavn was because my parents planned to foster me out to a family in Genoa before leaving for Australia. They did not want to take me with them. Apparently, Sigrid could not bear the thought of her little Antoinetta, who had lived with her since birth, being sent to a strange home with strange people. Hence her suggestion to my mother that I could be taken care of by her sister, Mia, in Tórshavn. Mother agreed to this alternative arrangement. No one

236

had ever told me about this fostering out plan, so this piece of weighty information was completely unexpected.

Even though I had accepted a long time ago that I was an unwanted child, I was still momentarily stunned by the extent of Mother's plans for me. For whatever reason, in 1949 I was clearly superfluous. No wonder Mother had in all these years resisted in filling in the blanks of our linked past. Before embarking on this adult journey I had prepared myself to be ready to uncover some of Mother's secretive past and known instinctively that what I may discover might not be all that palatable. Had I learned that Mother had wanted to foster me out when I first went to live with her, I know that my reaction would have been one of rejection and deep hurt. It may even have further eroded our already fragile relationship. Mother would have known this. There is also the possibility that something else was going on in her life at the time that I don't know about, besides my father's infidelities and the doubtfulness of a good future in Australia. The news certainly warranted another phone call to my son in Sydney to share with him yet another astounding discovery. We agreed, as we always do concerning my mother, that nothing could surprise us and concluded it was best that this latest revelation had come to me at this stage of my life, when I could handle it in a philosophical manner.

I decided to end the day by losing myself in one of the sagas. I had read the *Saga of the Faroe Islanders*, and my next favourite - yes, after years of disinterest in the Faeroes, I had even developed favourites - was the *Saga of the Gatebeards*, the richest and noblest family of the Faeroe Islands. The Gatebeards lived on the island of Eysturoy and were descendents of a great matriarch named Aud the Deep Minded. Aud was audacious and strong willed, sharing similar attributes with my mother, I thought.

Aud the Deep Minded was the daughter of a mighty Viking with the unfortunate nickname of Ketil Flatnose. She was married to the King of Dublin, one of three wives. After she became widowed and her son, Sigurd was slain in one of the usual Viking skirmishes, she found herself left without any protectors. Aud knew that her enemies would soon come for her, but rather than succumb to them, she dug deep into her mind and formulated a brilliant plan; she would have a getaway ship built secretly in a forest by the sea.

On a dark and moonless night she had the ship loaded with all her valuables, which included her grandchildren, and set sail, slipping easily past her enemies. The first port of call was the Orkneys, where she married off one of her granddaughters to an earl who ruled over the isles.

The next stop was the Faeroe Islands, where Aud arranged for another granddaughter to be married to the rich Gatebeards. That settled, Aud decided to sail on to Iceland, where two of her brothers were living. However, during a furious storm, her ship struck a reef and sank. She made it to the shore with her remaining grandchildren, companions and servants and all her precious cargo - Mother would also have seen to it that all her possessions were saved. Undeterred by this calamity, Aud found her way to the house of Helgi, one of her brothers, but he told her that he couldn't possibly accommodate her large entourage. After calling him by a few choice names - Mother would have done the same - she moved on to her other brother, Bjorn, who put her up for a while, no doubt to avoid her wrath.  But the call of the west was too strong and soon Aud set sail for Iceland. There, she acquired a great deal of real estate - my mother had also acquired a lot of property - by appropriating every free river valley she come across, dividing it generously among her family and companions.

Then, Aud married off her last granddaughter and also chose a wife for her grandson Olaf. She made arrangements for an immense wedding feast and guests came from far and wide. Forever the organiser, Aud the Deep Minded saw to it that all were provided for - just like Mother - then took to her bed. The next morning Olaf found her dead, not in a horizontal position, but sitting bolt upright. This fearless behaviour is typical of the stuff of these historical pioneers and promised to make my research thoroughly enjoyable.

## Chapter Thirty-Seven

SJÚROUR CAME TO the Hotel Tórshavn to take me for a drive to see the countryside; we planned to visit the historic hamlet of Saksun and some of the Viking sites that were of particular interest to me. This day would take me beyond my childhood boundaries, to places where Mia and I had never ventured, yet somehow everywhere I would find connections to my past. Taking a drive into the countryside normally means going inland away from the sea, but the Faeroe Islands are so narrow and mountainous that most roads run along the coastline. The average width of the islands is only about five kilometres, so one is never far from the sea.

At breakfast, I had watched from my favourite window as the Lutherans walked to the Havnar Church, feeling no pangs of guilt that I would not be joining them. It felt peculiar to be sleeping in a hotel instead of at Bakkahella 4, where I had spent every single night of my childhood without exception. And now, it came to me that the Hotel Tórshavn had been a *Sjómansheim*, Seamen's Home in my time. It was still called that by the locals, 'Oh, you're staying at the *Sjómansheim*.' I remembered that I would hurry past its entrance on one of my alternate routes back from school, fearful that a foreign seaman might emerge from its mysterious interior with not so mysterious intentions.

Sjúrður arrived accompanied by his daughter-in-law, Guðrið. He always brought an English-speaking family member with him on our outings, since he felt that his English was limited and knew my Faeroese was non-existent. Each day, I remembered more words, but not enough for any kind of conversation.

Not surprisingly, Tórshavn was covered by *mjørki*, the fine rain fog of summer.

Before long, the fog thinned and the sun came out, but typically, just for ten minutes. On the outskirts of Tórshavn, we drove into a heavy rainstorm that made the roads slippery and visibility poor. Despite Sjúrður's skillful driving, I looked ahead and not to the side, where there was a sheer drop into eternity.

The modern two-lane road system came as a surprise. When I lived here, extension of the road network had only just begun, and I never would have expected anything like this. Many tunnels had even been dug through the mountains, much to the displeasure of the Danes who had to foot the bill for what they considered unnecessary tunnelling.

In my time, the Smyril inter-island ferry service was our highway. Instead of traffic jams, we had to contend with delays due to bad weather, or treacherous docking in rough seas that would require several attempts to land. Travellers could be stuck on an island for a week or longer, and this was still the case today. We were not in the habit of going very far out of town by car either for our outings, as, in those days, we would have run out of road very quickly.

Road transportation was privately run in my time and Júst Senior provided this service with his classic Ford. Óli Arge operated the one and only bus service. Óli had two buses, painted a distinctive red, which ran from Vaglið, near the bookstore, to the hospital, to the TB sanatorium and on to Kirkjubøur.

Of course I was pleased to see the road improvements, but I selfishly would have much preferred everything to have remained as it was when I lived here. However, once away from the highway, the old footpaths connecting the villages were still there, though the cairns were not maintained and the habit of putting a rock on top of them no longer practiced. The solitary mountains, the lonely valleys and the rough sea had remained unchanged. This at least, was the same Faeroes of my childhood, a memory that I did not wish disturbed.

The natural pattern of work on the land had not changed either. Sowing is still done in March and April. The wool is sheared in June, although the old Norse habit of pulling off loose wool is no longer practiced. Fowling still takes place in the first part of summer and haymaking in August and September, depending on the weather. In October, the last outdoor work of the year is the slaughtering of sheep. Laura told me that she loves the hard and challenging work of the land and its long-standing customs: 'It is difficult to explain what it is that makes this work so exciting. It has something to do with the free life and having a strong connection to nature.'

Laura and her husband, Páll, want tourists to the islands to also experience the benefits of getting close to nature, and in summer visitors can walk to a hundred-year old wooden house that sits on their property. It was used formerly by the farm hands, who stayed overnight there when working in the outfields. It takes one and a half hours to get there by foot - the only way - from the nearest village. No modern facilities are to be found, only a lake, bird colony and magnificent views of the stone landscape. From this island, there is a ferry service to the smaller island of Skúvoy, where the Viking chieftain, Sigmund lies buried.

Sjúrður drove past steep grassy fields strewn with rocks on which sheep grazed precariously. One false step for sheep or man can mean certain death in this place, much like climbing Mount Everest. No one gets away with just a broken leg.

As we rounded a bend, the weather turned from rain to brilliant sunshine and the most majestic scenery, unspoiled since the creation of time, came in to view. Clean and colourful villages huddled on the few level areas along the shores. I kept exclaiming:

241

'Oh, my God. It's so beautiful.'

Ten minutes later, 'Oh, it's so beautiful.'

'Oh, it's so...'

I am certain that both Sjúrður and Guðrið must have thought to themselves, *She plans to write a book and that's all she can say!*

Words failed me, but not so the writer William Heinesen, who rightly described his island home as 'the navel of the world'. The landscape still looks as it must have millions of years ago, when the ravages of the Ice Age formed some twenty islands with mountains, deep valleys and narrow fjords of stark but incredible beauty out of the great North Atlantic volcanic region.

The resulting rock strata have given the mountains what is commonly described as a 'layer cake' look. The alternate layers of hard grey-green basalt shaped by submarine volcanic action and the softer reddish rock formed from volcanic ash cause this unusual appearance. They look like a multi-layered collapsed wedding cake turned green – no doubt something that would cause rather a nasty surprise on one's wedding day. Inland the terrain remains rugged and rocky with some low peaks down which pour narrow crystal clear streams, giving the appearance of a wedding veil torn into strips – the combination of the two images, not just the collapsed cake, but green at that and a shredded veil, would be enough to make any bride take flight!

No roads had existed in these areas in my time and Mia and I could certainly not have ventured this far by any other means. Our outings had been limited to *Havnardalur*, the Tórshavn Valley, through which ran a lovely river, just north of Tórshavn and another place called *Oyggjavegurin* (Island Road) up in the mountains. Tulla would pack a basket full of freshly baked cakes and a big thermos flask of coffee, while Mia would fret that some harm might befall me.

Now, as we drove through the valley at Mjøkadalur, Sjúrður pointed to a large building with a traditional turf roof, clinging to the side of a mountain. There were no other buildings around, nor any signs of it being a farm settlement.

242

'That is a military base built by NATO,' he told me. 'It was constructed during the Cold War years, when you were living here, as an Early Warning Station against possible missile launches by the Soviet Union.'

It is a sore point with the Faeroese that they were not consulted before Denmark, a member of NATO, agreed to the building of this base. The Faeroese parliament always maintains that the islands are neutral, but since affairs such as defence are not part of the Home Rule Act, the Danes need not consult them on such matters. Recently, archival records in the United States have revealed that the Faeroese Parliament might have been given misleading or erroneous information in earlier years and further research on the military significance of the strategically placed Faeroe Islands is planned.

We continued driving until we literally came to the end of the road. Here, between bright green hillsides, lies the sleepy, idyllic village of Saksun, unchanged by the advance of centuries. A 300-year-old stone and wood farmhouse stands here, which was still in use in my time. It has since been turned into an outdoor museum together with the adjoining barns. During the Black Death of 1349, the village was completely wiped out, except for a servant girl, who as sole survivor, so the tale goes, made her way to a nearby farm settlement and claimed ownership of the entire village. This was granted to her provided she married. She obliged and the village of Saksun was re-established.

Saksun was the location of the film *Barbara*, adapted from the novel by the Faeroese writer Jørgen Franz Jacobsen, which I had recently read as part of my new found interest in all things Faeroese. It tells a story of love and passion in eighteenth century Faeroe Islands and believe me, Saksun still looks like an eighteenth century village even to this day. The filmmakers would not have needed to build props. The novel is based on the part legendary, part historical character of beautiful Beinta Christina Broberg, who was born in Tórshavn in 1668. She married three pastors (not at the same time) and drove them all crazy. Her first husband, the minister Jonas Jonassen, was a widower and much older than her. She taunted him by placing soil from his first wife's grave under his pillow, which may have influenced his premature departure from this earth. The second husband, Niels Gregersen Aagard, was a minister on the island of Vágar. He was weak and gave into her wishes. They quarrelled a lot and it is said that she came at him with a candlestick holder. He also had an early meeting with his creator and there were suspicions that Beinta may have been responsible. Transcripts from the court hearing have survived attesting to this. A young priest, Peder Ditlefsen Arrheboe became the new minister in Vágar. He fell hopelessly in love with Beinta and they were soon married, but this *femme fatale* was more than he could handle. He suffered increasing periods of temporary insanity and was subsequently defrocked. This is about as wild as it gets among the Lutherans.

In the novel, Andreas Heyde, an old flame of Barbara's, the English translation of Beinta, returns to the Faeroe Islands and rekindles his interest in her. The capricious Faeroese weather also plays a part in the plot. Barbara's husband has to leave her to visit his flock on the westernmost island of Mykines, when bad weather sets in and he is stuck on the island longer than planned. Andreas takes advantage of Peder's absence and makes his move on Barbara. Things start to hot up. What happens next can be found out in the English translation of this novel. It makes for good reading.

As we were about to leave Saksun, a minibus arrived and out stepped a group of elderly people, propped up by walking sticks. Surely the Tourist Board in its enthusiasm was not catering for senior citizen tours in this difficult terrain?

'That's the Walking Club of Tórshavn. They walk in a different area each weekend,' Sjúrður offered. There was no such recreation in my time.

Our next stop was at the Viking burial sites of *Yviri í Trøð* at Tjørnuvík, the northern-most village on Streymoy. I particularly wanted to stop here, as I remember going to Tjørnuvík with Mia to view fragments of human bones that had been recently uncovered, but I don't recall how we got here. I remember there was a great to do about it at the time. Two small boys from the village had found the skeletal remains accidentally. Subsequently, twelve Viking graves had also been uncovered. I was very excited and a little apprehensive as it was going to be my first sighting of human bones. However, the bones were very clean as if they had been vigorously scrubbed. I had expected bits of red flesh, akin to whale meat, to still be clinging to them. They were displayed on a square patch of rich dark soil. The area was roped off and I marvelled at the dark-coloured soil, more than the bones. I wondered how the bones would stay there for any length of time, as they were so close to the open sea. I was too young to realise that they would soon be removed to the museum for safekeeping.

I remembered also there had been talk about caves between Tjørnuvík and Haldarsvík, the next village along the coast. The caves were thought to run through the mountains all the way to Saksun on the other side of the island, but no one had found them as yet. It is only a short distance as the crow flies from Tjørnuvík to the lonely Bay of Sjeyndir, but it required a trek over the mountains and a steep descent to the river that feeds into the bay, and we did not have time for such a hike. This was a shame as there is a legend about Sjeyndir, a place where old maids eventually end up. Such cruel fate! I wondered if Mia, Sigrid and Visa knew of their predestined circumstances. Had they ever performed the rite on 2 February, I wondered? That was the Pagan feast day of *Imbolc*, literally meaning 'in the belly', symbolising the womb of Mother Earth. The Christian name was Candlemas, or the Purification of the Blessed Virgin Mary, as the Catholic Church called it, never refraining from re-naming Pagan holidays. On the morning of Candlemas, unmarried girls from this part of the island would go down to the seashore and seek out a crow. In quick succession each maiden would throw three items at the unsuspecting crow: a stone, a jawbone from a cod and a piece of turf. If the crow flew out to sea, it meant she would marry a man from that direction. If it settled on a house, she would marry a man from that family, but if the crow stayed where it was, she would become an old maid.

245

The country abounds in legends. Tjørnuvík offers one of the best views of two famous sea stacks called Risin and Kellingin, the giant and his troll wife, also known as The Hag. The story goes that this lovely Icelandic couple liked the Faeroes so much that they wanted to tow them back to their homeland. The wife went to the top of the headland to place a rope around the northern end of the island, but it cracked; one can still see the split today. They quarrelled, as couples tend to do, as to the best way to tow the islands. By this time, day was breaking. Realising the consequences for trolls of being exposed to sunlight, the wife hurried down to the sea to her husband so that they could dive together into the depths of the fjord. Just as she got to him, the sun rose and they were both transformed to stone.

'And now we are going to cross the only bridge over the Atlantic Ocean,' said Sjúrður with a little chuckle. It sounded as though we were coming to the longest bridge in the world and I contemplated asking for a toilet stop, but the bridge only spans the narrow channel of Sundini between the two largest islands of Streymoy and Eysturoy. We crossed it in two minutes and I understood Sjúrður's subtle joke had relied entirely on his geographic definition. Sjúrður's claim could be challenged by the inhabitants on the island of Mykines, where there is an old footbridge – over the Atlantic – connecting that island to a nearby islet.

The sun burst out in full as we drove down a wide green valley towards the village of Gjógv (pronounced jag). From here we walked to the edge of the cliff, offering a dramatic view across the sea to the northern island of Kalsoy. The thick sea looked like mercury. The Sea Voice was mumbling under its heavy cover; several deep growls emanated from its wide watery mouth. The wind picked up and Kalsoy turned moody and blue. An eerie white light shone from behind its mountains. This was truly 'navel of the world' ambience and I marvelled at my good fortune to see it again.

Kalsoy had been the home of the legendary seal-wife, who lived in Mikladalur, the largest village on that island.

*Her story starts on the Twelfth Night, when once a year, mermen and mermaids would come ashore. They would take off their skins and, with their temporary human legs, dance away the hours – it is not recorded if they were sufficiently traditional to perform the Faeroese ring dance!*

*Watching from some distance was a young man from Mikladalur, who had seen the seals come ashore. He spotted a beautiful maiden among them and fell in love with her at first sight. He sought out her sealskin lying on the rock and took it. Suddenly the dance came to an end and all the sea folk put their sealskins back on and slid into the sea. The beautiful one could not find hers and so had to remain in human form. The young man took her home and married her. He locked the skin away in a big chest; the key to which he carried on him at all times. They lived happily together for some years and had several children.*

*One day, the husband went out fishing and realised that he had left the key behind. He rowed his boat home as fast as he could, but his heart sank when he saw a dark shape slipping into the water as he came ashore. When he got home his wife was gone, the chest was open, the seal skin missing. The children were safe as the seal-wife had thoughtfully put out the fire and hidden the knives.*

*Some time passed and the men of the village were preparing for a seal-hunt in a nearby cave. The estranged wife came to her husband in a dream and told him that her seal-husband (she had remarried) would be guarding the entrance of this cave and that her children, all of them seals, would be inside. She pleaded with him to spare her family. The husband did not heed her plea, as he was still angry with her for leaving him. That night the husband and his friends entered the cave. They had flares that were made out of linen dipped in melted tallow, but they concealed the lights until they reached the inner end of the cave. Then two of them jumped out of the boat with their clubs at the ready while another man held up the flares. The bull seal and smaller seals were all killed.*

*That evening, while the husband and his children were tucking into their seal burgers, the seal-wife called out to him that she had placed a curse that would result in many men being killed on the cliff, or lost at sea.*

Indeed, many men from the village subsequently met this fate while bird fowling or fishing, but now it seemed the curse had worn off. There was a family in Skálavik on the island of Sandoy, who were believed to be descended from the seal-woman. An indication of this was their very short toes. Sadly, the possibility of seeing bare feet in the Faeroes is rather limited, which leaves seekers of foot fables somewhat in the dark.

As we walked on the iridescent green pastures of Gjógv, I was surprised to come upon a deep and narrow cleft, more like a mini fjord. Oh, it was painfully obvious that I had forgotten the Faeroese language, otherwise I would have known what to expect, as *gjógv* means shore cleft or gorge in Faeroese. The sea was smooth inside the gorge and obviously provided good shelter for the local boats. However, nothing is easy here on the islands and the boats have to be winched up a steep track in order to be brought ashore. These cliffs are normally filled with birds at this time of the year, but on this day there was not a single bird in sight, as they were all out fishing for the day.

Sjúrður took us for lunch at a nearby restaurant, possibly the only restaurant on this side of the island. The place was packed, but the obliging owners made room for us at a window overlooking the bay. No sooner were we inside than the sun shone brilliantly in an almost cloud-free sky. One of the diners knew who I was, even in this place, so far from Tórshavn. I had forgotten the smallness of Faeroese society and how everyone knows everything about everybody. Yet this society is far from homogenous. Every island looks different and their inhabitants behave differently. Every village has its own dialect, although the differences are becoming less pronounced. But all Faeroese love to gossip. It all

248

started with milkmaids long ago. As they searched for wandering cows, they would catch up on the news from the next village when they met up with their friends in the outfields.

Some things never change: on the menu was thin soup with dumplings; boiled pork, boiled peeled potatoes and boiled carrots and for dessert a sort of sweet apple compŏte topped with sweet whipped cream, obviously the flavour of the month as it appeared in every eatery in Tórshavn. I said to Sjúrður,

'Oh, the food is just the same as it was forty-two years ago,' for which he thanked me sweetly. I really meant to say, 'What, I can't believe is that this food has not improved in 42 years', however, that would have been most unkind.

Back in town though, the food had improved considerably. This was evident at the Hotel Hafnia where Sjúrður and his wife Eyðhild took me for dinner the following night. It now offered a buffet service, and an à la carte menu of the best Nordic cuisine. The simultaneous translator on this occasion was daughter-in-law, Ann Mari. My choice of monkfish was truly delicious and the chef had shown great self-control in not drowning it with cream. Boiled peeled potatoes and carrots were miraculously nowhere in sight.

On my first evening in Tórshavn I had gone to a restaurant by myself, where I ordered a salmon steak, which came swimming in a mixture of cream and burned butter, the chef's attempt at *beurre brûlée*, I presumed. The salmon itself was delicious. I was looking forward to enjoying the beautiful taste of Faeroese water again, so I asked for a glass of water but was told that I would have to buy bottled water.

'Buy water, here in the Faeroes?'

The waitress explained that this summer there had been a drought – the last one was over a hundred years ago – with little or no rain for two months. So that was why the grass roofs were yellowed and dry.

Continuing on the Viking trail, Sjúrður, good-natured as always, drove on to the village of Leirvík. As with many of these sites that are no longer being worked by archaeologists, we were left with a neat arrangement of stones in varying formations, depending on the original use of the site, with grass growing in between. I knew from Símun Arge - Archeological Curator at the *Føroya Fornminnissavn* National Museum - that a complete Viking farm, providing a clear picture of the lives of the early Norse farmers, had once been here. Those hardy ancestors of the Faeroese lived in traditional Viking longhouses with extensive outward curved walls built in a typical Norse 'upside-down ship' style, the walls being made of dry stones covered with turf for protection against the strong winds. A sunken stone-lined open fireplace was in the centre. Furnishings were sparse, consisting of uncomfortable benches that also served as couches and beds. Judging by photographs that I have seen from the early twentieth century, this spartan life continued through the centuries with little improvement. Drains were constructed in all the buildings, as the settlement here was lower than the nearby stream. The poor Norsemen were not only pummelled by constant gale-force winds, but flooded as well. No wonder the modern Faeroese is resourceful and indefatigable.

The presence of animal bones on these Viking sites has suggested that pilot whales, seals and birds were part of the Norsemen's diet. Little has changed. Furthermore, bone material has brought to light their penchant for sucking marrow from sheep's feet. This quaint gustatory habit was still practiced into the twentieth century and was surely a forerunner to foot fetishism! The Vikings of Norway consumed large quantities of meat and no doubt the early settlers would have done so when available. Boiling and stewing meat was more common than roasting, a habit which unfortunately has carried through to today.

As we were leaving Leirvík, the sun disappeared once more, changing the light and mood of the place. We stopped to look across the sullen sea towards the rugged island of Borðoy, so close it seemed as if we could jump across to it. A mist drifted in, forming a thin line that came to rest exactly half way across the island, effectively cutting it in two. Another bank of mist was floating parallel to the surface of the sea. The clear sky had turned leaden grey. The air was thick with salt. A melancholy gloom set in and all conversation stopped. Not even the Sea Voice spoke to me. The noisy chirping of the oyster catcher suddenly broke the silence. We walked towards the car and continued along the wide fjord of Gøtuvík, home of *Trand* the famous Viking chieftain, who had opposed conversion to Christianity. Driving away from the coast, Sjúrður stopped the car at a particularly large boulder. The earth had been partly dug up from under it to make room for a dwelling and its tiny front entrance was flanked by a little stone wall. It looked deserted, but maybe not, as this was probably the home of a *huldufólk* family, who had made themselves invisible on our approach.

Guðrun had told me that when the plans for a new road necessitated the removal of large boulders, the road was moved to circumvent them, in order to avoid moving the houses of the grey people.

At the end of the day's outing, I had a new sense of the incredible beauty of the islands, one that I had not fully realised as a child. I appreciated the harshness of the land and the violence of the sea that had shaped not just the early Viking settlers, but also the modern Faeroese people as well. I took a walk alone along the rocky shore, rugged up in my winter jacket to keep out the chill of this summer's evening. As I approached the sea, I heard a familiar thumping noise followed by playfully malicious laughter. I was pleased that the Sea Voice was still talking to me.

## Chapter Thirty-Eight


$A$ SURPRISE WAS certainly in store for me when my school friend, Jórun invited me to her house for 7.00pm. I was sure it was for coffee, as Faeroese drink it all day and all night, but as my interest in coffee wanes by early afternoon, I asked if we could make it earlier and we settled for 5.00pm.

On entering the living room I noticed that it had not been set up for coffee. This was unusual, as a Faeroese hostess will always have the coffee service set out in advance on the table, as well as the traditional high cholesterol cake with cream. I noticed that the dining table was already set for dinner and I thought to myself how super efficient Jórun was to be ready so early for the family dinner. I sat down on the couch next to Jórun and her husband, Johan, but no coffee was served. After a while, I was invited to take a place at the dining table, where their son, Erling, joined us. Okay, I thought, we're having coffee here. Johan disappeared into the kitchen to fetch the coffee I presumed. After a long wait, I began to wonder if he had flown to Brazil for the coffee.

Earlier, I had met Jórun's brother, Jógvan at *Útvarp Føroyar*, Radio Faroe Islands. Jógvan was writing a series of books on the remarkable lives - I'd call it an endurance test - of the fishermen who in my time went to Greenland to fish and lived in *Føroyingahavn*. Here was a test of my memory and I failed it miserably as I drew a complete blank on my past association with him. It turned out that Jógvan had also gone to the Nuns' School.

Later, I spotted him in a photo given to me by Laura, where he was playing a shepherd in one of the inescapable Christmas Nativity plays. Jógvan was in a class below me, though we can be forgiven for not recognising each other after forty odd years.

Útvarp Føroya was founded in 1957, the same year that I left for Australia. Jórun's and Jógvan's father, Niels Juel, stopped driving the distinctive red buses for his family and joined Radio Faeroe Islands as a director.

Eventually Johan reappeared smiling, carrying a large serving tray, not a coffee pot. Quickly Jórun pulled out a camera, which she had concealed on her lap and pointed it in my direction. All eyes were fixed on me in anticipation of I knew not what. Was this the Faeroese version of The Mad Hatters' Tea Party? Sometimes I felt as bewildered as Alice did on her own adventures in Wonderland. The large serving tray, which had set everything in motion, was placed on the centre of the table. It was piled high with several sheep's heads, neatly cut in half along the nasal bone. I recognised the familiar dark brown skin and noticed their mouths half open in a half smile. A smile no doubt restrained by the disbelief of death and now divided further by the butcher. In the old days, the ears were left on the head so everyone could see by the nick marks that the sheep belonged to them and had not been appropriated in some disingenuous way from the neighbour. The practice of marking the ears is still performed as the sheep still graze on the common outfields. I was touched that Jórun had remembered that sheep's head had been my ultimate favourite food and it brought back fond memories of other local dishes. To appreciate this not so dainty delicacy, it is necessary to describe the unique preparation involved, although readers must be warned that it is not for the faint hearted.

First, ask your butcher for a sheep's head with the wool intact. Cut off the wool as much as you can with regular scissors and burn off the remaining wool over your gas burner. Every so often, stop and brush off the singed wool with a good strong brush. Be careful not to burn the head, just repeat this process until the head is smooth. Alternatively, do as the Vikings did: build a fire in the ground in your garden. Drive a stake into the sheep's head and hold it over the open fire, scraping the wool off with a knife. A unique way for families to bond.

Next, split the head in two along the nasal bone with an axe or a saw. Soak the split head overnight in cold water. The following day, rinse the head under running water and place in a saucepan, cover with water, add plenty of salt, and boil, covered, for one hour. Before it is ready, add potatoes and carrots to the water. Drain and serve. It is really delicious. However, Faeroese food is very much an acquired taste and not what could be described as epicurean.

On this occasion, instead of traditional boiled potatoes, Jórun served the sheep's heads with mashed potato in which the sheep's brains had, well, also been mashed. I enjoyed this meal enormously particularly the distinct different tastes of the various parts of the head - Johan told me there are seven, or maybe it was nine distinct flavours in the meat on the head - which brought back the taste sensations of the Faeroes that had lain dormant for more than forty years. It also stirred long-ago images of Tulla preparing sheep's head, as usual to perfection, and sensibly never attempted by Mia.

Another Faeroese treat was in store for me the next day, but not of the culinary kind.

## Chapter Thirty-Nine

*I* DECIDED TO catch a bus to the village of Kvívík, where I thought I had once gone with Mia. I checked with the Tourist Board about which bus to catch and was certain that I had got it right; however, after a short while, the bus driver stopped the bus on the main road and wordlessly indicated for me to get off. I was too stunned to do anything else. A few minutes later, I was directed by the bus driver to get on another bus. I made it to Kvívík. However, when I stepped off the bus, instead of a flashback of memory, the heavens opened and an almighty and prolonged downpour ensued.

Unperturbed, I made my way along the river in my turquoise galoshes. From the high basalt cliffs, the river rushed noisily through the length of the entire village. I waded towards a Viking site on which two modern junior Vikings were playing. Among the articles found on the site were cod-liver oil lamps, and I wondered if the tradition of administering a weekly dose of cod liver oil to children was already in practice then.

Looking towards the local church, I was reminded of the good Reverend Venceslaus Ulricus Hammerschaim, who long ago delivered a New Year's sermon to his congregation in the Faeroese language – at the time Danish was still the language of the church. Much to his dismay there was an uprising against him, as Faeroese was still regarded as a low peasant language, unfit for the word of

255

God. The poor pastor made no further attempts to preach in his own tongue.

The rain grew worse. As I looked out across the choppy oyster-coloured sea, large waves were rolling in. Though not as huge as the waves of winter, I remembered how as a child they had made me feel vulnerable and nervous.

I walked to the tiny bus shelter and wondered if a bus would ever turn up. I had asked the driver to stop at the village on his way back, but had received no acknowledgement. A young girl came to the bus stop and I asked her if she thought a bus, any bus, would eventually arrive.

'*Kanska,*' she said, meaning maybe. Faeroese have a fondness for the word *kanska*, and it creeps up several times in conversation, no matter the topic. I asked the girl if she could phone the bus company to double check – she was holding a mobile phone. This she did.

'And do you think a bus will come now?'

'*Kanska,*' was all she said.

'I wonder if the rain will stop?' I realised I was posing a question only asked by foreigners.

'*Kanska.*'

No wonder Earl Bradford named the Faeroes: 'Isles of Maybe' and Sydney Norgate, who was stationed here during the World War II, also called them 'The Land of Maybe'. It's not that the Faeroese themselves are indecisive. It is just that the weather is so unpredictable, making any plans involving outdoor activities or transportation totally dependent on weather conditions. These can change four or five times in one day, resulting in the best laid plans never coming to fruition.

In *The Atlantic Islands*, Kenneth Williamson relates the charming weather story of a pastor making his biannual visit to one of the rockiest isles. Not surprisingly, the weather was really bad, but one day there was a slight lull in the storm, so the pastor, having further ceremonies to perform on other islands, decided to leave while he could. He was due to perform another marriage ceremony in three days' time, but asked the young couple if they would agree to be married straightaway. This they did. Despite this change of plans, the wedding feast was still going ahead as originally scheduled three days later. After the marriage ceremony, as the pastor was rowing away to his next flock, the young groom chased after him in his boat with a pressing question.

'Will I be allowed to sleep with my wife before the wedding feast?'

By the time I returned to Tórshavn the rain had stopped and the sun was shining so I decided to cover some of my old tracks. I went into N.H. Jacobson bookstore and found to my delight that it had not changed at all. It was still packed with books and stationery. I asked the woman behind the counter if she was from the original Jacobsen family. At first she was a little taken aback, as though I had asked if she had been around since 1870 when the store first opened. She politely replied that she was no such relic and that the business had changed hands some time ago.

I continued walking around Tórshavn, retracing the steps of my childhood with notebook in hand and camera around my neck. On these solitary walks around this small capital, I hardly ever encountered a single soul. Certainly, there were people on the main street, but the other streets and alleyways were deserted. A lot of black and white cats were sitting outside their black and white houses, demonstrating a bizarre attempt at camouflage.

I noticed a football field just beyond the struggling plantation. Since my time, football had developed into the most popular sport. It all started in 1990, with a qualifying match for the 1992 European Championship Cup. The Faeroese team, recent members of the International Football Association, playing for the first time abroad beat the experienced Austrians 1–0, much to everyone's surprise. The Faeroes were at last put on the world map and the only time they are ever mentioned by the media in Australia is in connection with football.

Heading back to the harbour on the West Bay, I turned up Grím Kambansgøta, the road named after the first man to settle on the

257

Faeroe Islands – that is, according to the sagas. This time, several people were walking in groups and it wasn't even Sunday. They all appeared to be entering the same house, whose double doors were wide open. Curiosity got the better of me; I decided to follow one group in and found myself at the opening of an art exhibition. The artist was Elin Josephine Smith, a Faeroese who lives in Denmark. She counted among her famous relations her aunt, Ruth Smith, a talented painter of portraiture whose work is exhibited at the National Art Gallery in Tórshavn. Another noted relative was Janus Djurhuus, the lawyer-poet who had a great love for the classics, especially Greek ones. He translated the entire *Iliad* into Faeroese. When a Greek ship came into Tórshavn, Janus Djurhuus went on board and, seeking out the captain, recited to him the Odyssey in ancient Greek.

One of Elin Smith's aunts swam all the way between the neighbouring islands of Eystoroy to Tórshavn, not an easy feat given the strength of the currents.

'I do hope she was wearing a wet suit,' I said, reflecting on how tough this woman must have been. 'No, but she covered herself in duck oil,' was the reply. Her Uncle, Heri Smith, was in radio, where he gave notable impersonations of politicians - always a satisfying job.

As literature was flourishing in the Faeroes in my time, so were the visual arts. The first and most significant artist in the Faeroes was Sámal Joensen-Mikines, a contemporary painter when I lived there. He came from the island of Mykines, and was best known for painting some monumental canvases of his beloved wind-swept island and of its grieving and suffering people. Mikines journeyed to Norway, where he met Edvard Munch and to Paris, where he continued painting landscapes of Mykines, not of Montmartre. Eugene Delacroix and El Greco inspired him, but he always returned to his island and the cycle of life and death of his people. He was used to death from an early age as he sang at funerals and several members of his family had died of tuberculosis. Possibly that accounts for the grief-stricken themes of his paintings. Today, the Faeroese can boast some twenty professional artists and the highest publication of books per capita in the world.

I could only wonder with amazement that such a diminutive nation, with a population no larger than that of a medium-sized town in Scandinavia, could produce such a wealth of art and literature. It is almost as though anyone with talent feels responsible to develop it to its full potential in order to keep the identity of this small land firmly on the world map.

As the days passed, some of the uncertainties about my own history were being resolved, with the intervals between questions and answers leaving me in a state of restless anticipation and *kanska*. As details came to me, I realised that much of the familiar account of my early life was being upended, and that my childhood history was actually as foggy as the early history of the Faeroe Islands. One especially revealing fact emerged when I received a reply from Rachel in answer to my question as to why I had been included in Sigrid's passport a full year earlier than the time I went to live in Tórshavn.

Rachel wrote: *Sigrid came to Tórshavn in 1947 for a holiday and you were with her. You stayed for three or four weeks and then you both returned to Italy. Some time later, maybe in 1949, Mia went to Switzerland where she met Sigrid and you, and then she returned to the Faeroes bringing you with her. We were told that Sigrid was not able to keep you any longer at the clinic where she worked, and your parents were not in Genoa at that time. On the journey to the Faeroes you stayed for some days in Padburg, where Mia had some friends.*

I folded Rachel's letter, placed it back in the envelope and took a deep breath, but managed to quickly reconcile myself to this revised account of my past. After all, more than four decades had passed and I had long ago accepted my mother's reluctant approach to motherhood. During the great number of difficult years re-united with my mother, I had developed a low expectation of attachment from her, as she had possibly of me. Essentially, would it have made any difference to the way my life had turned out had I known earlier what I knew today? *Kanska*.

So, my early memory of arriving that day with Sigrid and being greeted by Mia in the hallway of the black house on Bakkahella went back to 1947, when I was only two and a half years old. Amazingly, I don't have any recollection of my second journey to Tórshavn in 1949, a year and a bit later, when Mia, not Sigrid, picked me up from Switzerland. But why Switzerland? Then I remembered that Mother told me she had secured part time work as a translator at the United Nations in Geneva. I now assume that my parents left Genoa for good, quite some time before their departure for Australia, and that they lived most of the time in Torino, where my father worked. Sigrid travelled with me from our hospital home in Genoa to Zurich to say our final goodbyes to my mother, before my departure to the Faeroe Islands with Mia. But why was Zurich and not Geneva chosen as the meeting point? No one seems to know. I have no idea what was going on in my parents' lives at that time and there is no one alive who can shed any light on their past.

Sjúrður's brother, Júst, had told me when I spoke to him recently on the farm about an incident at the border crossing into Denmark, when I was travelling with Mia from Zurich. When our train stopped at the border checkpoint, the Danish authorities questioned the authenticity of Mia's guardianship of me. Bearing in mind that I was stateless and held no travel documents of my own, it is entirely possible that whatever documents Mia had in her possession may have caused a mini chaos. Previously, I had been included on Sigrid's passport, but Sigrid was not travelling with me. The Danish police delayed the train by half an hour, while they sent a telegram to Tórshavn to ask for confirmation that the proper papers were on hand for my entry into the Kingdom of Denmark. The response from Tórshavn was apparently satisfactory. Júst said that on her return to Tórshavn, Mia dined out on this story for months.

So many pieces fell into place now: my mother and Mia greeting each other on the wharf when Mother came for the first time to Tórshavn, as though they'd met before - which now I knew they had, in Zurich. And in Padburg, I had stopped there overnight with Mia, not with Sigrid. Although Annalise, who sent the photo of me in her parent's garden, was correct in saying I came with my 'mother' – it was just not the mother she thought it was!

I suppose it was natural on my first trip to Tórshavn that previous year (1947), for Sigrid to have taken me on holiday with her, since we were living together as mother and daughter. It may also have coincided with the time that Mother took herself off to Argentina with friends for a spell of tango and *estancias*. I don't know how long she stayed away from Italy, but I know she enjoyed Buenos Aires enormously, because she often told me about this trip, carefully leaving out many details. I wondered later if she and my father would have been better off emigrating to Argentina, where the Latin temperament would have suited them so much better than the predominantly Anglo-Saxon culture in Australia.

At the time, Argentina was undergoing much needed social change under the presidency of Juan Perón, supported by his charismatic wife, Evita. Buenos Aires was a bustling city, the 'Paris of South America', teeming with European migrants, who had escaped the terrors of World War II, as well as a host of Nazi criminals, who had perpetrated this misery. The 1940s also saw the tango become a popular dance throughout the world. Mother had told me that every neighbourhood in Buenos Aires had two or three tango clubs and tango orchestras performed three times a night. I can visualise Mother so well, beautifully attired, surrounded by admirers, sitting on a bar stool smoking, drinking and tango-ing with the best of them, until the early hours of the morning and still managing to look fresh and glamorous. A good fit for her personality and background, but very un-Lutheran behaviour to my Faeroese mind.

I also remembered that, only recently, in a rare disclosure about her past, did Mother tell me that she got married a few days after my father proposed, the intention being to leave Belgrade immediately, though it did not happen that quickly. Finally, an explanation of her relatively casual attire in her wedding photos.

In the evening I looked through my folder containing the photographs and postcards that I had kept. My mother had carefully destroyed any paper trail leading to that episode of my past, except for one item that she must have overlooked. It was a certificate dated 20 March 1957 issued by the Chief of Police in the Faeroe Islands extending my permit to stay on the islands until 23 April 'as requested'. From this I can deduce that an extension had to be sought, as I had overstayed my visit. I could not have agreed more. However, I left Tórshavn with my mother only three days later, on 23 March. Presumably this had something to do with the crying episode when I did not want to leave Mia. Yet, another question mark in my past that would never be answered.

## Chapter Forty

*T*HE EVENING BEFORE my departure from Tórshavn on this
return trip, I couldn't wait to leave the islands. I couldn't explain
exactly why. Possibly it was a case of too much old and new
information being explored in such a short time. My feelings
towards the people who came to see me or called me remained shy
and somewhat remote. I could not rid myself of the old feeling of
not belonging. My next stop was New York, a city and culture at
the other end of the spectrum, but I knew that I would always feel
more at home and at peace there than I ever would in this small
tranquil place of my childhood. Only after I came back to Sydney
and set about recounting my story did I assuage much of that
shyness and recover some emotion about these people who were
important in so many ways during my early life.

The day arrived when my visit of rediscovery came to an end.
Much had changed since my childhood, especially my
understanding of the isolation of the Faeroe Islands. On the other
hand, some things about the Faeroes that I knew as a child had not
changed at all. Yet, what I gained was not just the experience of
revisiting the place where I had lived, but also a new perception of
the Faeroese people through adult eyes. I keenly felt the great
affection and understanding that they have for their unique
archipelago. Their stoic acceptance of the adverse elements of
nature was an inspiration. I admired their closeness to the natural

263

world, something that is lost to people living in steel and concrete cities. The Faeroese are ambitious, but contained. The islands have a small population of just over 47,000, but their people have a strong perception of themselves as an upcoming independent nation, blessed with their own distinct language, culture, history and national unity. They continue to be egalitarian and resilient and most importantly, they have not lost their distinct sense of place in the universe.

Nowadays, most people travel to Denmark by scheduled air services not unscheduled open boats. Even the remotest settlements enjoy the benefits of modern technology. Every citizen has a mobile phone and a car. Satellite dishes can be seen sticking out from traditional tuft roofs. The Internet is a way of life, but despite technological progress there are still occasions on the smaller islands with only a tiny landing site, when the inhabitants watch the modern ferry boat turn back after unsuccessfully trying to dock in rough weather. Even when the weather is good, the sea rarely remains calm for any length of time, proving that any amount of technological wizardry and advancement is still no match for the elements. The Sea Voice is fond of reminding us of the thousands that have drowned over millennia and it is a constant reminder to modern man that the sea has it own ageless, invincible powers.

From those early days of satisfying simple domestic needs, the Faeroe Islands have become a high tech fishing nation, with advanced shipping and fishing facilities, and equipment that rivals any country in the world. Despite this, there will still be one year when the fishing is good in one area and poor in another. The next year, the position will be reversed, so fisheries have to diversify their fleet and production in order to avoid financial losses. Yet the geographic location of these far-flung and barren islands leaves the Faeromen no alternative but to fish. In fact, some fishing is now even carried out on Sundays, much to the disapproval of the more devout Lutherans.

I left Tórshavn in sunshine. When I arrived at the airport on the island of Vágar it was blanketed in dense fog. I could only just make out the nose of the British Aerospace 146 aircraft on the tarmac. It's not unusual for the weather to be sunny on one island and pouring down with rain on the next. Still, we took off and, as we soared above the fog and swirl of mist, my optimism soared for the shining future of the Faeroe Islands and its people.

## Chapter Forty-One

**W**HEN I RETURNED to Sydney, I entertained my mother with amusing stories of my visit to Copenhagen and New York, which seemed to please her. If she suspected anything, she did not let on. However, it was not in her nature to hold back. In any case, it did not matter any more. I was not in the least disturbed by the recent discoveries of my childhood past that Mother had kept so well hidden from me. I had long ago come to understand and accept her ways, without necessarily comprehending the logic of them.

I reflected that her curious and harsh parental style had prepared me in some ways for the trials and tribulations of later life, though during the time that I lived with my mother and stepfather in Sydney, I felt more alone and cold than I had ever felt on those isolated rocky islands on the rim of the Arctic Circle. Looking back, I can see so clearly Mia's kindness, love and concern for me, which I so completely rejected – responding to her with a kind of perverse punishment for my mother having sent me away. I compensated by creating my own self-contained emotional world.

Later, once I was re-united with my mother in an equally far-away land, I wanted to undo this state, but it was not possible, as I found that I needed my self-created defences just as much in Australia. I had grown used to the ways of the Faeroese and had assumed the mantle of a 'northern temperament'. The Faeroese are reserved and restrained, conflicts are avoided at all costs. They are calm, not temperamental, and politeness is preferable to proving a point. In Sydney, I was plunged into a family of high anxiety, constant conflict and unrestrained tempers. This was *my* family and I belonged to it, come what may. Yet, despite my unhappiness, I did not want to return to the Faeroes, so much so that I almost totally obliterated all consciousness of them. Not until my return over forty years later, did I delve back into the memory of my life there, which in retrospect was actually far less unusual than my new life in Australia.

For many years, I continued to maintain a low wall of protection against the possibility of further physical and emotional dislocation. I can't say this is entirely bad, since my formative years in the Faeroes prepared me in many ways for life's uncertainties. Writing this book and recounting my story has helped to knock down that remaining wall of protection and I can now view my memories of a curious childhood in the Faeroe Islands in an entirely different and largely positive light.

Throughout her life Mother was the unaltered product of her upbringing - harking back to the family house where maids and valets attended her parents - and she perpetuated this particular late-Victorian grand style in her everyday activities. She was always impeccably groomed, kept the finest kitchen and bar; her home was always a cheerful and cared for place to come to, even though I often dreaded entering, and she had the inherited ability to preserve such a life style to the end. While health failed her in later years, her mind stayed sharp and clear and her tongue, as always, followed suit. She remained, until the end, the imperial granddaughter of Duke Radomir Putnik, Field Marshal of the Serbian Army; a man she never met, but so greatly admired.

Mother died on 15 June 2001, while I was writing this book, shortly before her 80th birthday, I have no regrets for not telling her about it, as I knew that she would have looked upon it as revenge for having sent me away to the Faeroe Islands. It is not in my nature to be spiteful, but she would not have believed me, such was the woeful state of our relationship. I would never have

267

wanted to hurt my mother and would have held off publication during her lifetime.

The morning Mother died in her sleep, it was still dark when I went to her apartment, where Roger joined me straight from the airport after his plane from Singapore landed. Only her favourite night nurse, who had called with the news, was with her. Now in that strange quiet that immediately follows a death, Roger and I both looked around and remembered the hundreds of times in the past thirty years we had come to this place with its eclectic appointments, its warm glow, cyclamens in silver buckets, a table beautifully set for a wonderful meal. Even though this was also the place of much unhappiness for me, my first memories were of the good times, of my elegant mother hosting dinner parties, cocktail parties and soirees.

I saw my mother adorned in jewels, holding court with her friends, champagne in one hand, cigarette in the other. Always the centre of attention, telling outrageous tales about her exploits that took poetic license to new heights. Everyone was laughing and agreeing with everything she said,

'Antonia, where are you? Bring us another bottle of Veuve Clicquot'.

How far I had come from being Faeroes' child.

268

## Historical Notes

Seafaring Monks – 600-800 AD

The popular theory on the early settlement of the Faeroe Islands is that of the seafaring monks. The mantle of mist that covers the Faeroe Islands kept them well hidden until the middle of the seventh century, when Irish monks came in search of solitude and lived among innumerable sheep and birds. The monks sailed in well-constructed boats, called *currachs*, roomy enough to hold at least twenty people plus provisions and livestock, such as the sheep found some 200 years later by the Norse settlers.

Some light on the earliest settlements was given by the Irish monk and scholar, Dicuil, who in a treatise on geography circa 825 AD, entitled *Libber de mensura orbis terræ*. (The Book of the Measurement of the Earth) wrote about first hand accounts of voyages made by Irish hermit monks in search of a religious refuge in the seas to the north of Ireland and Scotland. Some scholars concluded from Dicuil's writings that 'a set of small islands nearly all separated by narrow stretches of water and many diverse kind of sea birds' fitted the description of the Faeroe Islands.

The 'Northman pirates' mentioned by Dicuil, were taken to be the Vikings, who slaughtered the Irish hermits, leaving just the sheep.

Another theory put forward by philologists was the use of place-names. Although most of them were of Norse origin, which was to be expected, as immigrants tended to use names from their homeland, there were nevertheless names of Celtic origin. For example, the names of the two islands, Stóra Dimun and Lítla Dimun come from the Celtic word *dimun*, meaning two mountains. However, Símun Arge from the National Museum in Tórshavn points out that a closer look at the locations of some of the Celtic place-names where the Irish monks supposedly settled, improbably indicate areas of sheer basalt cliffs, facing the open North Atlantic.

The Intrepid Norsemen 800 - 1400

Norse pirates arrived circa 800 AD and either drove the original settlers off the island or slaughtered them. While there is no scientific or archaeological evidence to support any of the above, it is still a commonly held theory.

According to Símun Arge, who has written numerous papers on archeological findings in the Faeroes: 'A specific archeological investigation into the first settlement, the taking up of the land, or *Landnám* as it is called in Faeroese, has not been undertaken to date and systematic processing of archeological remains in tandem with pollen analyses is yet to be made'.

Símun Arge further points out that Dicuil's description of other islands and groups of islands in the ocean North of Britain', could equally apply to the Orkneys or Shetland. Furthermore, the number of sailing days used to establish the distances between groups of islands, in this case 'two days and two nights' was uncertain. This points to Dicuil being doubtful as a historical source.

'Therefore, when he is used, he should be treated with care!' Símun warns.

Símun Arge concludes that so far, archeological evidence indicates that the islands were settled by the Norsemen, not the Irish monks, during the Viking Age, between 900 and 1000 AD, but that recent pollen finds, still under investigation, suggest a possible settlement as early as 600 AD.

The Vikings were talented boat builders. Their robust 'cargo ships' called *Knörr,* fondly nicknamed 'goats of the sea' due to their ability to bound over the mighty waves, carried the first Norse settlers to the Faeroes. These ships could accommodate tons of cargo and at least forty people as well as livestock, fodder and all the basic gear needed to start a settlement from scratch. The conditions on board were cramped, but with clear weather, a favourable wind, and the powerfully strong Norwegian current, the journey from Norway to the Faeroe Islands would be over within two days' sailing. In foul weather it could take a week or end in tragedy. For these voyages of discovery over vast oceans to Greenland, Iceland and America, the early Norsemen relied on their ability to fix latitude.

The early Viking settlers are believed to have come mainly from West Norway sometime in the ninth century - but more about that later - and some also came via the Norse settlements on the Orkneys and Shetland, or as Nelson Annandale decorously wrote in *Island Life of the Faeroes and Iceland*, they were:

'Knit together by frequent though unorganised intercourse'.

History has given the Norwegians, Swedes and Danes the collective name of the Vikings to denote the period from the eighth to the eleventh century - the Viking Age. English historian, T. D. Kendrick, explains that the words *i viking* were used among the Northmen themselves meaning to go trading and plundering, or as he puts it:

'One who fared by sea to his adventures of commerce and of war'.

To be called a *vikinger mikill* - a great seafarer - by one's peers, was a true compliment. To the people, who bore the brunt of these Norsemen's adventures, *viking* meant raider and robber. However, the *vikings* did not plunder or raid the Faeroes, as there was nothing on the islands, except birds. The early Viking settlers on the Faeroes were farmers in search of arable land.

According to the sagas, written in Iceland in the vernacular around 1200, Grímur Kamban was the first man to settle in the Faeroes towards the end of the ninth century in the days of Harald Hárfanger, 'Fairhair' of Norway. The name Kamban is a

271

corruption of the Irish 'Camman', meaning bent or crooked, and it is thought that he might have arrived in the Faeroes by way of Ireland, where he could have been baptised. It is known that Harald 'Fairhair', was in power around the 880s, yet according to the sagas, Grímur Kamban's grandchild supposedly took part in the settlement of Iceland which has now been fixed at 874 AD!' This difficult chronological problem was explained away by some scholars by suggesting that two waves of emigration to the Faeroes took place: the early ninth century and towards the end of 1000.

Norse settlement of the Scottish islands took place in the first half of the ninth century and in the later half of the ninth century in Iceland. In Greenland, the first settlement began in 985 with Eric the Red. Possessing a natural talent for marketing, this red-haired fiery-tempered Viking called the land 'Greenland' in order to encourage settlement, even though 80% of it is covered permanently by Arctic ice. It worked, as farmers came in their thousands. They must have been angry when the first winter dumped so much snow on their dwellings that they had to dig tunnels in order to reach the surface.

In 999, these pagan Norsemen were blessed with Christianity. Whereas the settlements in Iceland and Greenland remained politically independent until late into the thirteenth century, the Faeroe Islands lost their independence as early as 1035, when they were incorporated into the Kingdom of Norway. They were once again 'blessed', this time by taxes collected by the king's sheriff, who also received fines payable to the crown and managed its properties.

During the Viking Age up to the thirteenth century, the Faeroe Islands experienced general economic prosperity together with the other Nordic countries. By the Union of Kalmar in 1380 Norway, together with the Faeroe Islands passed under the Danish Crown and Danish was introduced as the written language of the Faeroes. Later on, trade in the Faeroe Islands was taken over by the

Hanseatic merchants in Bergen. Around 1400, the original Viking *ting*, the parliament of free men, was reduced to a provincial court, known as Løgting.

## The See of Kirkjubøur

In the Middle Ages, the centre of power and learning on the Faeroe Islands was the bishopric at Kirkjubøur. Even though little is known about the history of the Faeroes during this period, it is known that bishoprics were set up in all the Norse countries as a means of extending Papal control and the tiny islands of the North Atlantic were not exempt. The Faeroes were made a separate bishopric of the Archdiocese of Nidarós (modern Trondheim) in Norway. Written sources indicate the names of some thirty bishops of Kirkjubøur, but little is known of their lives; however, many of them never even set foot on the islands. The few who did, lived on the working farms as was the norm.

The most celebrated of these bishops was Erlendur, who resided in Kirkjubøur and is credited with undertaking the construction of the Gothic cathedral. Not unusual for those times, Bishop Erlendur played an active political role as advisor to the king in Faeroese matters. He was also involved in making the Seyðabrœvið, Sheep Letter; in 1298 regulating the keeping of sheep and earlier Faeroese land laws, especially the joint use of outfields, which the crown accepted as local variations from Norwegian practice. The introduction of the Sheep Letter paved the way for the church to become the greatest landowner on the Faeroe Islands and consequently gave more power to the bishop. This wealth can be seen from the remains of St Magnus Cathedral and the bishop's place in Kirkjubøur.

The site of Kirkjubøur was probably chosen because of its favourably situated farm, which had good soil - as good as it gets in the Faeroes - and fields for sheep. The bay was an excellent site for collecting driftwood for all the buildings, of great importance in a treeless land.

Kirkjubøur also had a school where candidates were educated for the priesthood. Not much is known about the school itself; except that it groomed a famous pupil, Sverri Sigurdsson, who in 1177 became King of Norway. Sverri was born in Kirkjubøur, or at least spent much of his early years there, the illegitimate son of Gunnhild, a Norwegian lady of high birth, or a milk maid – we have a choice - and King Sigurd Munn of Norway. While he was still a small child, his mother married a Faeroese comb-maker and he was thus given the humble Faeroese name of Sverri. His uncle Rói was a bishop at Kirkjubøur and trained him for the priesthood. Only when Sverri graduated, did his mother finally tell him who his natural father was. Much, if not this entire story is thought to have been made up by Sverri himself. One suspects that he may have started his own legend. In any case, Sverri decided not to enter the priesthood but went instead to Norway to attain a higher office. After plunging Norway into a long civil war, he made himself king and established himself as a harsh, autocratic ruler with a strong centralised monarchy. He fought with the Church and was excommunicated. Despite open hostility towards him, he ruled until his death.

The Reformation

When the Reformation came to the Faeroes around 1538, the Norwegian church came under the authority of the Danish king, who asked the Catholic bishop, Ámund Olavsson of Kirkjubøur to accept the new doctrines, or leave. He left, and was replaced by Jens Riber, a Lutheran superintendent from Denmark. Riber's appointment was short lived, as he departed of his own accord, supposedly due to attacks by pirates who were plaguing the islands at the time. Four attacks in three years were just more than he could handle, though a more compelling reason may have been the reduced financial situation of the church, as all property was now assigned to the Crown. This change of property ownership also had a devastating effect on the livelihood of the Faeroese as this meant the taxes collected were leaving the islands.

The religious school in Kirkjubøur was closed down and a Danish Lutheran school opened in Tórshavn. Danish was introduced as the official language of the church, the state and of trade. The Danish ministers delivered their church sermons in Danish, which would have fallen on deaf Faeroese ears, until such time as the Faeroese had mastered the Danish tongue. Gradually, as Danish displaced the previous linguistic ties with Norway, Faeroese started to come into its own as a language.

The Trade Monopoly and the Period up to 1900

The trade monopoly started in 1553 and lasted for three centuries. It was one of the bleakest periods in Faeroese history. Sheep died and the fishing failed, the people went hungry, aggravated by the corruption of the feudal overlord, Christopher von Gabel and his son, who held the trade monopoly from 1655 to 1709, when the Danish government took it over with not much success. Much needed grain was prohibitively expensive and the people were underpaid for their goods. After the death of Frederick von Gabel, there was still no reprieve for the Faeroese, as they had to endure a royal monopoly, which operated on the premise of serving the country until its abolition in 1856. With this gloomy period over, trade expanded rapidly and Faeroese wool articles became an important export article.

Two forts, one in Skansin and one on the tip of Tinganes were built in Tórshavn to protect it from pirates, who started invading the island around 1500 and continued through to the 1800s. Pirates and hostile merchant ships swooped down on the Faeroe Islands, especially when Denmark was at war, which was quite often. Both forts were hopelessly inadequate and could not mount any kind of serious defense. In 1677, the French razed the fort to the ground. The fort was rebuilt but still remained inadequate to withstand determined attacks. In 1808, during the Napoleonic Wars, the British naval rig, *Clio*, captured the fort. The worst pirate attack was a raid by three Algerian ships on Hvalba on Suðuroy when the pirates carried off 30 people to be sold as slaves. The Faeroese were too poor to buy them back and the Danish coffers had been depleted by war.

The second fort, built on the tip of Tinganes near the Monopoly warehouse, has long since gone but the one at Skansin is still standing.

The Treaty of Kiel in 1814 saw King Christian VIII of Denmark sign Norway over to Sweden, to make reparations for having sided with Napoleonic France. As with many treaties, not enough care and time was given to drawing it up properly. Sweden was perhaps in a hurry to sign the treaty, or only interested in unifying the Swedish peninsula and attaining the Norwegian mainland, so they did not object when the Danes at the last minute asked for the Northern Islands, namely the Faeroes, Greenland and Iceland. There is no record of Faeroese reaction to this, but two years later the Faeroese *Løgting* (parliament) was officially abolished and replaced by a Danish judiciary. It was reestablished in 1852 as a county council with limited political powers. Before the Treaty of Kiel, the Faeroe Islands were never considered a Danish or Norwegian province, but rather a country still functioning under Norwegian law.

Birth of the Independence Movement

In the latter part of the nineteenth century, economic growth in the Faeroes fostered a development of nationalism that sought to protect the Faeroese language and culture. The first political parties were established in 1906. The *Sjálvstýrisflokkurin - impossible* to pronounce for a foreigner - better translated as the Self-Rule Party - wanted a greater Faeroese role in domestic affairs and the official use of the Faeroese language especially in schools.

On the other hand, the *Sambandsflokkurin,* or Unionist Party was for continuing close relations with Denmark. The political spectrum was broadened with the establishment in 1926 of the

276

Social Democratic Party, and in 1939 with the formation of the People's Party - a non-Socialist party - who wanted full autonomy. Some years later, when the *Løgting* was given more powers and could even propose legislation, the Danes quickly dismissed any notion of independence, as this was not exactly what they had in mind when providing assistance with development of the Faeroese economy.

The War Years 1940-45

On 9 April 1940, German forces crossed the Schleswig frontier and proceeded to occupy the whole of Denmark within a few hours. The Germans broke off all communication between Denmark and the Faeroe Islands, isolating them completely, but not for long. Realising the strategic importance of the Faeroes in the middle of the North Atlantic, British forces occupied the islands a few days later. On 11 April, the first Lord of the Admiralty, Winston Churchill, gave the House of Commons the following account of British naval action in the northern seas:

'We are also at this moment occupying the Faeroe Islands, which belong to Denmark and which are a strategic point of high importance and whose people showed every disposition to receive us with warm regard. We shall shield the Faeroe Islands from all the severities of war and establish ourselves there conveniently by sea and air until the moment comes when they will be handed back to Denmark, liberated from the foul thraldom into which they have been plunged by German aggression.'

At the peak of British activity, there were some 9000 troops stationed in the Faeroes, 6000 of which were on Vágar, where an airport was being built. This created a population explosion as the local inhabitants of the island only numbered about 2000. Security was tight and the locals had to carry identity cards. Visitors from the other islands had to apply for a permit from the British authorities before they could set foot on Vágar, an unheard of practice in the Faeroes.

One of the heaviest single losses sustained by the Faeroese during the war was that of the trawler *Nýggjaberg,* which vanished while on a fishing trip near Iceland, probably sunk by a U-boat. There were witnesses who recalled seeing black rats coming ashore before she set sail for Iceland in March 1942. Another trawler, the *Narðaberg,* was bombed between the Faeroe Islands and Scotland and the *Union Jack* (purchased from the British, hence the name) was sunk by a German U-boat off the Hebrides. To fend off attack by German aircraft, the British equipped the Faeroese boats with light machine-guns. Georg Joensen, the skipper of an old fishing boat, the *Thor,* from the village of Eiði (pronounced oy-yeh), succeeded in destroying a Henkel He 100 fighter plane from the *Luftwaffe.* The British decorated him with an MBE for his valour. Altogether 205 men lost their lives at sea and 25 vessels perished. A heavy toll for such a small population. On land, five Faeroese lost their lives as a direct result of enemy activity, air strikes being directed mainly at naval vessels and fishing boats. However, there was considerable property damage caused by mines and other explosive devices drifting into the bays. A German fighter plane took a swipe at the town of Klaksvik, only to plunge into the nearby pyramid-shaped mountain.

During a fearsome storm in December 1941, the British lost one of their own ships, the *Southerner,* which sank off the island of Fugloy, and all crew and passengers were lost. It was carrying Christmas gifts for the British soldiers. A diving team has attempted to salvage items from the 'Christmas Ship' as it is now called. In keeping with traditional rumours that surround shipwrecks, the Christmas Ship was carrying a cargo of rare coins.

So far, the divers have recovered a porthole, a telegraph machine and the ship's bell.

In the midst of all this bravery and tragedy, the Faeroes received a boost to their feeling of nationhood. The Faeroese had their own flag, the Merkið, but were not permitted to fly it on official occasions. When the war broke out the Faeroese ships naturally flew the Danish flag, and painted 'Danmark' on the ships' sides. However, so that the Allies would recognise them as neutral friendly ships, the British ordered the Faeroese flag, a blue-bordered red cross on a white background, to be hoisted and for them to paint 'Faeroe' on the ships. The Faeroese more than happily obliged. However, it turned out to be not such a good idea, as from a distance the *Merkið* looks similar to the white ensign of the Royal British navy and thus increased the risk of attack by the Germans.

So significant was this event that it was made into a national holiday - *Flaggdagur* or Flag Day, which is celebrated each year on 25 April. (Flags have a greater ceremonial and emotional importance for Scandinavians than for the British or Australians). Niels Juul Arge from Radio Faeroe Islands wrote several books entitled *Striðsárini 1940-45* (The War Years), providing a powerful insight into those five years on the Faeroes. Unfortunately, his books have not yet been translated into English.

The Faeroese fishing vessels supplied Britain with more than a fifth of all the fresh fish eaten in Britain during the five and a half years of war. In turn, the British paid the Faeroese handsomely for this assistance, enabling them to update their antiquated fishing fleet. However, this economic improvement came at a great cost to the Faeroese, who lost 150 at sea, representing about one and a half percent of the population.

Home Rule in 1948 to the Present

World War II also brought about a significant change in the Faeroes' political relationship with Denmark. It was unpalatable for the Faeroese, who had received plenty of experience in successfully running their own affairs during the war, to return to the old county status, which had been in effect since 1814. In fact, neighbouring Iceland, previously part of Denmark, was declared a republic during the war. Constitutional discussions were held between the three major Faeroese political parties and the Danish government. After a long period of negotiation, the Home Rule Act came into effect in 1948, whereby the Faeroe Islands function as a self-governing community within the Kingdom of Denmark with its own flag and Faeroese as a main language. The *Løgting* was reinstated with legislative and executive powers over all local matters. Education, health and social services are joint affairs, for which the home government assumes administrative responsibility. The Danish government handles the areas of defence, finance, justice and foreign relations. Danish legislation only takes effect in the Faeroes after ratification by the *Løgting*. The idea is to maintain a 'holy' union between the Faeroe Islands and Denmark, while fostering the uniqueness of the Faeroese culture. The Faeroes elect two members to represent them in the Danish parliament and a High Commissioner, rigsombudsmand, represents the Danish State on the islands. The areas that have been completely taken over by the Faeroese, such as communications, culture and industry are fully financed by the Faeroese themselves. The islands pay no taxes to the Danish treasury, but they contribute to the Danish economy by purchasing over two-thirds of their imports from Denmark.

As the Faeroese have been plagued by the fluctuation of fortunes in their fishing industry, Denmark provides an annual subsidy of about one-third of the islands' budget. Whenever talk of secession arises, Denmark has warned that this important subsidy will be withheld.

In the 1970s and early 1980s, the Faeroese enjoyed one of the highest standards of living in the world. Taxation was low, credit seemed to be limitless and many Faeroese took out large mortgages and loans. Then at the end of the 80s the bottom fell out of the sea so to speak. Heavy over-fishing, resulting from the use of high tech equipment caused a sharp drop in the once teeming North Atlantic fish stocks. Income dropped and the economy went into depression. There were numerous bankruptcies, not just in the fishing industry, and many lost their jobs. The national bank went into receivership. In 1992 the Danish government had to bail out the second largest bank. This was in addition to the subsidy, which the Faeroese receive annually. The Danish government has insisted on austerity measures and the economy has improved in the last few years. Many Faeroese still go abroad to work, mainly to Denmark, and young men find work on foreign fishing vessels. Oil finds in the immediate area of the Faeroes have given hope for a sustained period of economic prosperity in the future. The first drilling for the dark gold started in 2001 and a considerable amount of oil has been found. However, further tests will have to be done to determine if these amounts are sufficient for commercial development. Economic sustainability is an important factor in the Faeroese push for complete independence.

In recent years, discussions have been held in the Løgting over the proposal for a structured process towards a sovereign state, including the phasing out of financial subsidies from Denmark, whereby the Faeroese people will have to take full control of their own affairs.

## Glossary of Faeroese Words

*bindingarmynstur*  knitting pattern
*bøur*  infield, *viz* the cultivated land around a farm, enclosed by a fence
*bygd*  village, hamlet, settlement
*dansiringur*  circle of people dancing, or chain dance
*døglingur*  bottlenose whale; (nickname for) one-eyed person; badly made haystack
*Eysturoy*  East Island
*fleygingarstong*  net with long pole used for bird-catching
*fiskaknettir*  large fish balls
*frikadellir*  fish cakes
*frøkun*  Miss
*fuglabjørg*  bird-cliffs
*fuglakvæði*  Medieval bird ballad
*gøta*  road, street (in a town); path between two villages
*glasstova*  sitting room (in old houses) with glass windows
*grind*  school of pilot whales; meat of pilot whales
*grindaboð*  signal to inform people of the discovery of a school of pilot whales
*grindadráp*  whale slaughter
*grýla*  monster who lives in the hills
*hagi*  uncultivated land, outfield (as opposed to bøur, infield)
*hjallur*  storehouse or outhouse for air-drying meat and fish, etc.
*huldufólk*  'grey people' who live in the countryside and can make themselves invisible
*kanska*  perhaps, maybe
*klippfisk*  dried, salted cod fish
*knettir*  fish ball containing lumps of lamb's tallow
*kvæði*  heroic or folk ballad in Faeroese
*Løgting*  Faeroese Parliament
*lýsi*  light; cod-liver oil
*mjørki*  summer fog or mist
*múrurin*  walls (of St Magnus Cathedral)
*nykur*  water nymph, elf

*Ólavsøka*   St Olav's Day (29 July)

*-oy*   island in place-names, e.g. Sandoy,  Sand Island

*reyn*   stony soil, stony ridge

*roykstova*   kitchen and living room in old farm house with an opening in the roof ridge

*rullupylsa*   kind of sausage made of mutton

*ræst kjøt*   mutton which has been air-dried for a few months

*Sjómansheim*, Seamen's Home

*skadda*   thick mountain fog or mist (wet)

*skerpikjøt* one year old wind-dried mutton

*skipari*   lead singer of chain dance; captain, skipper

*skúla*   school

*Smyril*   merlin; name of inter-island passenger ferry line

*Streymoy*   Stream Island

*strond*   beach, (sea)shore

*terradropar*   scattered raindrops in dry weather

*Thór*   Norse god of thunder

*ting*   assembly

*tjaldur*   oyster catcher, national bird of the Faeroe Islands

*toskur*   large cod

# Bibliography

Annandale, Nelson, *The Faroes and Iceland: Studies in Island Life*, Oxford Press, London, 1905.

Arge, Símun V, (trans. Sheila Arnskov), *The Cathedral and other Historic Relics at Kirkjubour*, Feroya Fornminnissavn Foroya Fornminnagrunnur, 1989.

Gaffin, Dennis, *In Place: Spatial and social order in a Faeroe Islands Community*, Waveland Press, Inc., Ill., 1996.

Matras, Christian, (trans. George Johnston) *Seeing and Remembering*, Blood Axe Books Ltd., Newcastle upon Tyne, 1996.

Arge, Símun V., 'Vikings in the Faeroe Islands'. In *Vikings: The North Atlantic Saga*, Fitzhugh, William W. and Elisabeth I. Ward, Eds., 10:154-163, Smithsonian Institution Press, Washington, 2000.

Johnston, George (trans.) *Rocky Shores: An anthology of Faroese Poetry*, Wilfion Books, Paisley, Scotland, 1981.

Kendrick, T.D, *A History of the Vikings*, Frank Cass Co. Ltd., London, 1968.

Kershaw, N. *Stories and Ballads of the Far Past*, Cambridge University Press 1921.

Press, Muriel A.C, trans., *The Saga of the Faroe Islanders*, J.M. Dent & Sons. Ltd. London, 1934.

Tagel. Sven (ed) *Ethnicity and National Building in the Nordic World*, C. Hurst & Co. London, 1995.

West, John F, *Faroe The Emergence of a Nation*, C Hurst & Co. London, 1972.

Heinesen, William, trans. Anne Born, Arctis: Selected Poems 1921-1972. The Thule Press 1980.

Williamson, Kenneth, *The Atlantic Island*, Routlege & Kegan, London, 2$^{nd}$ ed. 1970.

Wylie, Jonathan, *The Faroe Islands: Interpretations of History*, The University Press of Kentucky, USA, 1987.

Wylie, Jonathan and Margolin, David, *The Ring of Dancers: Images of Faroese Culture*, University of Pennsylvania Press, Philadelphia, 1981.

Young, G.V.C., Clewer, Cynthia R., *Faroese-English Dictionary*, Mansk-Svenska Publishing Co. Ltd., Isle of Man, 1985.

## Articles and Papers

Arge, Eftir Jógvan, 'Tjaldur and Locatelli', *Atlantic Review*, November 1998, pp. 20-23.

Arge, Símun V, 'The Landnám in the Faroes', *Arctic Anthropology*, Vol.28, No.2, 1991, pp. 101-120.

Arge, Símun V, 'Site and Settlement Uppistovubeitnum Leirvík', *Fróðskaparrit* 45, bók, 1997, pp.27-44.

Arge, Símun V.and Niels Hartmann, 'Serprent. The burial site of við Kirkjugarð in the village of Sandur, Sandoy, *Fróðskaparrit* , 38-39 bók 1989-90.

Bradford Ernle, 'The Faeroes, Isles of Maybe', *National Geographic*, Vol. 130 No. 3, September 1970, pp. 110-442.

Hansen, Leo, 'Viking Life in the Storm-Cursed Faeroes', *National Geographic*, Vol.LVIII No.S, November 1930, pp.607-648.

Jones, W. Glyn, *Lecture*, 1974,'Faroe and Cosmos', University of Newcastle on Tyne.